The Book of Tennis

by Chris Bowers

D1649771

QUIET PLEASE!

"Anybody on for a game of tennis?"

GEORGE BERNARD SHAW 1856-1950

English writer and philosopher

Possible source of the phrase "Anyone for tennis?"

ten·nis (tns) *n.* 1. A game played with rackets and a light ball by two players or two pairs of players on a rectangular court, as of grass, clay, or asphalt, divided by a net. *Also called lawn tennis.* 2. Court tennis. Middle English tenetz, tenyes, court tennis, from Anglo-Norman tenetz, and Old French tenez; pl. imperative of tenir, to hold from Latin tenre. *See detain. Source:* The American Heritage ® Dictionary of the English Language, Fourth Edition.x

JWM PUBLISHING LIMITED

CONTENTS

INTRODUCTION
PAGE 5

1. THE HISTORY OF TENNIS
PAGE 7

A summary of the birth and development of tennis from the 1300s to today

Photograph: 19th century tennis rackets, by Michael Cole Camerawork

2. TODAY'S PROFESSIONAL TENNIS TOUR
PAGE 15

The governing bodies behind professional tennis, seedings and rankings, and maps of the four Slams

Photograph: Balls at the US Open, by Stephen Wake

3. COURTS & ARENAS
PAGE 37

The main tennis surfaces and the greatest tennis arenas

Photograph: Mark Philippoussis at Melbourne Park, by Tommy Hindley

4. OFF-COURT
PAGE 51

The array of off-court activity explained, from umpires and ballpersons to agents and pyschologists

Photograph: Line judges at the Ericsson Open, by Tommy Hindley

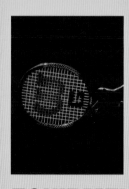

5. EQUIPMENT
PAGE 75

Rackets, strings, grips, balls, shoes and clothing

Photograph: Wilson logo on strings, by Stephen Wake

ACKNOWLEDGMENTS

We are very grateful to the following people
(and more), who have helped in the compiling of *The Book of Tennis*.

They appear in alphabetical order:

Gerry Armstrong, Janine Bailey, John Barrett, John Beddington,

Clifford Bloxham, Gayle Bradshaw, Roland Carlstedt, Andre Christopher,

Andrew Coe, Sian Crossland, Lynda Daley, John Dolan, Joe Favorito,

Stefan Fransson, Jane Fraser, Craig Gabriel, Jon Henderson, Mitzi Ingram-Evans,

Kurt Kamperman, Richard Kaufman, Beatrice Manzari, Frew McMillan,

David Mercer, Debra Miller, Sascha Miller, Roger Morgan, Mike Morrissey,

Jackie Nesbitt, Janet Page, Lynn Parker, Christophe Proust, Morven Rae, Brian Robins,

Chris Ronaldson, Nigel Sears, Lysette Shaw, Justin Smith,

Paul Smith, Audrey Snell, Alex Sofia, Jordan Sprechman, Barbara Travers,

Randy Walker, Eli Weinstein, Mark Young

tennis\Ten"nis *n. OE.*
tennes, tenies, tenyse; of uncertain
origin, perhaps fr. F. tenez hold or
take it, fr. tenir to hold *(see Tenable)*.
Court tennis, the old game of tennis
as played within walled courts of
peculiar construction; distinguished
from lawn tennis. Lawn tennis.
*See under Lawn, n. "His easy bow,
his good stories, his style of dancing
and playing tennis... were familiar to
all London"* – Macaulay *"A play in
which a ball is driven to and fro, or
kept in motion by striking it with a
racket or with the open hand"* –
Shakespeare Tennis court, *"a place
or court for playing the game of
tennis"* – Shakespeare. *Source:*
Webster's Revised Unabridged
Dictionary 1998.

INTRODUCTION

Welcome to *The Book of Tennis*!

Tennis should be fun, whether you're watching it, working in it, playing it as a hobby, or aspiring to greatness. But things are more fun when you know more about them, so the first thing I hope *The Book of Tennis* will do is provide you with entertaining stories and useful information about this wonderful sport.

I've often felt that fans, players, and those who work in tennis would like to have at their fingertips a work that gives them access to just about anything to do with our sport. Yet there has never been a definitive book which addresses all these needs, no matter from which part of the tennis spectrum you are coming from. Now there is: *The Book of Tennis*!

When I say 'definitive' I don't mean this book contains everything ever written about the sport. No book could do that without extending to countless volumes and a need for constant updating, probably daily. But our author, Chris Bowers, has put together a work that should give anyone who wants to get in touch with any branch of the tennis family an excellent first port of call.

The stories, like the information, are tremendously varied. Whether you are in need of contacts at your national tennis association, or one of the many companies that manufacture anything related to tennis. Or if you would like to know what size umbrella you should take to a tournament just in case you find yourself sitting on centre court when the rains come down. You will find it all in *The Book Of Tennis*.

We also plan to update *The Book of Tennis* at regular intervals, both in print form and on our website *www.thebookoftennis.com*, so even in a rapidly changing world, our hope is that the information will always be valid and current. And when visiting our website, check out our range of exciting and innovative tennis merchandise.

Chris and I are grateful to a number of people who have made *The Book of Tennis* possible, and the names of most of them appear facing page. But I am truly indebted to Chris Shaw of the Lawn Tennis Association in London, who took the trouble to introduce me to Chris Bowers, a writer and broadcaster who not only knows tennis at every level but has no less a passion for the sport than myself.

Tennis is truly global. The international tennis family stretches into well over 200 countries and territories. Whatever your involvement with tennis, have fun – and may *The Book of Tennis* always be by your side!

Jeff Wayne
Editor & Publisher
January 2002

tennis *n.* A game played with rackets by two or four players who hit a ball back and forth over a net that divides the court (syn: lawn tennis). *Source:* WordNet ® 1.6, 1997 Princeton University.

Written by Chris Bowers

Designed & art directed by Michael Bell Design

Edited by Jeff Wayne

Photography by Tommy Hindley of Professional Sport

Additional photographs taken by Chris Bowers, Alex Livesey, Stephen Wake and supplied by

Gianni Clerici, International Tennis Hall of Fame, Jeff Wayne and the Wimbledon Museum

Page 192 photograph (Chris Bowers interviewing Pete Sampras) by Gianni Ciaccia

Studio photography by George Taylor

Exercises modelled by Anna-Marie Wayne, Jemma Wayne, Zeb Wayne and Joab Wayne

Picture research by Chris Bowers and Marina Palmer

Additional research by James Kattan, Jemma Wayne and Jeff Wayne

ISBN 0 9541654 0 3

Order No JWM 15-30

Published and distributed by JWM Publishing Limited

Oliver House, 8/9 Ivor Place, London NW1 6BY, England

Telephone: +44 20 7724 2471

Fax: +44 20 7724 6245

E-mail: info@jeffwaynemusic.com

Originated by Hilite Reprographics Limited

Printed & bound in China by Excel Printing Company Limited

The Book of Tennis

www.thebookoftennis.com

info@thebookoftennis.com

1. THE HISTORY OF TENNIS

The idea of two people hitting a ball back and forth across some obstacle, with their hands, feet or some implement, has probably been acted out for centuries. Indeed, tennis historians who have looked hard enough claim to have found evidence of tennis in ancient Greece. But the first recognisable form of what we think of as tennis came in the 13th century, and the game we know today dates from the second half of the 19th century.

THE ORIGINS OF TENNIS

The first evidence of a game resembling tennis comes from 13th century France, where a game called *jeu de paume* (literally: game of the palm of the hand) was popular in royal circles.

Paume survived the blow to its prestige suffered when king Louis X died after a strenuous game in 1316, and its popularity was even carried on by many subsequent monarchs, becoming known as tennis.

By the early 16th century the first rackets were being used, and the English king Henry VIII built a tennis court at Hampton Court palace in the 1530s. While that court no longer exists, the one built there by Charles I in 1625 still remains and is probably the best-known 'real tennis' court.

The 16th century version of tennis is still played today, but only in four countries: France where it is still known as *jeu de paume*, Australia where it is called 'royal tennis', Great Britain where it is 'real tennis' (a corruption of 'royal'), and America where it is 'court tennis'. All three English terms reflect the sport's popularity among Europe's monarchies, and it might have died out without royal support. In fact the royals brought the sport indoors from its origins in streets and fields (those tennis 'purists' who disliked the introduction and rapid popularity of indoor tennis in the 1960s, 70s and 80s missed the point that indoor tennis returned the sport back to some of its early roots more than many other modern developments).

The real tennis court itself is a little like a cross between today's tennis and squash courts, and the game itself looks like something of a mixture.

Right: Real Tennis, around 1632 – the court looked something like a room in a palace or monastery, and the rules of the sport still specify that a real tennis court should have a protruding wall where the gallery would once have been

The net exists but players can bounce the ball off the walls, and the rules are considerably more complex than either tennis or squash.

Though real tennis has long been succeeded by today's form of tennis as a mass spectator and participation sport, it still has a thriving following, and some of the biggest tournaments held today are played at the Queen's Club in London.

The origin of the word 'tennis' is unclear, though the most plausible theory is that it comes from the French 'tenez', from the verb 'tenir' meaning to take or to hold. 'Tenez' is the command, and the theory is that a server or umpire would have shouted 'tenez!' to a receiver just before the serve, in the sense of 'take this!'. In the royal games, the server was always a servant, as it was considered improper for a monarch to start a point – this may explain the origin of the word 'service' as the shot which starts a rally.

LAWN TENNIS

It is unclear when the first attempts were made to take tennis out of doors, but it was certainly happening by the end of the 18th century.

Whatever attempts were made, it was not until the 1870s that an outdoor form of tennis really took off. The key figure was an English army major Walter Clopton Wingfield, who if not the inventor of today's form of tennis certainly deserves his place in the sport's history as the man who did most to kick-start it.

Wingfield's brainwave was in designing, patenting and manufacturing the equipment for tennis, and selling it in boxes for people to buy and put into practice on their own lawns. A box cost five guineas (5.25 British pounds or around $8 at today's rate), and included two net posts, a net, rackets, and India rubber balls, plus instructions about laying out the court on a lawn, and how to play the game (with a scoring system resembling the rackets or squash rule of first to 15 points).

*"When we have match'd out racket to these balls,
We will, in France, by God's grace play a set"*

WILLIAM SHAKESPEARE 1562-1616

English playwright and poet, from Henry V (1599), referring to real tennis

Above: Walter Clopton Wingfield

Left: A Sphairistike court around 1874 – note the hour-glass shape of the court

1873

AS WALTER CLOPTON WINGFIELD WAS INTRODUCING LAWN TENNIS AT HIS GARDEN PARTIES, KING AMADEUS OF SPAIN ABDICATED AND SPAIN BECAME A REPUBLIC

The name he gave it was 'Sphairistike' from the Greek word for ball games, and it had a subsidiary name 'lawn tennis' because it was like tennis but played on a lawn. While the game was very well received among many of the papers and periodicals that reviewed it – in good part because it offered the chance for women to play as well as men – the one thing that was heavily criticised was the name, and Wingfield soon recognised that 'lawn tennis' was a much better description for his otherwise successful invention.

AS THE FIRST WIMBLEDON TOOK
PLACE, RUSSIA HAD DECLARED
WAR ON THE OTTOMAN EMPIRE,
AND IN AMERICA THE BELL
TELEPHONE COMPANY WAS
ABOUT TO BE INCORPORATED

Wingfield launched Sphairistike at a party in Wales in 1873, and the fact that the boxes were easily exportable meant the game spread. Two brothers, Clarence and Joseph Clark, took a box to America in 1874, and it caught the attention of a Mary Outerbridge, whose brother Emilius organised what is believed to be the first major tennis event in the USA. Another box arrived at the Massachusetts summer home of William Appleton where another tournament took place in Nahant in 1876. Boxes also reached Paris, where the game still called *paume* had been fading in popularity.

The early regulators of lawn tennis were the Marylebone Cricket Club, the governing body of English cricket. In 1876 the MCC rewrote a number of Wingfield's rules (with Wingfield's support), notably replacing the 'first to 15 points' rule with the scoring system used in real tennis with deuce and advantage, and giving servers two serves instead of one. The MCC handed over control to the All England Club in Wimbledon after the first championship there in 1877.

INTERNATIONAL CHAMPIONSHIPS

If not quite the first official tennis tournament, Wimbledon certainly set the international ball rolling – astonishingly less than four years after Wingfield had patented his practical outdoor version of the sport. There tends to be an assumption among Wimbledon visitors that lawn tennis rather invaded the ancient traditions of croquet, a genteel lawn game played by hitting wooden balls through hoops with a mallet.

But though croquet had been popular in England for many years prior to the 1870s, the All England Croquet Club was only founded in 1870. So it was hardly against a background of long-standing tradition that Henry Jones (who wrote for 'The Field' magazine under the name 'Cavendish') introduced lawn tennis to the All England Croquet Club in 1875. A croquet lawn was given over to lawn tennis, four more were added in 1876, and in 1877 the first tournament was held, won by Spencer Gore who will have suspected little of the line of great champions he was to head.

In 1881 the second of the four events that were to form the Grand Slam was founded. Seven years before the British got round to establishing a tennis association to govern the sport, the United States National Lawn Tennis Association was founded, and promptly launched its National Championship the same year, though restricted to American residents. It was held at Newport, Rhode Island, and was won by Richard Sears, who went on to win the first seven stagings of the event.

While Wimbledon suffered the only decline in its history during the 1890s, the game spread across Europe. In 1891 the French national championships were held in Paris, the sport had also taken root in Belgium, and in 1896 Germany held its first national tournament.

The growth of the Davis Cup, which started in 1900 as a challenge between America and Great Britain, added to the international competitive scene. By 1905 a team from Australasia (Australia and New Zealand) was competing, and won it in 1907, and the Australasian National Championships began in 1905.

DROP *SHOTS!*

Success in tennis doesn't guarantee a successful run in life, as St Leger Goold's tale confirms. Goold, who hailed from Waterford in Ireland, was the Wimbledon runner-up to John Hartley in 1879, but ended up as the tournament's only finalist to become a convicted murderer.

He and his wife were in France in 1907 when they were approached by a woman asking for repayment of a debt. A fight ensued, and the woman died as a result of her injuries. Goold and his wife were both convicted of murder, she was sent to Montpelier prison, he to Devil's Island where he died two years later.

Right: Richard Sears – winner of the first seven US titles, and never beaten

QUIET PLEASE!

"A vain, idle and sinful game at which there was much of the language of the accursed going on"

JAMES HOGG 1770-1839
Scottish poet

Left: Early tennis advertising from the sports catalogue of the tennis equipment manufacturer F H Ayres in 1886, and (above) product placement and image transfer using tennis to advertise lawn mowers

They were not the first international event in Australia – that honour is held by the Victorian championships of 1879, when the seven states which make up today's Australia were independent colonies.

In 1913 an international umbrella organisation, the International Lawn Tennis Federation, was founded in order to guarantee that the sport would grow with uniform scoring and without diverging too much from country to country.

Above: Worple Road, Wimbledon – a packed house for the seventh Wimbledon final between Willie and Ernest Renshaw in 1883

The ILTF had 13 members representing 14 countries, a sign of how far the sport had taken root in the mere 40 years since Wingfield's boxes were first marketed.

MEMORABLE MATCHES
Suzanne Lenglen v Helen Wills Challenge Match 1926

On 16 February 1926 the Carlton Hotel in Cannes, southern France, staged the only match ever played between Suzanne Lenglen, who dominated tennis for the first decade after the first world war, and Helen Wills, who dominated the second decade.

It was a fiercely competitive match, which Lenglen was on the point of winning when there was great drama. At 6-3 6-5 40-15 Wills hit a crosscourt forehand, the cry of 'out' was heard, Lenglen rejoiced, the players shook hands, and Lenglen was showered with flowers. But then it became clear the line judge was signalling that he had not called the ball out, and that the call had come from the crowd.

The match referee Commander George Hillyard, the former secretary of the All England Lawn Tennis Club, ordered the two players back onto court to replay the point. To add to the drama Wills saved both match points (one on a double fault, said to be one of only six in Lenglen's entire career) and broke back to level at 6-6. Lenglen then took the next two games to win 6-3 8-6, and collapsed with exhaustion.

These days it is unthinkable that they would not have had a rematch, but they never played again.

'OPEN' TENNIS

The growth of tennis was hit by the first world war but the sport continued to grow afterwards, largely thanks to the irresistible appeal of Suzanne Lenglen, the French player whose peak came between 1919 and 1925. Many tennis watchers who saw her, even those who watched tennis for another 60 years afterwards, said she was the greatest ever female player, combining remarkable and relentless accuracy with balletic elegance.

The end of her amateur career was hastened by a misunderstanding at Wimbledon in which she inadvertently kept the king and queen of England waiting – when she was blamed for this she was so upset she said she wouldn't return to Wimbledon, and didn't.

But by then the French were getting excited about a new generation of heroes, four outstanding players in the late 1920s and early 30s who won most of the major titles and brought the Davis Cup to France. They were Jean Borotra, Jacques Brugnon (nicknamed 'Toto'), Henri Cochet and René Lacoste, and they became known as the Four Musketeers.

It was also the era of Big Bill Tilden from America, Fred Perry's dominance in the mid-1930s, and the first Grand Slam for Donald Budge in 1938.

But in the 1930s a problem began to emerge that was to haunt the sport for another 30 years and make it impossible to work out the greatest-ever players. The official tennis circuit was amateur, but such was the appeal of the game that there was money to be made away from it, and most of the top players were offered money to desert the amateur ranks and play for money in non-official professional tournaments. Perry turned professional after winning the 1936 US championship, but by that time he had won eight Slam singles titles (a career Grand Slam but never a calendar Grand Slam, see page 17).

QUIET PLEASE!

"What a polite game tennis is.
The chief word in it seems to be 'sorry' and
admiration of each other's play crosses the net as
frequently as the ball"

J M BARRIE 1860-1937
Scottish novelist and playwright

By the late 1940s and throughout the 1950s anyone who won Wimbledon was immediately approached to sign for a professional circuit, which explains why so few major champions of that era ever won more than once. One of the leading figures on the professional scene was the American Jack Kramer, who intended to turn professional in 1946 but felt he needed the tag of Wimbledon champion, so he stayed an amateur until he had won the 1947 title. After earning his money for a couple of years as a player, Kramer began signing up players for his own professional tour in the early 1950s.

By the late 1950s it was impossible to judge who the best players in the world were.

The great Australian coach Harry Hopman churned out champions year after year, but then they turned professional and disappeared from the official circuits.

There were many other charismatic figures, such as Pancho Gonzales, Tony Trabert, Ken Rosewall and Alex Olmedo who were plying their trade away from the top tournaments. In addition, many amateur players were receiving questionable payments from their national associations so they would continue to play the official events, making the concept of the amateur a sham and leading to the word 'shamateurism'.

So a motion was put to the ILTF's 1960 annual meeting that the two circuits should merge and tennis go 'open'. It was approved by 134 votes to 75, but it needed a two-thirds majority and fell just five votes short – it later emerged that three supporters of open tennis had missed the vote for risible reasons: one was in the toilet, one had fallen asleep, and one was arranging that evening's entertainment on a riverboat down the Seine.

The 1930s were dominated by Fred Perry (left) and Donald Budge, but one of their leading rivals was the German baron Gottfried von Cramm (above)

1938

THE YEAR DON BUDGE WON THE FIRST GRAND SLAM, ORSON WELLES CAUSED PANIC IN THE USA WITH HIS CONVINCING BROADCAST OF H G WELLS' SCIENCE FICTION STORY THE WAR OF THE WORLDS

1968

AS TENNIS WENT 'OPEN', STUDENTS RIOTED AT EUROPE'S UNIVERSITIES, MARTIN LUTHER KING WAS ASSASSINATED, AND THE FIRST MOON ORBIT TOOK PLACE

1977

THE INTERNATIONAL LAWN TENNIS FEDERATION DROPPED THE WORD 'LAWN' FROM ITS NAME IN THE SAME YEAR THAT ELVIS PRESLEY WAS FOUND DEAD

Rod Laver – seen here winning Wimbledon in 1969, the third leg of what proved the first 'open' Grand Slam and still the only one ever completed in men's tennis

It took another eight years for the deadlock to be broken, and it came when, at the end of 1967, Wimbledon announced it would open its 1968 championships to contract professionals, whether the ILTF sanctioned it or not.

The USLTA announced it would do the same for its 1968 championships, and the ILTF backed down, starting the 'open era' at the Bournemouth claycourt tournament on the English south coast in April 1968. Mark Cox, a British Davis Cup player, became the first amateur to beat a professional when he defeated Pancho Gonzales, a legend of the professional circuit by then aged 40, in the first match. Ken Rosewall, a professional, went on to win the tournament.

The merging of the two circuits brought about the first totally credible Grand Slam by Rod Laver in 1969 (he had become the second man after Budge to win a Grand Slam when he was an amateur in 1962). A year later Laver's fellow-Australian Margaret Court became the second woman (after Maureen Connolly in 1953) to complete the feat. The Grand Prix circuit for men, another of Jack Kramer's ideas, began in 1970. But 'open' tennis didn't end the political troubles.

In 1971 the Texan oil millionaire Lamar Hunt organised his World Championship Tennis circuit which was not sanctioned by the ILTF, and the top players Hunt had signed up missed the 1972 French and Wimbledon championships.

And in 1973, shortly after the formation of the first players' union, the Association of Tennis Professionals, 79 of the top players boycotted Wimbledon over the banning of Nikki Pilic, who was not allowed to compete at Wimbledon because he had not played Davis Cup for Yugoslavia when asked.

There have been other developments in the modern history of tennis whose true significance can't yet be assessed but which nevertheless warrant a mention. The growth of the women's game led initially by Billie-Jean King and continued in stateswoman-like fashion by Chris Evert and Martina Navratilova. The advent of the tiebreak in 1970 which gained universal acceptance within 20 years. The breakaway founding of the ATP Tour in 1989. And even the ILTF's dropping of the word 'Lawn' from its name in 1977, thereby effectively confirming that lawn tennis had become the legitimate successor to the earlier forms of tennis.

2. TODAY'S PROFESSIONAL TENNIS TOUR

Tennis in the first decade of the third millennium is a highly organised, ultra commercialised sporting circus taking in thousands of tournaments covering 52 weeks of the year. Though not as diffuse as boxing with all its world championship authorities, the global tennis circuit nevertheless has four authorities running the game: the ITF, the ATP, the WTA Tour, and the Grand Slam Committee. In recent years the level of cooperation among them has increased, and there is sporadic talk of them uniting to nominate a 'tennis commissioner' to run the sport.

THE GRAND SLAM

The Grand Slam is the term used to denote the four major tournaments around which the tennis year evolves and which tend to provide greatest motivation to the top players: the Australian Open, les Internationaux de France (French Open or Roland Garros), Wimbledon and the US Open.

The term came into use in tennis thanks to one of the leading tennis journalists of the 20th century, the New York Times' correspondent Allison Danzig. In 1938, as Donald Budge closed in on becoming the first player – man or woman – to win all four major titles in a calendar year, Danzig turned to the terminology of the card game Bridge to describe Budge's impending achievement as 'a Grand Slam in tennis'.

Since then, the four events have become known as Grand Slam tournaments, or in tennis slang as 'Slams', though purists could argue that the events themselves are just the majors, with only the achievement of winning all four deserving of the term Grand Slam. Nevertheless, officials of the four events liaise closely through the Grand Slam Committee, and the name was given to the Compaq Grand Slam Cup (see Drop Shot), a controversial 1990s tournament for men in which entry was reserved for the 16 players who had performed best at the year's four majors (a smaller version of the event was held in 1998 and 99 for women).

It is generally accepted among tennis connoisseurs that a pure Grand Slam has to involve winning the four events in the same year. By that criterion, only two men and three women have achieved it: Donald Budge (1938), Rod Laver (1962 & 69), Maureen Connolly (1953), Margaret Court (1970), and Steffi Graf (1988).

In the 1980s the International Tennis Federation offered a $1 million financial bonus for winning four titles in succession, a bonus claimed by Martina Navratilova, who won six in a row from the 1983 Wimbledon to the 1994 US Open.

DROP *SHOTS!*

The memory of the Compaq Grand Slam Cup (1990-99) stands as testimony to the way the ATP Tour and the Grand Slam tournaments fell out in a big way. When the Association of Tennis Professionals turned themselves into the ATP Tour, it changed the year-ending Masters tournament into the ATP Tour World Championship. Yet the four Slams staged their own rival year-ending event, the Grand Slam Cup.

Most players might have turned their back on it had it not been for $6 million prize money to be shared between 16 players and two reserves. And the fact that $2 million of the cup's profits went to tennis development meant the cup understandably claimed some moral high ground.

The ATP Tour's rejection of the cup went as far as to not include results from it in head-to-head data for the first eight years, and there was never any question of Grand Slam Cup matches earning a player ranking points.

Yet in 2000 common sense prevailed, the two events were merged into the Tennis Masters Cup (which does give ranking points), and as if to prove that this should have happened 10 years earlier, the first Tennis Masters Cup in Lisbon achieved something fitting for the event which neither the ATP Tour World Championship nor the Compaq Grand Slam Cup had ever managed – the year's four Grand Slam singles champions becoming the four semi-finalists (Agassi, Kuerten, Sampras and Safin).

Right: Allison Danzig

Far right: Don Budge

But the fact that she never won all four in the same year means technically she never achieved the feat (though she did win three women's doubles Grand Slams with Pam Shriver, 1984-85 and 87). The term 'Career Grand Slam' is used for players, like Andre Agassi, who win all four during their career, and when Steffi Graf won her Grand Slam and topped it by winning the 1988 Olympic gold medal for singles, many referred to it as the 'Golden Slam'.

ATP

The ATP runs the top two levels of the men's professional set-up: the ATP tour and the Challenger circuit. It obviously liaises with the one major tier above it, the four Grand Slam tournaments, and the Satellite and Futures circuits below it which are run by the ITF.

The ATP in its current incarnation has existed since 1990 (it was known as the 'ATP Tour' for its first 11 years) though the term 'ATP' goes back to 1972. The Association of Tennis Professionals was the original male tennis players' trade union founded in 1972 at the height of conflict between the traditional top-level tournaments and the rebel World Championship Tennis circuit run by the Texan oil millionaire Lamar Hunt.

For the first 19 years of its existence the men's Grand Prix circuit was run by the Men's International Professional Tennis Council (MIPTC), a committee of nine made up of three players, three tournament representatives and three representatives from the ITF.

But in 1989, frustrated at a perceived inability of the sport's authorities to improve prize money and expand the men's circuit, the ATP launched its own tour, which came into existence at the start of 1990. Its launch was highly theatrical, an impromptu announcement by Hamilton Jordan – the ATP Tour's first chief executive officer who had run Jimmy Carter's successful US presidential election campaign in 1976 – in the car park of the US Open at Flushing Meadows because the US Tennis Association had refused to make a room available indoors.

The Association of Tennis Professionals thus became the 'ATP Tour' in 1990; in 2001 it returned to the name 'ATP' but still as a tour body. In 1990 it turned the year-ending Masters tournament, which had been born with the Grand Prix in 1970, into the ATP Tour World Championship and moved it from Madison Square Garden in New York to Germany, first Frankfurt (1990-95) and then Hannover (1996-99).

Though it was called a world championship, it was probably the only one not to call its winner 'world champion'. The event is now the Tennis Masters Cup (see Drop Shots) and changes its venue every year.

In 2000 the ATP Tour was made up of 69 events on the full tour, and 122 Challenger events. The most prestigious events are the nine Tennis Masters Series tournaments, formerly known as the 'Super Nine' – Indian Wells, Miami/Key Biscayne (formerly known as 'The Lipton', now officially the 'Ericsson Open'), Monte Carlo, Rome, Hamburg, Toronto/Montreal, Cincinatti, Stuttgart and Paris.

Many of these tournaments are today's incarnation of some of the most traditional events in the sport – for example, the Monte Carlo Open, German Open and Italian Open, which used to form the build-up to the French Open, are now part of the Tennis Masters Series and are known officially just as TMS – Monte Carlo, TMS – Hamburg, and TMS – Roma.

At the start of 2000 the ATP introduced a new ranking system (see page 28) to make the most important events count for more.

ATP
Headquarters:
201 ATP Tour Boulevard
Ponte Vedra Beach
Florida 32082
USA
Telephone: +1 904 285 8000
Fax: +1 904 285 5966
Website: www.atptennis.com

**MARGARET COURT'S FIRST
GRAND SLAM COINCIDED WITH
THE BREAK-UP OF THE BEATLES
AND THE INTRODUCTION OF
COMPUTER FLOPPY DISKS**

The men's end-of-year championship, the Tennis Masters Cup, is no longer owned solely by the ATP but jointly with the ITF and the four Grand Slam tournaments though it maintains the format of the old ATP Tour World Championship in which eight players play three matches each in round robin format before semi-finals and a final.

In 1999, 248 players earned $50,000 or more in prize money. The original ATP players' union is now a sub-section of the ATP known as the ATP Player Council.

WTA TOUR

The WTA Tour – currently the Sanex WTA Tour thanks to a sponsorship deal with the skin care and beauty products company that runs from 2000 to 2004 – administers the top level of the women's professional circuit. Like the ATP it liaises with the one major tier above it, the four Grand Slam tournaments, and the Satellite and Futures circuits below it which are run by the ITF.

The Sanex WTA Tour in its current form began at the start of 1995 when the Women's Tennis Council (up to then the administrators of the women's tour) and the Women's Tennis Association (which represented the players) merged to form the WTA Tour.

The Women's Tennis Association pre-dated the Association of Tennis Professionals by two years. After many years of women's tennis being treated as a very poor relation to the men, a rebellion took place in 1970 which led to the formation of the WTA.

*Above: Gladys Heldman –
effectively the founder of the
women's professional circuit*

Resentment was running high when Margaret Court, in completing the Grand Slam at the 1970 US Open, picked up just a third of the prize money that the men's champion Ken Rosewall collected. Additional disgust on the part of Billie-Jean King and Rosie Casals at the way they were being treated by tournament officials failed to cool tempers, and when the prize money disparity at the Pacific Southwest Championships in Los Angeles in September 1970 favoured the men by a ratio of 8:1 ($12,500 to $1,500) the rebellion happened.

**WTA
Headquarters:
1266 East Main Street
Stamford
Connecticut 06902-3546
USA**
*Telephone: +1 203 978 1740
Fax: +1 203 978 1702
Website: www.sanexwta.com*

The publisher of 'World Tennis' magazine Gladys Heldman signed up nine of the top women players for a token one dollar and set up an alternative women's circuit – the nine were King, Casals, Peaches Bartkowicz, Mary Ann Curtis, Judy Dalton, Nancy Richey, Kerry Melville, Valerie Ziegenfuss and Heldman's daughter Julie Heldman. Although the nine were initially barred from the traditional circuit (including the four majors), they were soon reinstated as it became clear the WTA had a tour that was not going to go away.

Court's prize money for winning the 1970 US Open had been $3,000; by 1973 it was $25,000, and the 2001 champion Venus Williams picked up $850,000 (same as the men's champion).

In that time women's tennis has been boosted by a handful of names who have become known well beyond the boundaries of tennis, notably King, Chris Evert, Martina Navratilova, Steffi Graf, Monica Seles, and now a new generation headed by Venus and Serena Williams, Martina Hingis, Lindsay Davenport, and the magnetically marketable but so far much less successful Anna Kournikova.

In 1995 the WTA transformed itself into the WTA Tour, with the original players' union becoming the WTA Tour Players' Association.

In 2001 it ran 62 of its own tournaments, split into five tiers and the year-ending championships. Of the five tiers, the top consists of the nine events offering more than $1 million in prize money: Tokyo (indoor), Indian Wells, Miami/Key Biscayne, Berlin, Rome, Montreal/Toronto, Moscow, and Zürich. The year concludes with the WTA Tour Championships, which up to the end of 2000 were held at Madison Square Garden, New York, and from October 2001 moved to the Olympiahalle, Munich. The WTA Tour started out as the 'Virginia Slims Circuit' under an extension of women's tennis' long-standing sponsorship by companies owned by Philip Morris, and later became the 'Kraft Tour'.

It has since had two principal sponsors: the computer company Corel (1995-98) and Sanex (2000-04).

QUIET PLEASE!

*"She's a great player, for a gal.
But no woman can beat a male player who knows what he's doing.
I'll put Billie Jean and all the other Women's Libbers
back where they belong – in the kitchen and the bedroom"*

BOBBY RIGGS 1918-1995

Hall of Fame page 126

Quoted in 1973 before the match with King

INTERNATIONAL
TENNIS FEDERATION

The ITF is the world governing body of tennis, the umbrella organisation for 198 national tennis associations which looks after everything from the rules and court specifications to the development of tennis in the third world.

1 9 7 3

THE INTRODUCTION OF
COMPUTER RANKINGS
HAPPENED AS THE USA
WITHDREW ITS ARMED FORCES
FROM VIETNAM

In the years before the first world war, the increasing worldwide popularity of lawn tennis made national associations feel they should cooperate globally to ensure the sport was uniformly structured. A conference was held in Paris in 1913, at which the International Lawn Tennis Federation was founded.

Above: Philippe Chatrier –
possibly the most influential
president the International Tennis
Federation has ever known and
the man who started the ITF's
development programme, pictured
with Steffi Graf

The 13 founder members were: Australasia (Australia & New Zealand), Austria, Belgium, Denmark, France, Germany, the British Isles, the Netherlands, Russia, South Africa, Spain, Sweden and Switzerland. The official ILTF rules of tennis were not drawn up until 1923 and came into effect in January 1924, though they were essentially a confirmation of Wingfield's rules from the 1870s. The ILTF found itself in the middle of much of the controversy surrounding the separate amateur and professional circuits in the 23 years after the second world war, and had the narrow vote at its 1960 annual meeting gone in favour of allowing professionals to compete at ILTF events, the 'open era' of tennis would have begun eight years earlier than it did.

ITF
Headquarters:
Bank Lane
Roehampton
London SW15 5XZ
England
Telephone: +44 20 8878 6464
Fax: +44 20 8878 7799
Website: www.itftennis.com

Even after the circuits merged in 1968 the ILTF had its hands full, first with the breakaway women's circuit organised by Gladys Heldman in 1970, then with World Championship Tennis in 1971-72, and most publicly with the boycott of Wimbledon over Nikki Pilic's refusal to play Davis Cup in 1973.

In 1976 it embarked on its development programme to introduce and nurture tennis in third world nations, a programme boosted by the sponsorship of the Davis Cup in 1981; and it shepherded tennis back into the Olympic Games in 1984, firstly as a demonstration event, then in 1988 as a full medal sport after a 64-year absence. It dropped the word 'Lawn' from its name in 1977 to become the ITF.

The ITF has roles in five areas of the sport:

• **Administering and regulating tennis –** *the ITF is responsible for the rules of tennis, (page 134) including the technical specifications for courts and equipment. It also liaises with the ATP and WTA Tour to agree calendar dates, and it runs the sport's anti-doping programme.*

• **Organising international competitions –** *it controls the major international team events for all age groups and for wheelchair tennis, including the two largest annual team sports events in the world, the Davis Cup and Fed Cup. It also runs the Olympic tennis event.*

• **Structuring tennis through international circuits** – *this includes running the junior world ranking circuit, the men's and women's Satellite and Futures circuits (the professional levels below ATP/Challenger and WTA Tour levels), veterans events, and the wheelchair tennis tour.*

• **Developing tennis** – *managing the Grand Slam Development Fund around the world, which includes regional junior training centres and competitions like the African Junior Championships, the oldest 'development event' which dates from 1976.*

• **Promoting tennis** – *the ITF markets tennis through television, public relations activities, event management, and sponsorship.*

The ITF's anti-doping programme has to a large extent kept tennis free from accusations of drug abuse among the top players, with generally only a handful of cases of social drug abuse coming to light (the fact that tennis involves not just strength and endurance but also tactics, technique and adaptability to surfaces means there is less scope for performance-enhancing drugs to make a massive difference to a player's ability than in some other sports). The breadth of the anti-doping programme includes drugs tests at and outside tournaments, the imposition of penalties for doping offences, and providing support and assistance to players when applicable.

Notable players to test positive in recent years include two Grand Slam title winners, Mats Wilander (for a social drug) and Petr Korda (for an illegal substance to reduce the effects of an injury). In both cases it proved the end of their top-level playing careers.

Wheelchair tennis has been part of the ITF's remit since the mid-1990s (see page 92). It is the only form of tennis for disabled people that the ITF presides over, though some national associations supervise tennis for people with other disabilities (for example, the British LTA runs tennis for deaf people).

There are six regional associations which represent groups of countries and are semi-autonomous from the ITF but work in some areas as in-between agencies between the ITF and national associations. Their areas of competence include organising junior and veterans' events – sometimes with different eligibility rules than those of the ITF – and coach education.

The six are:
Asian Tennis Federation (ATF)
Confederation of African Tennis (CAT)
Confederacion de Tenis de Centroamerica Caribe (Central America and Caribbean, Cotecc)
Tennis Europe (until recently ETA)
Confederacion Sudamericana de Tenis (South America, Cosat)
Oceania Tennis Federation (OTF)

Details are listed under Associations, page 162.

Above: Presidential approval – the wheelchair tennis world champions are always honoured at the annual ITF champions dinner in Paris; ITF president Francesco Ricci Bitti with Esther Vergeer of the Netherlands at the 2001 dinner

THE GRAND SLAM COMMITTEE

An informal gathering of representatives of the staff and committees of the four Grand Slam tournaments, plus representation from the ITF. It normally consists of 10 representatives, two each from the four events, and two from the ITF.

It meets five times a year: at the four events and at the men's year-ending singles championship (now the Tennis Masters Cup). It generally acts as a forum for the exchange of information among the four tournaments, and generates a sense of solidarity which means it is very rare for one Grand Slam event to take a decision which adversely affects another.

Pete Sampras v Jim Courier Australian Open Quarter-Final 1995

Perhaps the most dramatic match in the Australian Open's history took place between 9pm and 1am one Tuesday night, 24 January 1995.

The top seed Sampras renewed his rivalry with Courier, his predecessor as world No1, having just learned that his coach and friend Tim Gullikson had been diagnosed with a brain tumour and given only months to live (the crowd knew Gullikson had returned to America for tests but knew neither diagnosis nor prognosis).

With the quality of tennis superb, Courier took the first two sets on the tiebreak. Sampras sneaked a break early in the third, which allowed him to take that set, but with Courier leading 4-2 in the fourth Sampras looked beaten. But then Courier tightened, Sampras reeled off four games on the run and levelled the match. In the first game of the fifth set, a spectator shouted "Do it for your coach, Pete," at which point Sampras burst into tears.

The drama was heightened when Courier, who was beginning to get cramp and wanted to relieve the tension of the moment, shouted across the net to Sampras: "I'm not feeling too good myself, how about we come back and finish this tomorrow?"

Sampras played the whole of the final set with tears streaming down his face, but in a superb effort that showed the human side to this very private man, he captured an incredible victory 6-7 6-7 6-3 6-4 6-3.

Right: Boris Becker with the 1996 Australian Open title

THE GRAND SLAM TOURNAMENTS

The four members of tennis' elite series of tournaments have always been the championships of Australia, France, England and the USA, though the tournaments have changed in character, name (notably after the 'open era' began in 1968), and facilities. In the 1980s tentative attempts were made to strip the Australian Open of its Grand Slam status and replace it with the International Players tournament in Key Biscayne (now the Ericsson Open), but the Australian Open had begun a revival after a slump in prestige, and the moves came to nothing.

AUSTRALIAN OPEN

The youngest of the four majors, the Australian Open is enjoying a renewal of fortunes following a period sometimes referred to as the dark ages which ran from the early 1970s to the mid 1980s.

It started in 1905 as the Australasian National Championships (in 1906 and 1912 they were held in New Zealand; women were admitted from 1922), and the championships alternated between five grasscourt venues: the Kooyong Club in Melbourne, White City in Sydney, Milton Ground in Brisbane, Memorial Drive in Adelaide, and King's Park in Perth, before settling on Kooyong in 1972.

Decreasing attendances followed the reluctance of many of the top players to travel to Australia in the 1970s and early 80s, and the tournament became the first of the majors to have a title sponsor (Marlboro cigarettes 1974-84, Ford motor company 1985-97). A move in the tournament's date from January to December to avoid a clash with the year-ending Masters tournament resulted in two Australian Opens in 1977, but it was moved back to January in 1987 (meaning no event during 1986).

The dark ages ended with the decision to leave Kooyong and move to a purpose-built National Tennis Centre closer to the Melbourne city centre, which has hosted the Open since 1988. That meant a move away from grass to the rubberised hardcourt Rebound Ace.

The tournament is run by the Australian tennis association Tennis Australia, but despite the country's great tennis tradition home winners have been thin in the 'open' era. Mark Edmonson was the last Australian men's singles winner in 1976, Chris O'Neil the last woman in 1978, both coming through depleted international fields.

The men play for the Norman Brookes Challenge Cup, the women for the Daphne Akhurst Memorial Cup.

Official website: **www.ausopen.org**

FRENCH OPEN

The French national championships were just that – national only – until 1925, when entry was opened up to players not affiliated to French clubs. Today the tournament is known as 'Les Internationaux de France', but is referred to in the English-speaking world as the French Open, even if the French Tennis Federation (FFT) tends to like it known more as 'Roland Garros' for marketing purposes. It is run by the FFT, whose headquarters are at the stadium and tennis centre complex known as the Stade Roland Garros.

The men's championships began in 1891, the women's in 1897. The tournament was given a new lease of life in the late 1970s under the FFT presidency of Philippe Chatrier, who later became a highly influential president of the ITF.

Since the era of the four French 'Musketeers' who dominated world tennis in the late 1920s and early 30s (Borotra, Brugnon, Cochet and Lacoste), only two French men have won at Roland Garros: Marcel Bernard in 1946, and Yannick Noah who gave the stadium its most ecstatic moment in 1983.

Five French women have won the Paris title since 1925: Suzanne Lenglen, Simone Mathieu, Nelly Landry, Françoise Durr, and Mary Pierce. The men play for the Coupe des Mousquetaires (Musketeers cup), while the women play for the Coupe Suzanne Lenglen (though Lenglen never played at the Roland Garros stadium).

Official website: **www.rolandgarros.com**

WIMBLEDON

The first of the four championships, it began in 1877, with the first women's championships in 1884. It has always been played on grass in Wimbledon, the SW19 postal district of London, though the championships didn't move to their current site until 1922.

As well as playing a major part in the early history of lawn tennis, Wimbledon was the leading activist in bringing the amateur and professional circuits together in 1968 by declaring that it would admit professionals to the 1968 championships, even if the ILTF refused to authorise it (the ILTF eventually backed down and 'open' tennis began).

It is run by the All England Lawn Tennis and Croquet Club for the British tennis authority, the Lawn Tennis Association. It has not had a British singles winner since Virginia Wade in 1977, and the last British men's winner was Fred Perry in 1936. Though it guards many of its traditions fiercely, like the grass courts and the rule that players can only play in 'predominantly white' tennis clothing, it has moved with the times and is still arguably the most prestigious of the four majors among players from all but the most clay-court-dominated of countries.

The tournament is officially called the All England Lawn Tennis Championships, but the All England Club markets the event under 'Wimbledon' and 'The Championships'.

Official website: **www.wimbledon.org**

1979

MOTHER THERESA WAS GIVEN THE NOBEL PEACE PRIZE AND SONY INTRODUCED THE WALKMAN THE YEAR WORLD TEAM TENNIS COLLAPSED

Left: French ecstasy – June 1993, Yannick Noah becomes the first Frenchman to win the French title since Marcel Bernard in 1946

Above: Wimbledon in the 1930s – a heyday for the centre court in the era of Fred Perry, Bunny Austin and Don Budge (pictured)

US OPEN

The US national championships began in 1881 (first women's event in 1887), and became the US Open in 1968. From 1915 to 1977 it was played at the West Side Lawn Tennis Club in Forest Hills, a private club in the Queens district of New York. Up to 1974 it was played on grass, but for the 1975 event the club switched the surface to American clay.

However, in 1977 the US Tennis Association (USTA) began construction of a new National Tennis Center on the site of the 1964 World Trade Fair just outside Flushing, also in Queens. The US Open moved there in 1978, becoming a hardcourt tournament. The changes allowed one of the most charismatic figures in the tournament's history, Jimmy Connors, to win on all three surfaces. American winners of the US Open are much less rare than home winners of the other three Slams.

The tournament is run by the USTA, whose headquarters are also in New York state but not at Flushing Meadows (see page 169).

Unlike the Australian, French and Wimbledon, it did not have breaks for the first and second world wars, and unlike the other three it does have tiebreaks in final sets.

Official website: **www.usopen.org**

THE DAVIS CUP

The Davis Cup is the premier team competition in tennis. It is played annually, the winner being decided in a final which currently marks the end of the tennis year at the highest level. It is for men only – the women's equivalent is the Fed Cup.

Dwight Filley Davis (1879-1945) was a Harvard University student, who loved tennis and played it to a high level. In 1899 he persuaded the United States National Lawn Tennis Association to invite some of the best players in the British Isles to cross the Atlantic for a challenge match. That match took place at the Longwood Cricket Club in Boston in 1990, and Davis got a Briton, Rowland Rhodes, who worked for a New England silver company, to make a cup which he named the 'International Lawn Tennis Challenge Trophy'.

It is still officially called that, but no-one refers to it as anything other than the Davis Cup. Davis later carved out a career for himself in politics; his most notable achievement was as governor-general of the Philippines (1929-31) from where there came tales that he played tennis with Filipinos as a way of breaking down barriers.

HISTORY OF THE COMPETITION

The Americans and British contested the first three Davis Cups (1900, 1902 and 1903), but in 1904 France and Belgium came in, in 1905 the southern hemisphere was represented through Australasia, and the competition has grown steadily since then. A total of 143 nations entered the 2001 competition, the full members of the ITF – around 25% of the ITF's affiliate countries are associate members, generally developing countries with poor tennis infrastructure and players of insufficient calibre to compete in the Davis Cup (see page 170).

Until 1974, only the big four Grand Slam nations had won the cup, but since then six more have been champions: South Africa, Sweden, Italy, Czechoslovakia, (West) Germany and Spain.

The USA has won the cup 31 times in the 90 stagings of it (up to the end of 2001), Australia 27 times, and Great Britain and France 9 each.

There are many notable dates in the history of the Davis Cup, but 1972 and 1981 are probably the most significant. Up to 1972, the holders gained automatic entry into the Challenge Round (today's final), but a knockout system was introduced in 1972.

QUIET PLEASE!

*"Ask Nureyev to stop dancing,
ask Sinatra to stop singing -
then you can ask me to stop playing tennis"*

BILLIE JEAN KING
Hall of Fame page 121

This was further refined for the start of the 1981 competition, the year the Davis Cup took on its current format.

The World Group was established in 1981, which meant a country had to start the year in the 16-nation elite group in order to win the cup that year. 1981 also saw the start of a 22-year sponsorship deal with the Japanese electronics giant NEC, which not only ensured the continued growth of the Davis Cup but also provided a source of money for the development of tennis in the third world. NEC's title sponsorship stopped at the end of 2001, succeeded by the Paris-based bank BNP Paribas. The tiebreak was introduced to Davis Cup in 1989.

FORMAT

The Davis Cup is administered by the International Tennis Federation. The World Group is a 16-team knockout competition played over four weekends. The World Group is fed by regional zones in Europe/Africa, the Americas and Asia/Oceania, which have three levels. It therefore takes a nation at the bottom level of the Davis Cup structure a minimum of three years to reach the World Group and thus be in a position to win the cup. There are matches within the groups at the start of the year, and then inter-group matches to determine promotion and relegation.

In theory it is possible for no team to be promoted or relegated from any division in a given year, though this is highly unlikely to happen as it would involve a highly specific series of results allied to a draw for the qualifying round which would pit all existing World Group teams against nations from lower divisions.

Each team must name four players, though only two need play. A tie is played over three days: two singles on the opening day (one team's first player against the other team's second, and vice versa), a doubles on the second day, and the reverse singles on the third day (generally the two top players against each other, followed by the two second players against each other).

Each live match – or 'rubber' – is the best of five sets, with a tiebreak in the first four; matches played on the third day when the overall outcome is clear are called 'dead rubbers' and are best-of-three sets with tiebreaks in all three. The home team chooses the venue, surface and balls for a tie, subject to approval from the ITF.

Home advantage works on an alternating basis, in that when two teams are drawn to face each other they play in the country which was away the last time the same two countries played each other. In the few cases where two teams have never played each other, or not since 1970, home advantage is drawn out of a hat (the reason for the 1970 cut-off is that prior to then there were many matches played on neutral territory, and not all records of teams which did play home/away before 1970 are reliable).

Some rule changing is occasionally applied to the bottom divisions to see whether ideas being considered are viable or not. Recent examples of this include trying out the 'no ad' rule (at deuce the player to win the next point wins the game with the receiver choosing which side of the court their opponent serves from) and the 'no let' rule (a serve touching the net and going in is not retaken).

There is an additional rule under which a home team can be deducted one point at a time if its supporters are considered by a tie's referee to have overstepped the mark of legitimate support.

Above: The Spanish and Australian teams meet for the draw for the 2000 Davis Cup final in the majestic city hall of Barcelona; from left Juan Balcells, Alex Corretja, Juan-Carlos Ferrero, Albert Costa, Javier Duarte, John Newcombe, Lleyton Hewitt, Patrick Rafter, Sandon Stolle, Mark Woodforde

Above: The Davis Cup – the cup itself was the one commissioned by Dwight Davis; the three plinths have been added since to record the names of the winning nations

MAUREEN CONNOLLY WON
THE FIRST WOMEN'S GRAND
SLAM IN THE YEAR MARSHAL
TITO BECAME PRESIDENT OF
YUGOSLAVIA, JOSEF STALIN DIED
AND DNA WAS DISCOVERED

FED CUP

The Fed Cup is the premier team tennis event
for women. Founded in 1963 as the Federation
Cup to mark the 50th anniversary of the
International Lawn Tennis Federation, it was
widely known as the 'Fed Cup', and that became
its official name in 1994. In its 38-year history
it has attracted the best players in the women's
game, but with the exception of a few ties, it has
never caught on the way the Davis Cup has.

FORMAT

The ITF has changed the Fed Cup's format
several times over the last few years in an attempt
to get fans more interested. From 1992-99 it
featured the best eight nations competing in a
World Group. Until 1994 the event was held in a
single week in a round-robin format in a given
country, the last three years in Germany.

*Federation Cup's finest hour –
one of the great moments in the
premier women's team tennis
competition happened in 1986
when the ITF accepted
Czechoslovakia's bid to stage the
event in Prague on condition the
nation allow Martina Navratilova
to play – Navratilova returned to
a heroine's welcome 11 years after
defecting at the 1975 US Open,
and helped the US to win the cup*

*Below from left:
Marty Riessen (captain), Martina
Navratilova, Zina Garrison,
Chris Evert and Pam Shriver*

That was fine for fans of the home country, but
it meant only one of the eight teams was at home,
and if the home team wasn't doing well,
spectator interest dropped. So in 1996 a change
was made to give more teams home advantage.

The eight-nation World Group became a
knockout tournament of three rounds (quarter-
finals, semi-finals and final) played over three
separate weekends, with teams hosting the
visitors over the best of five rubbers (four singles
and a doubles) played over two days.

In 2000 the format changed again, expanding
the World Group to 13 nations: the reigning
champions plus 12 others. This involved the
12 challenger nations being divided into three
groups of four and playing a round-robin format
to decide which country would go through to the
four-nation final week. This meant only one
of the four nations was at home, and spectator
interest levels didn't improve.

So in 2001 the format changed again, with
the World Group expanding to 16 nations.
Eight teams played the four first round ties over
a given weekend with four teams having home
advantage. Then the four winners played second
round ties against four nations who had byes in
the first round (also over one weekend with four
of the teams enjoying home advantage).

Then the four winners (minus the USA which
pulled out citing security reasons) joined a further
four teams for the final week, which has an
identical format to the men's World Team Cup
(see facing page). All first and second round ties
are the best of five matches (four singles and a
doubles), and ties in the final week are over the
best of three matches (two singles and a doubles).
This format will remain largely unchanged for
2002. In 2001, Belgium won its first-ever Fed Cup
title.

In 2000 a record 102 nations took part in
the Fed Cup. Like with the Davis Cup, there are
regional qualifying matches. The regional
zones are: Europe/Africa, the Americas, and
Asia/Oceania.

OTHER TEAM COMPETITIONS

There are a handful of other team competitions, most of them run on a bilateral basis, but two are global:

The **World Team Cup**, currently sponsored by the German insurance company Arag, is run by the ATP and always held on the red clay courts of the Rochusclub in Düsseldorf, Germany, the week before Roland Garros. It involves eight teams divided into two groups of four; each team plays the other three in their group over three matches (two singles and a doubles), with the two group winners playing the final.

It has often attracted some of the top men in the sport, because it guarantees players three matches in the week before the sole Grand Slam tournament on clay. Spain were the first winners in 1978.

The **Hopman Cup** began in December 1988 as a private initiative by Paul McNamee, the former Australian Grand Slam doubles champion who is now tournament director of the Australian Open, but in 1996 it became an official tournament under the ITF's auspices. It is a mixed men's/women's competition following a similar format to the World Team Cup, the main difference being that the two singles matches are one women's and one men's, and the doubles is a mixed doubles involving the two singles players. It is always played in Perth, Western Australia, during the week which includes New Year, as a curtain-raiser to the new tennis year.

Among the many team competitions that no longer exist, the **King's Cup** and **Wightman Cup** are the two with the longest history. The King's Cup started when in 1936 king Gustav V of Sweden donated the cup for an indoor equivalent of the Davis Cup. But it never went beyond a European team competition, and by the mid 1980s few countries were selecting their best players. In 1986 it was renamed the European Cup, but while it is still held at the end of the year, it is now used as an event to give representative experience to younger players.

The Wightman Cup ran from 1923 to 1989 and involved a seven-rubber match between women's teams nominated by Great Britain and the USA. It eventually disappeared because of the disparity of strength between the two nations, and attempts to resurrect it in the style of golf's Ryder Cup by making it a Europe v America match came to nothing.

Above: The Burswood Dome in Perth, home of the Hopman Cup

A number of team tennis leagues go back many years, probably the most successful being the German **Bundesliga** (run by the German Tennis Federation, see page 165), which still attracts players from the world's top 100 for its brief season in the European summer.

The most high-profile attempt at a team tennis league came in the 1970s, when a company called **World Team Tennis** signed up many of the world's top players for a league based around America's top cities. Its season ran for nearly four months with a three-week break for Wimbledon (thereby depriving the French Open of many star names), the scoring system was simplified, the courts were marked with coloured squares instead of lines, and spectators were encouraged to cheer and shout during points. It ran for six seasons (1974-79) before going bankrupt, and subsequent attempts to recreate team tennis have been successful only at a more minor level.

RANKINGS & TOURNAMENT ENTRY

The Association of Tennis Professionals introduced computer-generated rankings in 1973 in an attempt to create a fair system to decide which players could play in which tournaments.

Until then the only rankings in existence tended to involve a committee of tennis watchers subjectively choosing a top batch of players for a given year.

Those top players had no problem getting into tournaments, but for most of the rest it was frequently a lottery, and in some cases players who were liked by tournament directors got into an event at the expense of players who were arguably better but less popular. Since 1973, the ranking systems used in the men's and women's games have undergone changes, and the debates still rage over whether all a player's results should count towards a ranking (as opposed to just the best 14 or 18 tournaments), whether seedings for a tournament should be dictated strictly by rankings, and even whether rankings should be published.

RANKINGS

The men's rankings underwent a major change at the start of 2000. The name 'ranking' was dropped to make way for two lists, known as the Entry System and the ATP Champions Race.

The Entry System is similar to the old ranking system, in that it serves the purpose of seeing which players are eligible for tournaments, and which players should be seeded.

A player earns Entry System points based on his results, and then keeps those points for 52 weeks. That is fine in terms of working out eligibility for tournaments, but the 52-week rule means the Entry System has a built-in capacity for a player who wins a tournament to drop down a few places the following week (especially if he did well at the same tournament the previous year) and for a player who just wins a couple of rounds to move up (if he missed or did badly at the same tournament the previous year).

Concern that this feature was confusing spectators and thus discrediting the rankings led to the introduction of the second classification, the ATP Champions Race. This is like a league table, where only a player's results in a given calendar year count (in other words everyone starts with no points at the start of the year).

The women's rankings work like the men's Entry System: on a rolling 52-week basis. Whereas the men effectively operate a 'best of 18' system in which players competing in more than 18 tournaments a year are allowed to ignore their worst showings at tournaments, the women have a 'best of 17' rule – but the women can ignore any bad result, while the men can only drop results from tournaments outside the Slams and Masters Series.

The women also get bonus points if they beat an opponent ranked inside the top 500, a system abandoned by the men after 1999. The Sanex WTA Tour runs a league system which up to the end of 2000 it called 'The Race to the Chase', but this was publicised more as a qualification table for the year-ending Chase Championships than as a players' league championship.

TOURNAMENT ENTRY

A player can enter a tournament one of three ways: through their ranking being high enough for direct acceptance six weeks before the tournament (a cut-off date established to give people time to plan schedules), through the qualifying tournament, or as a wildcard.

Tournaments with 32 players in the singles draw tend to have 25 places for direct acceptance, 4 qualifying places, and 3 wildcards, while for the 128-draw Grand Slams the division tends to be 104 by direct acceptance, 16 qualifiers and 8 wildcards. So if a player's ranking is 104 or better six weeks before a Grand Slam tournament, he/she is guaranteed entry into that event, and allowing for a few withdrawals through injury and other reasons, most players ranked in the top 110 on the cut-off date get into the draw.

Right: Pete Sampras has spent longer as world No1 than any other male player

(The only case in which a player ranked 104 would not get into the main draw at a Slam would be if there were one or more players with 'protected rankings'. This is a system whereby if a player suffers a serious injury, on comeback he/she can qualify for entry to up to six tournaments at a ranking close to what he/she had when the injury occurred, so in theory there could be 106 players ranked in the top 104 for tournament entry purposes.)

Wildcards tend to go to players from the country where the tournament is taking place (to add home interest) or to big names whose ranking doesn't allow them direct acceptance (perhaps a charismatic figure, or a player returning from injury). Entry to qualifying tournaments is on a similar basis to the main draw, with the majority of players directly accepted on the basis of their ranking, plus a few wildcards.

SEEDINGS

Seeding is a way of ensuring that the top players don't play each other in the early rounds.

Just as a seed is planted in the earth in a way that will enable it to grow, a seeded player is 'planted' in a certain part of the draw for a tournament to give him/her the best chance to advance to the later rounds.

In a tournament with a 32-player draw, eight players are seeded. In a 64-player draw, 16 are seeded. In the 128-player Grand Slam singles draws, 16 players were seeded until the middle of 2001, but that has now changed to 32. The change came about when Wimbledon agreed to take the top 32 players from the 52-week rankings, and seed them according to performance on grass and other fast surfaces. The US Open followed with 32 seeds, and the Australian and French Opens will do the same in 2002 (though only Wimbledon will deviate from the rankings for the order in which it seeds the top 32 players).

So now every fourth player at a Slam is seeded. On the experience of two tournaments, it has made for better second weeks but fewer upsets in the first week.

No1 RANKINGS
Player and number of weeks.

MEN

Only twenty men players have attained the world No1 ranking since the men's computer rankings began in 1973.

Pete Sampras 286 weeks	
Ivan Lendl 270	
Jimmy Connors 268	
John McEnroe 170	
Björn Borg 109	
Andre Agassi 88	
Stefan Edberg 72	
Jim Courier 58	
Gustavo Kuerten 41	
Ilie Nastase 40	
Mats Wilander 20	
Boris Becker 12	
Marat Safin 9	
John Newcombe 8	
Lleyton Hewitt 7*	
Thomas Muster 6	
Marcelo Rios 6	
Yevgeny Kafelnikov 6	
Carlos Moya 2	
Patrick Rafter 1	

WOMEN

Only nine women players have attained the world No1 ranking since the women's computer rankings began in 1975.

Steffi Graf 377 weeks	
Martina Navratilova 331	
Chris Evert 262	
Martina Hingis 209	
Monica Seles 178	
Lindsay Davenport 37*	
Tracy Austin 22	
Arantxa Sanchez-Vicario 12	
Jennifer Capriati 3	

* No1 as of 31 December 2001

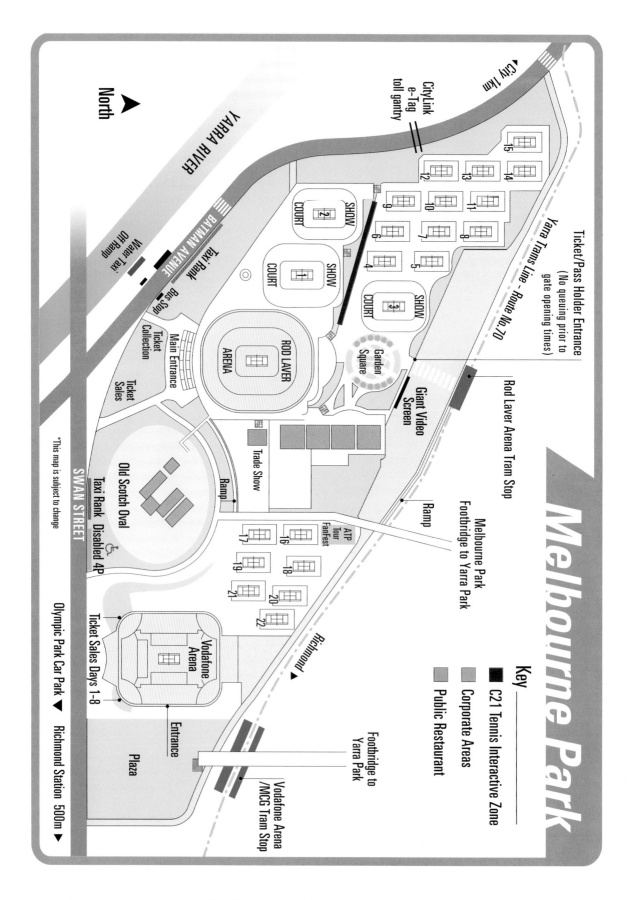

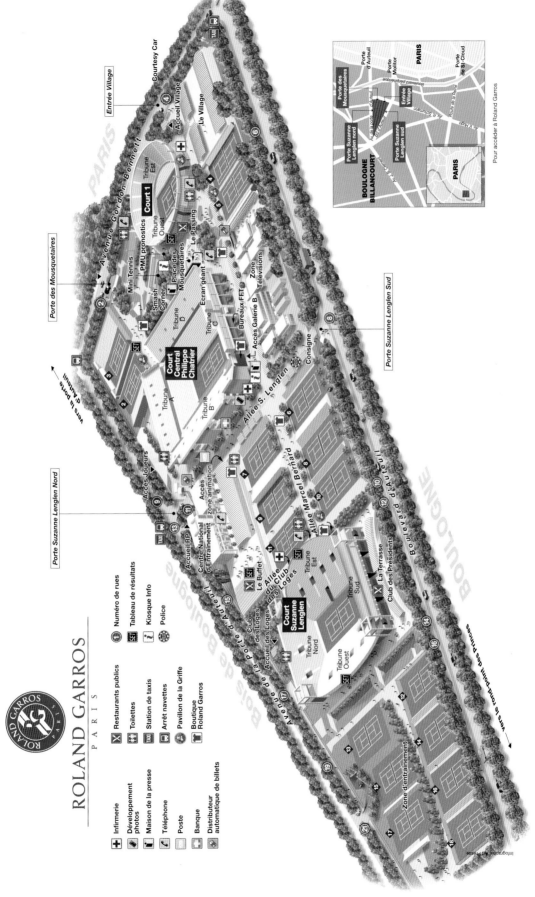

ROLAND GARROS
PARIS

Infirmerie
Développement photos
Maison de la presse
Téléphone
Poste
Banque
Distributeur automatique de billets

Restaurants publics
Toilettes
Station de taxis
Arrêt navettes
Pavillon de la Griffe
Boutique Roland Garros

Numéro de rues
Tableau de résultats
Kiosque Info
Police

Courtesy Car
Entrée Village
Accueil Village
Le Village
Avenue Gordon Bennett
PARIS
Porte des Mousquetaires
Tribune Est
Court 1
PMU pronostics
Tribune Ouest
Le Passing
Mini Tennis
Smash Corner
Place des Mousquetaires
Ecran géant
Zone Télévisions
Bureaux FFT
Vers la porte d'Auteuil
Tribune D
Tribune C
Accès Galerie B
Court Central Philippe Chatrier
Tribune A
Tribune B
Allée S. Lenglen
Consigne
Porte Suzanne Lenglen Sud
Accès Joueurs
Accès zone animation
Allée Marcel Bernard
Porte Suzanne Lenglen Nord
Accueil RP
Centre National d'Entraînement
Boulevard d'Auteuil
BOULOGNE
Le Buffet
Allée du Club des Loges
Tribune Est
Court Suzanne Lenglen
Tribune Sud
Club des Présidents
La Terrasse
Tribune Nord
Tribune Ouest
Avenue de la Porte d'Auteuil
Bois de Boulogne
Club des Loges
Accueil des Loges
Zone d'entraînement
Vers le Pont des Princes

Porte des Mousquetaires
Porte d'Auteuil
Porte Molitor
PARIS
Porte de St-Cloud
Porte Suzanne Lenglen nord
Entrée Village
Porte Suzanne Lenglen sud
BOULOGNE BILLANCOURT
PARIS
Pour accéder à Roland Garros

Infographie : 11 Presse

The *Book of Tennis* 31

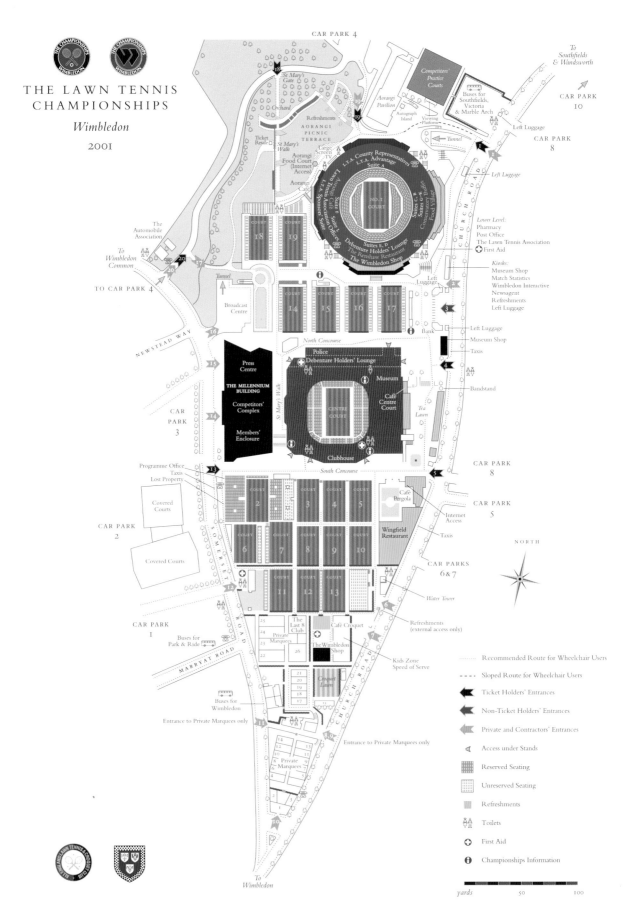

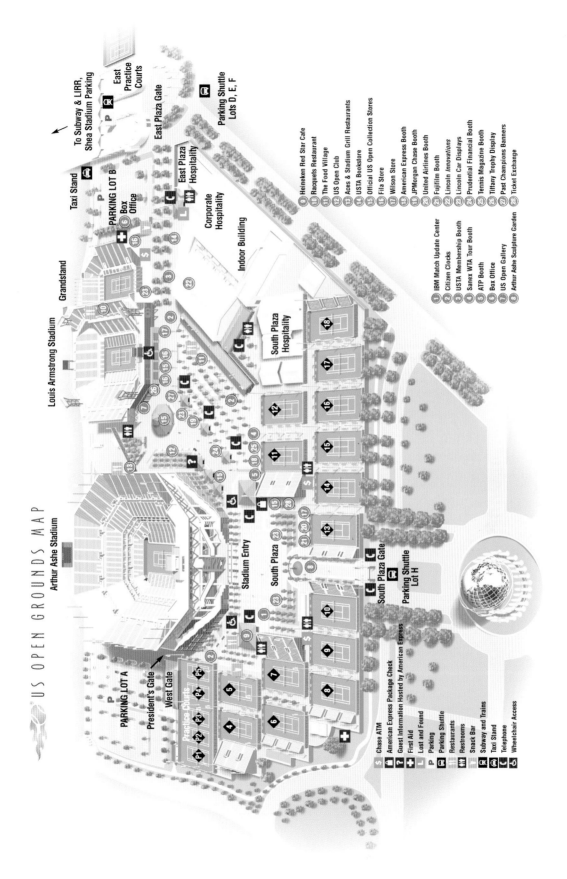

US OPEN GROUNDS MAP

Arthur Ashe Stadium

Louis Armstrong Stadium

Grandstand

Taxi Stand

To Subway & LIRR,
Shea Stadium Parking

East
Practice
Courts

East Plaza Gate

Parking Shuttle
Lots D, E, F

PARKING LOT B

Box
Office

East Plaza
Hospitality

Corporate
Hospitality

Indoor Building

South Plaza
Hospitality

South Plaza

Stadium Entry

Parking Shuttle
Lot H

PARKING LOT A

President's Gate

West Gate

Practice Courts

South Plaza Gate

- ⑤ Chase ATM
- ❓ American Express Package Check
- ❓ Guest Information Hosted by American Express
- ✚ First Aid
- Lost and Found
- P Parking
- Parking Shuttle
- Restaurants
- Restrooms
- Snack Bar
- Subway and Trains
- Taxi Stand
- Telephone
- ♿ Wheelchair Access

- ① IBM Match Update Center
- ② Citizen Clocks
- ③ USTA Membership Booth
- ④ Sanex WTA Tour Booth
- ⑤ ATP Booth
- ⑥ Box Office
- ⑦ US Open Gallery
- ⑧ Arthur Ashe Sculpture Garden

- ⑨ Heineken Red Star Cafe
- ⑩ Racquets Restaurant
- ⑪ The Food Village
- ⑫ US Open Club
- ⑬ Aces & Stadium Grill Restaurants
- ⑭ USTA Bookstore
- ⑮ Oficial US Open Collection Stores
- ⑯ Fila Store
- ⑰ Wilson Store
- ⑱ American Express Booth
- ⑲ JPMorgan Chase Booth
- ⑳ United Airlines Booth
- ㉑ Fujifilm Booth
- ㉒ Lincoln *Innovations*
- ㉓ Lincoln Car Displays
- ㉔ Prudential Financial Booth
- ㉕ Tennis Magazine Booth
- ㉖ Tiffany Trophy Display
- ㉗ Past Champions Banners
- ㉘ Ticket Exchange

Above: Basking in the sun – spectators in the Rod Laver Arena in Melbourne sitting in direct sunlight could do with a parasol, but as this picture shows, to have one would involve blocking the view of a number of other spectators, so sunhats and sunblock have to do the job

GOING TO A TOURNAMENT?

Going to watch a professional tennis tournament is a great experience, but if you've never done it, here are a few useful tips:

1. Take sunscreen and a sunhat with you if it's an outdoor tournament. If you're not sure you have a seat that is in the shade, take sunscreen with at least a protection factor 12, and in places like Australia and Florida take at least factor 15. A sunscreen with a protection factor of 15 will allow you to stay in the sun up to 15 times longer than you could without any protection. The sun can be vicious!

2. Take an umbrella, but not a large one. If the tournament is on clay, play can continue during light rain for more than an hour before the court gets too heavy, but if you have a large umbrella you won't be able to use it during play because it will either block someone else's view or invade their space. As a guide, look for one that when open is hardly wider than a normal sized chair (which is about 50 centimetres wide, or 20 inches).

3. If you're taking a picnic – which is often a good idea because food at tennis tournaments can be expensive – take your food and drink in a soft bag. Some tournaments, for example the Australian Open, ban cool boxes (known in Australia as 'eskies').

4. Some tournaments ban alcohol. If you don't know for certain that it's allowed, it's best not to take any.

5. If you're taking a camera which has an automatic flash, make sure you know how to turn it off. Umpires are always having to ask people not to use flash photography as it disturbs the players and other spectators.

6. The other thing umpires are always asking for is for people to turn off their mobile phones. Most tournaments ban use of mobiles in the stadiums, and tennis is supposed to be fun, not a different place for a telephone conference. If you really can't turn it off, then leave it at home!

7. It's OK to bring a radio if you're at a big tournament where there's radio coverage of lots of different courts. It's terribly frustrating to be sitting by one court and hearing the crowd at another court going ecstatic and you don't know what's happening. It's also acceptable to bring small portable televisions if you like to see instant replays or to see if the line call currently being disputed by one of the players is right or wrong. If you do bring a radio or TV, don't forget to bring headphones as not everyone around you will be keen to listen with you.

8. If it's an outdoor event in hot weather, bring lots to drink. Tournament medical staff have to treat dozens of people for sunstroke and dehydration. Water or certain isotonic sports drinks replace the electrolytes, potassium and sodium lost by perspiration. When you're watching tennis players drinking from bottles with funny coloured liquid in it, you can bet it is for just that purpose. Remember also that alcohol dehydrates.

9. Tennis is not good for non-humans, so bring an insect repellent, especially for outdoor tournaments in hot weather. Also leave any pets at home – you may have seen players like Arantxa Sanchez Vicario, Martina Navratilova, Monica Seles and Venus Williams bring their dogs to tournaments, but while they can get away with it (though maybe not for much longer) you won't be able to.

10. Always take The Book of Tennis with you – you're bound to want to refer to it!

3. COURTS & ARENAS

SURFACES

There are probably somewhere between 600,000 and 750,000 tennis courts in the world today. They cover a multitude of surfaces, from the most impromptu sand in parts of Africa to the highly sophisticated scientifically designed carpet and hard courts.

There are four officially recognised surfaces in tennis: clay, hard, grass and carpet. Within those categories there are variations, and there are other surfaces that were used in the past which are not officially sanctioned today (eg. wood).

CLAY

Clay is by far the most favoured surface on the mainland of Europe and South America, and until the 1980s there were virtually no courts in countries like Spain and Italy that were not clay.

Clay essentially has two variants: red clay, which is found predominantly in Europe and South America, and the grey 'Har-Tru' clay favoured in North America. However, there are a couple of other lesser-used variants, like shale which is made up of a coarser grain and still found in many countries, and anthill which is a soil-like court still to be found in Australia and South Africa.

Claycourts are a complex cross-section of up to six different layers, with the top dressing we think of as clay sometimes making up just 6 millimetres ($^1/_4$ in) of a 20 centimetre (8 in) deep surface (see page 42).

Clay needs water – a feature of clay courts is that they need regular watering in hot weather, occasionally during matches on really hot days

The top dressing on European red clay is mostly crushed roof tiles – without it the court would be a pale yellow. It is known in French as 'terre battue' which means 'beaten earth'.

The American clay top dressing is made from basalt, which is a natural material which needs mining and crushing. Clay can in theory be used all year round, though it is more susceptible to the weather than hard courts, especially to frost which makes it a viable surface for only eight or nine months of the year in many developed countries.

When a ball hits a claycourt, it digs into the powdery top dressing and loses a lot of its speed. This means clay favours the players who have the greatest fitness and patience, as it is much harder to produce winning shots than on 'faster' surfaces. Among the greatest exponents of clay are Björn Borg who won Roland Garros a record six times, Chris Evert who won it seven times, the French 'Musketeers' notably Henri Cochet and René Lacoste, and countless players from Spain and South America, among them Manolo Santana, Sergi Bruguera, and Arantxa Sanchez Vicario from Spain, and Brazil's Gustavo Kuerten. The most successful American claycourt men were Frank Parker, Tony Trabert and Jim Courier.

HARD

Hardcourts come with many different names, surface textures and colours, but they can essentially be broken down into two categories: porous and non-porous or impervious.

All hardcourts are built on a base of bituminous macadam (known in the building profession as 'bitmac'), which can either be built to be porous – ie. letting the water pass through, or be soaked up – or impervious to water. On top of it, a hard-court surface is added, which is either porous or impervious to match the base. The base is made from quarried materials.

The cross section of a hardcourt may also include a cushioning substance near the surface to offer a little 'give', and the top layer is normally an acrylic paint (leading some people to call the court 'acrylic' rather than just 'hard' – see page 43).

It was not until the late 1940s that the first hard courts hosted official tournaments. There were events before the second world war called 'hard court tournaments', but they were played on clay.

Above: Not so hard – hardcourts are known for their 'true' bounce and generally offer the kind of tennis that allows for both baseliners and attackers to thrive. Ivan Lendl won 40 of his 88 titles on hardcourts

Hardcourts have gained in popularity at clubs and public parks because of their ability to be used in a variety of weather conditions.

The two major hardcourt surfaces that are most commonly used on the international circuit are known as DecoTurf II, a concrete-like surface used widely throughout North America including the US Open, and Rebound Ace, a rubberised surface made mainly from recycled car tyres, which is used at the Australian Open.

Rebound Ace was supposed to be the ultimate surface, in that it gives a true bounce with a mild cushioning, but experience in Australia has shown that in hot weather it can sometimes get sticky, which has been blamed for injuries to leg and ankle joints. DecoTurf II has virtually no 'give', but many players like it as it is the only surface that gives a totally true foothold without sinking or sliding.

The pace of hardcourts can vary, but they are thought of as medium to medium-fast, in other words benefiting the players who have big serves and powerful groundstrokes.

Courts that are floodlit tend to be mainly hardcourts, as the surface is unaffected by dew or other night-time climatic features (which explains why Wimbledon can't have floodlit play). Some players who are very comfortable on hardcourts have difficulty playing under lights – the reason Björn Borg failed to win the US Open is often put down to his relative discomfort under lights, and players who wear contact lenses frequently lose a little confidence under lights.

GRASS

In theory grass is the most natural of tennis's surfaces, though most grasscourt ground staff will say that the way they treat grass to make a tennis court embodies everything that should not happen in the care and nurturing of a lawn.

As a living organism, it is the most idiosyncratic of the four surfaces, playing differently from country to country, region to region, club to club, and frequently from day to day at the same tournament. When a grass court is new, it can often be soft and slippery, but as it gets played on and the colour goes out, it can frequently play better as the absence of sap and chlorophyll can make for a better grip under foot. In a prolonged period of hot sun, the surface gets more 'baked', thus harder, so the ball tends to bounce higher.

Since the demise of wood, grass has been acknowledged as the 'fastest' of tennis's four recognised surfaces, benefiting players with big serves and natural volleys, and the relatively low and skid-like bounce means the sliced shot is particularly effective.

Up to 1973 the international circuit was predominantly grass-based, with three of the four Grand Slam events played on grass (the US Open went to clay for three years, 1975-77, and hard thereafter; the Australian Open went to hard in 1988). These days, Wimbledon is by far the top grasscourt event, supported by a number of

grasscourt tour events in London, Nottingham, Eastbourne, Birmingham (all Great Britain), Halle in Westfalen (Germany), s'Hertogenbosch (formerly Rosmalen, Netherlands), and the one remaining tour-level grasscourt tournament in America, Newport (Rhode Island).

There are still a number of arenas in Australia that are used for top-level grasscourt tennis, notably the former Australian Open stadium at the Kooyong Club in Melbourne, Memorial Drive in Adelaide, and the ANZ stadium in Brisbane, but as Australia no longer has a tour-level grasscourt tournament, these arenas tend only to host Davis Cup matches.

Different types of grass and different cross-sections of court strata are used in different arenas, depending on local factors. Until the early 1990s Wimbledon used four types of grass. These days it uses mainly rye grass, mown to a height of eight millimetres ($^1/_3$ in).

In the mid 1990s amid concern that the power of the top players was ruining men's tennis on grass, Wimbledon experimented with allowing the grass to be mown to 8mm, in contrast to the 6mm ($^1/_4$ in) that had previously been the norm. Hardly any players noticed the difference, but 8mm is today's norm.

The grass in Halle, also 8mm, is grown in 400 palettes, each 1 metre x 2 metres (3ft x 6ft), and imported into the 12,300-seater Gerry Weber Stadium three weeks before the mid-June grasscourt tournament starts.

Because grass gets very slippery in rain and takes a long time to dry, grasscourts need covers. The generally accepted method is to have a waterproof textile sheet which is stored at the side of the court; when it rains, about eight members of the ground staff drag it across the court, and in prolonged rain or over night, it is inflated to form a dome-like balloon, thus enabling the grass to 'breathe'.

At Wimbledon, the centre and No1 courts are not inflated but raised in a structure similar to a ridge tent, so the flow of air underneath can be regulated more flexibly.

DROP SHOTS!
Because rain can make grass courts dangerously slippery in a short time, court coverers have to be quick. Wimbledon's are so quick they frequently have the court covered less than 30 seconds after the decision to suspend play. Their record is believed to be 22 seconds, though head groundsman Eddie Seaward says any faster is just not practical because they cannot get the players off quickly enough!

The Gerry Weber Stadium in Halle has no cover because the 88 seconds it takes to close the roof is almost as quick as using a ground-level cover.

CARPET

The name 'carpet' is somewhat misleading in tennis these days. Perhaps 'mat' would be a fairer term, as 'carpet' refers to most of the synthetic surfaces used in indoor arenas (though the fact that some of them are effectively hard courts has now been recognised by the tour bodies which now differentiate between 'indoor carpet' and 'indoor hard'). The first carpet court was called 'Sportsface' and was a genuine 'pile' carpet, but in the 1970s 'Supreme' became the first of the rubber mat surfaces to become widely accepted.

There are still a number of 'pile' tennis surfaces available today (soft bristles sticking up from a matted base, like a standard domestic carpet), used both indoors and out, often at clubs.

However, the term 'carpet' in professional tennis effectively means rubber mats. There are a number of different carpet surfaces, of which three – Supreme, GreenSet, and Taraflex – are the ones most commonly used on the professional circuits.

Though all three have characteristics that make them quicker or slower, the defining factor about the speed of the carpet is the surface on which it is laid. If it is laid on wood, it will tend to play fast; if it is laid on a softer undersurface, it will play slower. Having said that, top players generally feel that indoor courts play fast, mainly because the absence of wind and clouds makes the ball fly through the air somewhat faster indoors than out.

Advances in carpet court technology spelt the end for wood as a recognised surface, as today's carpets are easy to lay, and provide fairer playing conditions than the ultra-fast characteristics of wood.

The need to accommodate television schedules and maximise playing time outside standard working hours has led to an explosion in indoor tennis over the past 30 years, both on the professional circuits and in leisure play.

Above: Grass for volleys – grass has allowed some of the great volleyers in tennis to flourish, notably Billie-Jean King

In 2000, 17 of the 75 events on the men's circuit, and 18 of the 63 on the women's were played in indoor arenas. In addition, the principal stadiums hosting four outdoor tournaments – Australian Open, Hamburg, Halle and Tokyo – have sliding roofs, which enable some matches to be played indoors in rain or extreme heat.

With no wind or sun to contend with, some players have posted their best results on indoor courts, especially those with big serves. The best example is Boris Becker, who won 30 of his 49 career titles indoors. Ivan Lendl also did well indoors, partly because with a very high toss on his serve he was less vulnerable to wind.

TENNIS COURT SURFACES

The following diagrams show how the court surfaces mentioned in the previous pages are broken down as cross sections (data supplied by LTA, London).

CLAY (RED): TRADITIONAL FRENCH

CLAY (GREY): AMERICAN FAST DRY (HAR-TRU)

1. 6mm American Clay top dressing

2. 25mm American Clay

3. 30mm levelling course of crushed stone

4. 125mm non-frost susceptible stone sub-base

5. Geotextile membrane and drainage system (if required)

---

1. 2 tons of crushed brick per court

2. 40-50mm compacted depth of crushed limestone

3. 60-100mm cinders or volcanic rock (pouzzolane)

4. 0-600mm compacted depth non-frost susceptible carboniferous limestone or granite course

5. Geotextile membrane and drainage system (if required)

Excavate to remove topsoil compact formation

CARPET: INDOOR POLYMERIC OR TEXTILE

1. Polymeric carpet

2. 25mm compacted depth dense macadam wearing course

3. 40mm compacted depth dense macadam course

4. 200mm compacted depth non-frost susceptible carboniferous limestone or granite course

5. Geotextile membrane (if required)

HARD:
OUTDOOR
PAINTED POROUS
MACADAM

HARD (ACRYLIC):
OUTDOOR
AMERICAN

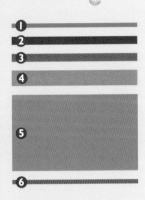

ARTIFICIAL GRASS:
TEXTILE OR
SAND FILLED

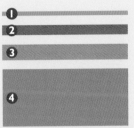

GRASS

1 Colour coat

2 25mm open grade porous macadam 6mm diameter aggregate wearing course

3 40mm compacted depth base course porous macadam

4 150mm compacted depth non-frost susceptible carboniferous limestone or granite course

5 Geotextile membrane and drainage system (if required)

Excavate to remove topsoil establish 1:120 fall to formation in a single plain cross fall or lengthways compact formation

1 Acrylic paint system

2 Shockpad (if required)

3 25mm compacted depth dense macadam wearing course

4 40mm compacted depth dense macadam base course

5 200mm compacted depth non-frost susceptible carboniferous limestone or granite course

6 Geotextile membrane (if required)

Excavate to remove topsoil establish 1:120 fall to formation in a single plain cross fall or lengthways compact formation

1 Textile carpet or sand filled artificial grass wearing course

2 25mm open grade 6mm diameter aggregate porous macadam

3 40mm compacted depth base course porous macadam

4 150mm compacted depth non-frost susceptible carboniferous limestone or granite course

5 Geotextile membrane and drainage system (if required)

Excavate to remove topsoil establish 1:120 fall to formation in a single plain cross fall or lengthways compact formation

1 Wearing course of selected grasses

2 100-150mm topsoil, sand soil mix or sand depending on ground conditions

3 50mm coarse sand grit binding layer

4 6-10mm grade permable backfil with perforated plastic drainage pipes

1928

THE OPENING OF THE
ROLAND GARROS STADIUM IN
PARIS COINCIDED WITH THE
DISCOVERY OF PENICILLIN
AND THE FIRST MICKEY MOUSE
CARTOON

*Below: Rod Laver Arena –
opened as Flinders Park in 1988,
now the Rod Laver Arena*

*Right: Court Philippe-Chatrier –
balloons being released as part of
70-year celebrations in 1998*

STADIUMS

The four principal tennis stadiums are the
centre courts at the four Grand Slam events, but
there are others with a past and present in
top-level tennis. Which to include and which to
leave out will always be a matter of subjective
judgement – those featured here are either the
top arenas purpose-built for tennis, or multi-
purpose stadiums which contribute to tennis lore.

ROD LAVER ARENA
MELBOURNE PARK, MELBOURNE

The home of the Australian Open, it was built
as the centrepiece of the new National Tennis
Centre and was used for the first time in January
1988. It pioneered the idea of a sliding roof, which
can close in 20 minutes, giving the impression
of an indoor arena.

In fact the amount of indoor events that take
place between Australian Opens make it seem to
the Melburnians more like an indoor arena with
a roof that can open, while the tennis world sees
it more as an outdoor arena with a roof that
can close. It has a seating capacity for tennis of
15,000, and now has a little sister, a 10,000-seater
lookalike multi-purpose Vodafone Arena which
in January 2001 became the Australian Open's
second stadium court.

Known for the first 10 years of its life as Flinders
Park (after the navigator Matthew Flinders
who charted the coast of southern Australia),
it changed its name in 1998 to Melbourne Park as
local politicians sought to give added publicity to
the name of the city. Its surface is Rebound Ace,
a rubberised hardcourt.

Melbourne Park has its own tram stop on the
Melbourne city tram network. Nearest railway
station: Flinders Street (15 minutes walk).

The other 50 weeks: The Rod Laver Arena is
a multi-purpose arena in the middle of the
National Tennis Centre, at which courts can be
hired outside the Australian Open fortnight.

COURT PHILIPPE-CHATRIER
STADE ROLAND GARROS, PARIS

The home of the French Open, the stadium
underwent a major refurbishment for the
2000 championships. The north and east stands –
called stands A and D – were rebuilt to give
the stadium a more uniform look, even though
this reduced its capacity by over 900 from
15,995 to 15,059.

DROP *SHOTS!*

While the referees at the
Australian Open, Wimbledon
and US Open are in regular
contact with local weather
bureaux, the organisers
of the French Open aren't –
because they have their own
weather station. Located
under the west stand of the
Philippe Chatrier court, it is
a fully equipped meteorological
centre which can pinpoint
with a fair degree of accuracy
when the next rain is going
to hit the Stade Roland Garros.
Fans can look through the
windows from the covered
walkway under the stand.

Though the French championships date from 1881, the stadium was only built in 1928, and then for the Davis Cup challenge round against the United States at the height of the four French tennis Musketeers (see page 12).

The city donated the original 15 acres of land on the western outskirts of Paris, on condition that it bear the name of Roland Garros, an aviator who died five weeks before the end of the first world war (the fact that he was much keener on rugby than tennis has been conveniently ignored).

On a sunny day it is a magnificent arena, but it has virtually no cover from the rain. In 1994 a new second court was opened at Roland Garros, now called the Court Suzanne Lenglen, though Lenglen never played at the Roland Garros stadium. Its surface is European red clay.

Nearest stop on the Paris Metro network: Porte d'Auteuil (10 minutes walk).

The other 50 weeks: The Roland Garros complex houses the French Tennis Federation's national tennis centre, where French players practise all year round. From late 2002 it will also feature the 'Tenniseum', a museum of French tennis.

CENTRE COURT
WIMBLEDON, LONDON

The arena itself has changed little since it was first built for the 1922 championships.
For the first 74 years of its existence it had the ground's second show court, Court No1, attached to its west stand, but following that court's demolition as part of the current Wimbledon redevelopment programme, the centre court is now a self-standing stadium.

Until 1990 part of the east and west stands had standing room, but when that was abandoned in 1990 in favour of an all-seater stadium, the capacity was reduced slightly and something of the 'carnival atmosphere' of the centre court was lost. Today it holds 13,800 spectators, and first-time visitors are normally surprised how intimate it is.

Though part of a club with many grass courts, the centre court grass is played on for just the two weeks of the championships, plus two traditional occasions: a women's doubles the day before the championships start to 'play in the court', and the chairman's invitation afternoon normally on the Tuesday after the finals weekend.

MEMORABLE MATCHES
Vitas Gerulaitis v Björn Borg Wimbledon Semi-Final 1977

A match that took everyone by surprise because it came amid such other interest.

It was Wimbledon's centenary year, home interest was taken up by Virginia Wade's quest for a first title, Maria Bueno and Billie-Jean King had returned to singles action, 14-year-old Tracy Austin made her debut, and faced world No1 Chris Evert, who later beat King in the quarter-finals. And on the same day as the Borg-Gerulaitis match, an ill-mannered but highly talented 18-year-old John McEnroe made history by becoming the first unseeded semi-finalist.

After McEnroe's eight-match run had been ended by Jimmy Connors, few expected much of the second semi between the reigning champion and the colourful, brazen but ultimately fragile New Yorker of Lithuanian origin. But from the start the quality of tennis was superb on a beautiful early summer's evening.

The quality lasted throughout, but the drama came in the fifth set. Gerulaitis broke for 3-2 with the help of a dubious line call that caused one of the very few demonstrations of dissent in Borg's career. The American had a point for 4-2 but Borg broke back, and using the advantage of serving first he capitalised on Gerulaitis' fragility to break in the 14th game for victory, 6-4 3-6 6-3 3-6 8-6. It was three hours of superb tennis, perhaps the pinnacle of Gerulaitis' career, together with winning that December's Australian Open.

Borg beat Connors in another five setter in the final two days later.

When the All England Club conceived its redevelopment programme, it was anxious to keep the new Court 1 smaller than the Centre Court, to preserve the supremacy of arguably the most charismatic arena in tennis. The redevelopment also included a range of new facilities, including a network of underground tunnels to improve security for players moving between locker rooms and courts.

In recent years the question of a roof over Centre Court has been increasingly raised; so far the All England Club has resolutely said no, saying it hosts an outdoor event which should remain outdoors, but it is constantly reviewing the situation, and pressure from television rights holders might force a change before long.

Nearest stops on the London Underground network: Wimbledon, Wimbledon Park & Southfields on the District Line (25 minutes walk, shuttle service available.

The other 50 weeks: The centre court is the centrepiece of the the All England Club, a private club where only members and invited guests can play. However, it also houses the Wimbledon Lawn Tennis Museum, which is open to the public 52 weeks a year, though its main exhibit, a look into Centre Court, is obviously closed during the championships' fortnight.

Museum telephone: +44 20 8946 6131.

DROP *SHOTS!*

The Williams sisters Venus and Serena have stamped their authority on the Arthur Ashe arena, winning the singles titles in 1999 (Serena), 2000 and 2001 (Venus).

Guided by their father Richard, they have made the name Williams synonymous with the growing appeal of women's tennis. But did you know the name Richard Williams was already established in the history of tennis? Richard Norris Williams (known as Dick Williams) sailed on the 'Titanic' in 1912, a journey in which his father died but Dick survived.

Next year he helped the USA win back the Davis Cup, one of five winner's medals he collected, and in 1914 he won the first of his two US Grand Slam singles titles, the other coming in 1916.

ARTHUR ASHE STADIUM
FLUSHING MEADOWS, NEW YORK

The biggest stadium purpose-built for tennis, the 23,000-seater arena looks like a salad bowl from the number seven Subway train as it rolls between the USTA National Tennis Center and the legendary Shea Stadium, home of the New York Mets baseball team. It was opened in 1997 as part of a major reshaping of the National Tennis Centre site (which itself dates from 1978) in the grounds of Flushing Meadows and Corona Park. On opening, it took over from the Louis Armstrong stadium, which used to hold 18,000 spectators but has now been reduced to 10,000.

The Arthur Ashe Stadium offers spectators no protection from the rain, and has no covers, so that after rain a team of around 50 court staff get down on their hands and knees and rub the surface dry with towels. The surface is DecoTurf II, a concrete-style hardcourt. The site originally hosted the World Trade Fair in 1964, and an artistic metal globe left over from the fair forms a focal point for photographers and television companies just outside the gates of the National Tennis Center.

Nearest stop on the New York Subway network: Willetts Point – Shea Stadium on the No 7 line (5 minutes walk).

The other 50 weeks: The USTA National Tennis Center is open to the public when the US Open is not being played. Telephone: +1 718 760 2000.

Above: Arthur Ashe Arena – opened in 1997 with a parade of champions and Whitney Houston singing 'One Moment in Time'

INDIAN WELLS TENNIS GARDENS
INDIAN WELLS, CALIFORNIA

The second-largest stadium primarily used for tennis in the world (by capacity) with 16,100 seats, it was opened for the 2000 staging of Charlie Pasarell's tournament in the southern California desert which was also the launch event of the ATP's Tennis Masters Series.

The playing surface is 11 metres (36ft) below ground level, creating a sunken effect. The stadium was built to respect traditional 'south-western' architecture, but has all the amenities of a modern tennis complex. The site has a cosy, almost surreal feel, with grassy expanses and young palm trees set against the backdrop of the snow-capped mountains of southern California.

On the Sun Bus network in the Palm Springs area; stop during tournament: Miles Avenue.

The 14,000-seater octagon-shaped arena is the crowning glory, the focal point on a 30-acre expanse that spends 50 weeks of the year as a public tennis facility. Though more than half the seats are permanent, the fact that 6,500 are not means there is no shelter from the rain.

Nearest stop: Brickell on the Miami Metrorail.

CRANDON PARK
KEY BISCAYNE, FLORIDA

One of the most impressive modern arenas, it came into operation for the 1994 staging of the tournament known variously as Key Biscayne, Miami, the Lipton, the International Players Championships and now the Ericsson Open.

The event was founded by the former American Davis Cup player Earl 'Butch' Buchholz and played for the first time in 1985 as the only tour event held over two weeks – though it is now only 11 days, it is still the biggest tennis tournament after the four majors in terms of days and size of draw (96 for men's and women's singles).

MONTE CARLO COUNTRY CLUB
MONTE CARLO, MONACO

The site of one of the most historically prestigious tournaments outside the four majors, the Monte Carlo Open, it is a remnant of the days when most tennis tournaments were played at private clubs – and a highly spectacular one!

The Monte Carlo Country Club is situated on the eastern edge of the principality of Monaco, with some courts in Monaco and some in France (the on-site phone numbers are on the French telecommunications system, not the Monagasque). The clubhouse, a regal building with marble pillars and engraved roll of honour boards, stands at the northern end of the main court, and has spectacular views over the court in the foreground, Monte Carlo beach in the middle ground and the vast expanse of the Mediterranean Sea beyond. Most of the 7500 spectators sit in temporary seating.

Nearest rail station: Monaco (30 minutes walk).

Above: The most spectacular tennis venue in the world? – the Monte Carlo Country Club

Left: Crandon Park, Key Biscayne, whose Ericsson Open is still recognised alongside the men's and women's year-ending championships as the biggest event outside the Slams

1997

WHEN THE ARTHUR ASHE STADIUM WAS OPENED IN NEW YORK, HONG KONG HAD JUST RETURNED TO CHINA, SCIENTISTS HAD JUST CLONED THE FIRST SHEEP, AND PRINCESS DIANA WAS KILLED IN A CAR CRASH WHILE THE STADIUM HAD ITS FIRST SATURDAY EVENING SESSION

ROTHENBAUM
HAMBURG

The home of one of the longest-standing tournaments, the German Open (now Tennis Masters Series – Hamburg on the men's circuit), this modern 13,000-seater stadium is one of the four tennis arenas to have a roof.

Unlike the other three (Melbourne, Tokyo, Halle) it is not a metal sliding roof but a tent-like structure with a membrane made from translucent synthetic canvas. Opened in 1998, it cost 33 million deutschmarks (around $17m), and slides on cables from its bunched-up central resting place like an umbrella being opened, taking seven minutes to completely cover the court.

Nearest station on the Hamburg U-Bahn underground network: Hallerstrasse (1 minute walk).

FORO ITALICO
ROME

A stadium heaped in tennis and historical tradition. It was built in the 1930s as part of a massive project to the north of Rome called 'Foro Mussolini' after the fascist leader of Italy Benito Mussolini.

When the fascist era ended in 1945, the area, which includes the Academy of Physical Education and the Marbles Stadium, became known as the Foro Italico. The original centre court was built in 1933-34 with marble steps and adorned with 18 marble statues of athletic figures, aimed at recalling the architecture of the Roman Empire.

It hosted the first 'Campionati Internazionali d'Italia' in 1935, but with a capacity of just 4000, it ultimately proved too small for the burgeoning Italian Open, especially once it became a Super Nine event in the 1990s. So a new centre court was opened in 1997 with 10,400 seats, with the old centre court now the site's second court. The old court is now called 'Stadio della Pallacorda', *pallacorda* being the Italian name for *jeu de paume*, the name used for tennis during the middle ages.

Nearest station on the Rome underground: Ottaviano on Line A though 2km away (1.25 miles), nearest bus stop: Lungotevere Cadorna.

PALAIS OMNISPORTS
DE PARIS-BERCY
PARIS

A multi-purpose indoor arena by the River Seine just to the east of the Paris city centre, it was not used for tennis until the Paris Open tournament began in 1986, but it has quickly become established as one of the great arenas in the sport. The timing of the tournament in November has for many years helped it attract some of the best male players looking for ranking points to qualify for the year-ending men's championships (now the Tennis Masters Cup). As one of the nine Masters Series events on the men's tour, it is now compulsory for all players who qualify to enter.

Nearest stop on the Paris Metro network: Bercy (1 minute walk).

ARIAKE STADIUM
TOKYO

A 10,000-seater stadium in the Kotu-ku suburb of Tokyo used for the Japan Open, a tournament featuring men and women. It earns inclusion on the basis of having a retractable roof, though not one which most people consider pleasing to the eye. It isn't just a moving roof as in Melbourne or Halle, the whole cover is on girders that track along the ground, dwarfing the whole stadium.

Nearest railway station: Toyosu on the Yurakucho Line.

Below: The Pallacorda at the Foro Italico – the former centre court, now the second court, is surrounded by 18 marble statues

QUIET PLEASE!

*"They should send Borg away to another planet.
We play tennis. He plays something else"*

ILIE NASTASE

Hall of Fame page 124

GERRY WEBER STADION
HALLE IN WESTFALEN

A slightly incongruous 12,300-seater stadium in a small country town of barely 20,000 inhabitants, it was the brainchild of fashion entrepreneur Gerhard Weber, whose company Gerry Weber gives its name to the stadium and the tournament played there in June. In 1994 it became the first to host tour-level tennis on grass under a closed roof, and in 1995 it became the first multi-purpose grasscourt stadium, with the grass spending 48 weeks of the year on pallettes outside the arena to allow for a full summer programme of sporting, cultural and social events.

Nearest railway station: Gerry Weber Stadion (on a branch line from Bielefeld, 8 minutes walk).

SCANDINAVIUM
GOTHENBURG

No longer a regular tennis venue, it nevertheless deserves its place in tennis history for being the first indoor arena to stage top-level tennis on a makeshift clay court. In 1984 Sweden chose clay for its Davis Cup final against the USA, and built a court in the 12,300-seater arena.

The final was hugely hyped as the USA picked its two top players John McEnroe and Jimmy Connors, but Sweden led 3-0 after two days, and the event will be remembered more for the two Americans' boorish behaviour than for Sweden's dominance – the USTA banned Connors and McEnroe from representing the USA for the following year.

The precedent set by the Scandinavium for indoor clay has been adopted on numerous occasions in the subsequent two decades.

Nearest stop on Gothenburg's bus and tram network: Korsvägen.

KOOYONG
MELBOURNE

The stadium that held the Australian Open as late as January 1987 looks a relic of a by-gone era, yet it wasn't because of the stadium that the Australian Open moved to Melbourne Park but the sheer lack of infrastructure.

The stadium holds 17,500 spectators, 2,500 more than the Rod Laver Arena at Melbourne Park, largely because it has space for two courts – in the first week of the Australian Open both courts were used, and in the second week the relatively untouched grass between the two was used as the sole court. But the stadium is the only major structure in the grounds of the private Kooyong Club on the north-eastern outskirts of Melbourne, and even in the mid-1980s all corporate hospitality and media activities were catered for in tents.

The stadium still has its grass, but the highest-profile event it stages these days is the Colonial Classic exhibition warm-up tournament for the Australian Open, when a temporary Rebound Ace court is laid (the tradition of lorry drivers honking as they pass Kooyong on the Dandenong highway when the tennis is on is still partly observed during the Colonial Classic's week).

Kooyong hosted the Davis Cup finals in 1946, 53, 57, 61, 66, 83 and 86 and in theory it could still host Davis Cup ties, but that is now unlikely as Tennis Australia's deal with Melbourne city authorities is that Melbourne Park must stage any home final that Australia ever reaches.

Nearest stop on the Melbourne tram network: Glenferrie Road (2 minutes walk).

1975

THE YEAR ARTHUR ASHE BECAME THE FIRST BLACK MAN TO WIN WIMBLEDON, THE INFAMOUS POL POT BECAME DICTATOR IN CAMBODIA, AND THE MICROSOFT CORPORATION WAS FOUNDED

Above left: A roof with a view – the Gerry Weber Stadium in Halle, Germany, which has achieved what was previously thought impossible: tennis played on grass under a closed roof on a rainy day

Below: Hard on grass – the centre court at Kooyong as used for the Colonial Classic tournament in which a Rebound Ace hardcourt is laid on top of the grass

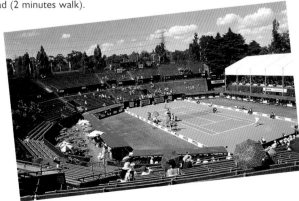

A classic case of the old but fading champion trying to defend his throne from the young pretender. Tilden, now 34, had lost his six-year unbeaten run at Forest Hills to Henri Cochet the year before, but was now desperate to get his title back, equal Dick Sears' record of seven titles, and thwart the French takeover of men's tennis.

Lacoste, 23, had won the title the previous year, was French champion, France were Davis Cup holders, and Cochet was Wimbledon champion. Tilden was the out-and-out attacker, Lacoste had perfected a new line in defence that wore down opponents. Though a straight sets result in seven minutes short of two hours, the great New York tennis correspondent Allison Danzig said: "It was a match the like of which will not be seen again soon... the reaction of the gallery at the end was that it had seen the best that tennis can offer."

Had Tilden converted one of the three set points he had in the first set the outcome might have been different, but he lost them. He then let a 3-1 lead in the second slip as Lacoste won five games on the run. In the third Tilden, pouring iced water on himself to keep cool, led 5-2 and had two set points, but Lacoste stormed back to lead 7-6.

Tilden saved two match points and then levelled for 7-7 as the 14,000 crowd went wild. Lacoste broke for 9-8 and again served for the title, but Tilden broke back to love. But his strength was waning, and the relentless accuracy of Lacoste's deep groundstrokes saw him to victory 11-9 6-3 11-9. It was the height of Lacoste's career, but Danzig said of Tilden: "It was one of the most ennobling fights a former champion ever made to regain his crown." Tilden did win his seventh US title two years later, and won a third Wimbledon title in 1930 aged 37.

MADISON SQUARE GARDEN
NEW YORK

Now a slightly sad and faded indoor arena, 'the Garden' is no longer a regular tennis venue following the move of the year-ending WTA Tour championships to Munich, yet it has a major place in the history of professional tennis.

Many amateur champions made their pro debuts there during the years of split amateur and pro circuits, notably Jack Kramer in 1947 against Bobby Riggs in the December snow. In 1970 the first year-ending men's 'Masters' tournament was played there, rounding off the new professional Grand Prix year (pictured above), and the Garden hosted the men's finale until 1989. But it has a greater place in the lore of women's tennis, having hosted the year-ending tournament from 1972 to 2000.

The first Virginia Slims championships in 1972 marked the first major women-only event in a major arena for the fledgling women's tour, and from 1984 to 1998 its final was the sole best-of-five-sets match on the women's circuit.

The first Madison Square Garden was in Madison Square on the junction of 26th Street and Madison Avenue, an old rail station that had life as a circus venue for PT Barnum and other things, like flower shows (hence the name 'Garden'). It began business in 1879 hosting concerts, flower shows, dog shows, and the New York Athletic Club's first winter meets.

The current Garden on 8th Avenue has hosted a range of sports, most memorably the Muhammad Ali v Joe Frazier boxing fight in 1971, and it is still home to basketball and ice hockey teams.

Nearest stop on the New York subway network: Penn Station (2 minutes walk).

WEST SIDE TENNIS CLUB
FOREST HILLS, NEW YORK

The former home of the US championships and US Open, the name 'Forest Hills' was shorthand for the tournament the world over. Like Kooyong in Melbourne, it is something of a monument to how tennis has changed in recent years. It is a private club, founded in 1892, which hosted the top US tennis event from 1915 to 1977. It has a mock-Tudor clubhouse built in 1914 where liveried doormen and dark panelled walls hark back to the 1920s.

The main stadium, built in 1923, is horseshoe shaped and holds 14,000 spectators. Amid complaints about the quality of the grass, the club changed its showcourts to American clay (Har-Tru) for the 1975 championships, but within a year the US Tennis Association had decided it wanted to take tennis to a wider public, and a private tennis club was just not the place for its showcase tournament. Even though the US Open has been at Flushing Meadows just a few miles from the West Side Tennis Club since 1978, there are many who still refer to the tournament as 'Forest Hills', and the club still receives a few ticket enquiries and even the occasional tennis fan thinking the US Open is still played there!

Nearest stop on the New York Subway network: Forest Hills (10 minutes walk).

4. OFF-COURT

The global nature of the professional tennis circuit these days is such that there is a massive off-court operation. This ranges from the administration and running of tournaments through the commercial side of tennis to efforts to spread the gospel into parts of the world where the sport is relatively unknown.

COACHES & OTHER TRAVELLERS

People who watch tennis on television will be aware that behind most players is a coach, or at least someone who goes by the name of coach.

The cameras frequently 'cut away' to a player's entourage sitting in the stadium, and most players have someone who travels with them as a companion, hitting partner, or proper coach.

Below: Brad Gilbert & Andre Agassi – one of the longest-standing and successful player-coach relationships dating back to April 1994

Bottom: Tim Henman & Larry Stefanki – one of the newer coaching arrangements, it dates from July 2001 after Henman split with his coach of nine years, David Felgate

There are many variations on how players can be coached, but essentially they can be broken down into three unofficial categories:

• **The convenience coach** – *an arrangement more popular on the women's circuit because there is less prize money and this is a cheaper option. As our name suggests, the coach is someone who is conveniently placed to help the player. It could be a parent, boyfriend/girlfriend, or just a good friend.*

Or it could be an experienced coach who is always at the major tournaments and can lend a hand. As such the arrangements can be permanent or ad hoc. In many cases the coach is just happy to be with the player, booking practice courts, picking up balls during service practice, etc, but there are some who revel in the glory of being coach to a touring professional.

For financial reasons this kind of relationship is more common among players ranked outside the top 50, but there are one or two high-profile examples.

Arantxa Sanchez Vicario being coached by her brother Emilio, a former top 10 player, is one, as is Patrick Rafter's occasional coaching relationship with Tony Roche (though neither Roche nor Emilio are prone to claiming great credit for their player's successes).

• **The rookie coach** – *a more serious arrangement for players who either don't have much money to pay a coach, who have found a young coach they feel comfortable with, or are between two experienced coaches and want to buy themselves time to think about who their next coach should be. Such coaches are often ex-Satellite circuit or college players aged 20-30 who are happy to work for around $500 a week because it gets them onto the tour, and they hope for a major break through in coaching, especially if their player does better than people expect.*

Recent examples include Mary Pierce working with Michael DeJong, Lisa Raymond with Olive Messerli, and even Martina Hingis with Rikhard Bergh and David Taylor in April/May 2001 as she experimented with not having her mother as her coach.

• **The experienced coach** – *the genuine arrangement that spectators think is the norm but which is surprisingly rare, especially on the women's tour. This is when a player takes on someone who has either proven experience as a coach, or has played at a high level and who has a good rapport with the player. Such coaches offer advice on technique, fitness, tactics (especially after having scouted unknown opponents), and the mental side of the game, and generally make sure their player goes on court in the right shape and frame of mind.*

"Sometimes a defeat can be more beautiful and satisfying than certain victories.
The English have a point in insisting that it matters not who won or lost, but how you played the game"

ARTHUR ASHE
Hall of Fame page 114

Examples of this include Andre Agassi with Brad Gilbert, Lindsay Davenport with Robert van't Hof, Pete Sampras with Tim Gullikson and – going further back – Björn Borg with Lennart Bergelin.

There are a variety of ways the experienced coach can be paid. A common arrangement is a salary plus a percentage of the player's prize money (normally 6-10%). A variation on that is a salary plus defined bonuses for certain levels of performance, eg. reaching the quarter-finals of a Grand Slam, a certain ranking, etc.

Some players want to pay their coach a flat week-by-week rate, which obviously offers little job security for the coach, while a few of the top coaches ask for a fixed annual payment which bears little relation to the amount of work they need to put in or the results their player achieves.

Not every player pays their coach directly. Some national tennis associations pay part or all of a coach's fee, there are sponsors who may fund a player's coach in return for, say, having their company logo worn on the player's sleeve, and occasionally individual benefactors offer to fund coaching for an up-and-coming player for a given period. Sometimes players approach someone they want to coach them, though with the younger players the choice of coach is often left to their management company, or sometimes to parents in the case of under-age players (or pushy parents).

Most players will hit for at least an hour on the morning of their match, though work on fitness and changes of technique will be done during weeks when the player is not at a tournament. According to the Rules of Tennis, coaching is not allowed during a match, unless it is a repre-sentative event where a team captain is allowed to chat to their players at changes of ends. However, a number of coaches try to work out a code of gestures to communicate to their player a change of tactics mid-match (like scratching their ear when they want the player to go more to the net). Some coaches refuse to do this, not just because it's illegal, but because it encourages the player to remain dependent on their coach. Other coaches do it for exactly the same reason.

Occasionally a player gets an official warning for receiving courtside coaching – even though the player is the innocent party and the coach has committed the violation, the player still receives the warning, and if it happens again a point penalty. Recent players to have received such warnings include Martina Hingis and Anna Kournikova.

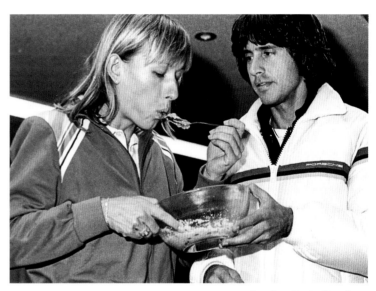

Haas diet – Martina Navratilova (left) dominated women's tennis in the 1980s, her fitness fed by adherence to the Haas diet pioneered by Robert Haas (right)

OTHER SPECIALIST PRACTITIONERS

The more successful players frequently have other specialist practitioners travelling with them. The most common example is a ***fitness trainer***. When in 1995 Pete Sampras looked to have a physical weakness in long matches, he engaged the services of the then ATP Tour trainer Todd Snyder to be his personal travelling fitness adviser. No-one can say for sure what it did for Sampras, but contrast his fourth-round five-set defeat against Jaime Yzaga at the 1994 US Open with his quarter-final victory over Alex Corretja in 1996, a match in which he vomited during the final set tiebreak – many observers believe that without Snyder's assistance Sampras would never have got through the Corretja match, and certainly not gone on to win his fourth US Open title.

1992

AS THE 11-YEAR-OLDS MARTINA HINGIS AND ANNA KOURNIKOVA WERE BEING SIGNED UP BY IMG, THE END OF THE COLD WAR WAS OFFICIALLY DECLARED, AND THERE WAS RIOTING IN LOS ANGELES AFTER THE VERDICT IN THE RODNEY KING TRIAL EXONERATED THE POLICE OF EXCESSIVE VIOLENCE AGAINST HIM

Other fitness trainers who have travelled with top players include Pat Etcheberry, Walt Landers, and Kieran Vorster.

Martina Navratilova worked with the **dietician** Robert Haas who introduced her to his Haas diet; Boris Becker used to travel with his own **stringer** (as well as a nanny when his ex-wife Barbara used to bring their son Noah to tournaments); Andre Agassi's powerfully built friend Gil Reyes is always with him without his role ever being clearly defined, perhaps to act as a bodyguard if fans get too close to Agassi; and Pat Rafter, who is the seventh of nine children, always has at least one member of his family with him.

There are also a number of specialists for various injuries who enjoy a good reputation among players, and while they don't travel as members of a player's entourage, they frequently receive visits from players. Perhaps the best example is the German joint specialist Hans Müller Wohlfahrt, who has worked with Steffi Graf, Boris Becker and various other top names (see Different Approaches pages 101-102).

Another figure that can sometimes turn up in a player's entourage is a **psychologist**, either travelling or just in practice weeks. With so much of tennis played in the mind, the need to steal an advantage in a highly competitive sport has led attention to fall on what goes on in the head of the player.

Timothy Gallwey published a book 'The Inner Game of Tennis' in 1975 which first put the psychology of tennis on the map. But the name most readily associated with tennis psychology is Jim Loehr, a psychologist from Colorado, who in the 1970s opened the Athletic Excellence Institute in Denver.

He later worked with a number of players, including Sergi Bruguera, Jim Courier, Aranxta Sanchez Vicario, and also Tim Gullikson who passed on some of what he had learned when he coached Pete Sampras in the three years before his death in 1996.

For many years Loehr was the international tennis family's sole recognised psychologist, but he seldom submitted his methods to academic review or empirical testing, so tennis psychology has been thought of a bit as 'pop psychology'.

Bob Nideffer, best known on the tennis circuit as the husband of former top-15 player Rosalyn Fairbank, developed a tennis-specific Test of Attentional and Interpersonal Style back in 1976, and though it has since been criticised for being psychometrically flawed, his explanation of it was the first tennis-specific article to appear in a mainstream psychology journal until the late 1990s.

More recently, Roland Carlstedt, who is known to some tennis fans for having devised a series of 'Psycho World Rankings' which appeared in a number of newspapers and magazines, has studied links between brain functioning, personality, and performance in tennis players.

Carlstedt is also the founder of the American Board of Tennis Psychology which aims to further the use of psychology in tennis and to share information.

AGENTS & PLAYER MANAGEMENT

Agents are so much a part of today's professional tennis world that it's hard to believe that just 40 years ago even the top players didn't have people managing their business affairs. That started to change in the mid-1960s when a Yale Law School graduate Mark McCormack became the agent of the top golfer Arnold Palmer, and quickly expanded his range of interests to include tennis, other sports, and these days even the arts.

McCormack's International Management Group (IMG) was soon rivalled by ProServ, started in the late 1960s by Donald Dell, Frank Craighill and Lee Fentress. Like McCormack, Dell was a great visionary, but his vision was matched by a volatile personality which set him on a collision course with many he did business with, and by 1982 Craighill and Fentress had split from Dell to form Advantage International.

Above: Mark McCormack – founder and chairman of IMG

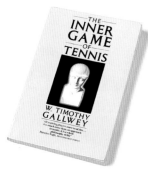

Above: Tennis psychology – one of the first and most influential books on tennis psychology was Timothy Gallwey's 'The Inner Game of Tennis'

American Board of Tennis Psychology
Telephone: +1 917 680 3994
E-mail: abspsychology@aol.com
Website: www.americanboardofsportpsychology.org

QUIET PLEASE!

"I don't know that my behaviour has improved that much with age. They just found someone worse"

JIMMY CONNORS
Hall of Fame page 117
Referring to John McEnroe's on-court behaviour

These three firms are still the leading management companies in tennis, though ProServ is now called SFX and Advantage is called Octagon, and in terms of the number of top players represented, IMG and Octagon are now some way ahead of SFX, and IMG is well ahead of Octagon certainly among male players.

There are still a few top players who are either managed outside the big three (the best example being Boris Becker who was managed by Ion Tiriac and later by the legal firm of the late Munich entrepreneur Axel Meyer-Wölden), or not formally managed at all (like Pat Rafter whose brother Steve looks after his financial and promotional interests).

The management companies look to sign up players when they are very young. Both Martina Hingis and Anna Kournikova were signed up at age 11 (both by IMG, both now with Octagon), though the companies generally try to avoid such early contracts, not just for reasons of social responsibility but also because too big a deal at too young an age could send a player the message that they have already made it and thus diminish their competitiveness.

Classic examples of targets are players aged 16-20 who look good prospects, and those who are likely to become the top player in their country even if they don't make it to the top 30. The management companies report that it is generally harder to get good deals in women's tennis – the top eight or 10 'marquee names' who regularly make the quarter-finals of the major tournaments are very marketable, but most women outside the top 20 have little market impact, so the deals available to them are much less favourable.

Every deal between a player and a management company is different, depending on the player and his/her entourage. For promising players from countries or families with little knowledge of tennis, the assistance could mean anything from getting a racket deal so the player can actually play, to arranging a top-level coach to take them from being good at junior level to making it on the international professional circuit.

Clifford Bloxham, group director of Octagon's London office, says: "Whatever the player's circumstances and personality traits, you need a strategy. You need to know what you want to achieve and how you're going to achieve it."

Above: A family affair – a young Steffi Graf pictured with her father Peter when he managed all Graf's tax affairs; mismanagement on his part landed him in jail

A delicate matter for management companies can arise when a player's family claims some expertise which may not be fitting for the big bad world of professional tennis. For example, numerous players have run into difficulties having had parents who have some experience in finance but can't begin to contemplate the complexities of international tax, investments, etc (the best-known case in recent years being Steffi Graf).

Top players in particular, who earn lots of money find plenty of people willing to 'help' invest it, so seek advice from experienced sources, and while this doesn't automatically mean they need a management company, there are few places to get that advice other than the companies that deal with top players' interests 52 weeks of the year.

The image of the management companies among the tennis watching public ranges from the negative to the non-existent.

1967

THE FIRST PLAYER MANAGEMENT COMPANIES IMG AND PROSERV GREW UP AGAINST THE BACKGROUND OF CHE GUEVARA BEING KILLED AND THE SIX DAY WAR IN THE MIDDLE EAST

1981

THE DAVIS CUP'S FIRST
SPONSORSHIP DEAL BEGAN IN
THE SAME YEAR THE AIDS VIRUS
WAS DISCOVERED AND THE
PERSONAL COMPUTER
WAS INTRODUCED BY IBM

Those fans who know that the companies exist tend to view them with the same suspicion as they might view money lenders or real estate agents, and the media frequently blames management agents for restricting access to players. Yet the nature of the modern international professional circuit means players will inevitably seek assistance for their off-court interests, and many firms can thank player management companies for deals which have been good both for them and the sport.

For example, after Anna Kournikova did a poster advertisement in 2000 for a brassiere marketed by Berlei, the company reported a sales increase of 150% and one of the most charismatic tennis players had her face (and upper torso) on the streets of numerous towns and railway stations the world over.

Management companies normally earn their money by taking a percentage of the deals they arrange for their players. Investment in a young player might include a deal where the company's percentage increases as the player's on-court earnings increase, and in some cases the income may include a share of prize money.

When Boris Becker won Wimbledon as a 17-year-old in 1985, his manager Ion Tiriac had done a deal with Becker's parents that he would pay them a lump sum in return for all Boris's prize money up to the age of 21. The deal was subsequently readjusted after Becker's sudden rise to prominence, but it is a financial model Yevgeny Kafelnikov is trying to use for an initiative to boost young tennis talent in Russia.

For management companies contact details see page 177.

Above: Wimbledon champion at 17 – Boris Becker's parents had already signed up their son with the Romanian management impresario Ion Tiriac when he won Wimbledon in 1985 and moved the talented teenager from his home in Leimen, Germany, to Monaco

Below: On-court television cameras are these days a feature of all the top tournaments

ADMINISTRATION OF TOURNAMENTS

The 69 tournaments that appear on the full ATP tour and the 62 that make up the Sanex WTA Tour look just like a list of cities, but each one represents a 52-week operation that has a budget starting from something around $2 million.

The Grand Slam events have a budget around 20 times that – the US Open's operating budget is between $45 and $50 million.

Many tournaments are listed together with their prize money, but the prize money frequently makes up only 20% of a tournament's total budget. The rest is made up of facilities hire or maintenance, staff costs, advertising and promotion, providing hospitality for officials, players and the media, and general bills like heating, lighting and electricity.

A tournament's income comes from a variety of sources, of which the sale of television rights is normally the biggest.

However, these days some of the smaller tournaments prefer to give away their television rights or sell them cheaply in the hope of gaining more from on-court advertising, the thinking being that they can get better deals from the on-court advertisers if the advertisers get good television coverage.

The source of income the fan sees most readily is the ticket or admission price, but this often makes up a small percentage of a tournament's total income. And while true tennis fans rightly moan at the corporate hospitality ticket holders who seem to enjoy eating and drinking more than watching top-quality tennis, the reality for the tournaments is that corporate hospitality tickets bought by sponsors bring in on average 20 times more income than ordinary tickets sold to the public. (At most events the only companies entertaining clients are those who sponsor the tournament, but Wimbledon is an exception – it is so prestigious that companies that have no sponsorship involvement still pay for a corporate hospitality tent.)

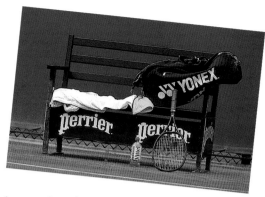

There was a time when the tournament director was normally also the impresario who put the money down and stood to gain or lose heavily depending on the success of the event.

Due to the advance of big business, and the precarious nature of running an event that could depend very heavily on the weather for its profitability, there are very few of those around these days – the remaining ones include Tommy Buford at the men's indoor event in Memphis, and Gerhard Weber at the men's grasscourt event in Halle (though his son Ralf is nominally the tournament director).

The biggest player management companies in tennis, IMG and Octagon, each own five tournaments, but competition rules restrict them from owning any more.

Many tournaments are owned by national tennis associations, and the players who receive wildcards (see page 28) at these events are frequently those to whom the associations want to offer competitive opportunities at full tour level. For tournament directors' contact details see page 182.

PROMOTIONS, MEDIA & MARKETING

Every tournament needs to make sure it is properly promoted, though all the major tournaments are these days part of bigger series and tours, so much of it is done under a corporate image. For example, the top tier of tournaments on the men's circuit, the Tennis Masters Series, has a uniform image, with eight of the nine tournaments having the same name and adopting their own variation of the uniform shield logo.

To promote Davis Cup and Fed Cup ties, the ITF publishes a massive publication 'Promotional Toolkit' aimed at national tennis associations and telling them about every aspect of promoting home ties.

There are really four constituencies a tournament needs to address in promoting itself:

• **Sponsors** – who pay for advertisements around tennis courts are frequently the biggest sources of income for a tournament, so they need to be kept happy. The best-known sponsors in tennis are those companies that have stuck with a tournament for the longest number of years, notably Lipton (at Key Biscayne), Family Circle (Hilton Head/Charleston), Bausch & Lomb (Amelia Island), Stella Artois (London Queen's), NEC (Davis Cup), and BNP (French Open).

• **Television** – the income from television rights is also a significant percentage, so there has to be a good rights deal. But television is also vital for exposure, so the most lucrative deal isn't always the best overall, because if sponsors want to see their advert on television and the tournament is on a cable channel with low viewing figures, the sponsors won't be happy.

The specialist sports channels ESPN in America and Eurosport in Europe are examples of stations that might not pay the largest fees for rights, because their reach (especially Eurosport's into central and eastern Europe) means tournaments get coverage over a wider area than they might from a channel willing to pay more money.

• **Other media** – radio, newspapers, magazines and the internet are important not for the money they can bring in to the tournament but for the publicity they can give it. This can be in the form of news stories (eg. 'Kuerten signs up for Smithtown Open', 'Safin injury could threaten participation in Smithtown Open'), direct advertising, or competitions with tickets or VIP trips to the tournament as prizes.

• **Spectators** – the amount of money the paying public brings in is a relatively small percentage of the overall tournament income, but if the seats are empty then television doesn't like it, the atmosphere isn't good so other potential spectators might be put off attending, players might decide not to come back next year, and the event begins to lack credibility. And spectators rarely pay only their ticket fee – they normally buy other things while at the tennis, such as T-shirts and refreshments.

Various ways of getting a brand name noticed at a tennis tournament

Clearly all these factors are strongly interlinked. A sponsor might be able to promote the event by advertising it on its products; television coverage keeps the sponsors happy; and if there is a title sponsor, the tournament needs to convince journalists to use it at least once in their reports (eg. 'Gustavo Kuerten breezed through his first round match at the Fizzpop Smithtown Open').

Players are a major 'tool' in promoting a tournament, and it is common for the biggest names to agree to do interviews and promotional appearances to help the tournament reach a wider public.

MERCHANDISING

An increasingly important part of tennis's income comes from merchandising. Everything from mugs and key rings to books and T-shirts are sold with official logos, pictures and text on them.

National associations, the tour bodies, the Slams and other major tournaments do particularly well from sales of official souvenirs. Wimbledon has its merchandising campaign based around a big 'W' logo, with products on sale 52 weeks a year well beyond the perimeter fence of the All England Club. And the reason the French Tennis Federation want their Slam known as 'Roland Garros' rather than 'French Open' is that its merchandising is built around the name 'Roland Garros'. 'Roland Garros', which works in French and other languages, is now also the name of a car marketed by the Peugeot company, which is one of the French Open's sponsors. The US and Australian Opens also have merchandise for sale all year round (see their websites, pages 22-24).

Some merchandise is given out as gifts to tournament staff and members of the media, both as a thank you for their involvement, but also to help promote the event.

MEDIA

Reporting of tennis in newspapers, radio, television and increasingly on the internet is a vital part of keeping tennis in the public eye and therefore keeping the large sums of money that can be brought in from sponsorship and television contracts. At every tournament there is the host television broadcaster with responsibility for sending the 'feed' to all other television companies with the rights to show the tournament.

The host broadcaster generally has commentators on site, but there is obviously only so much room for commentary boxes, so some secondary rights holders receive just the pictures and have to use commentators sitting off site in studios. Very few tennis fans watching on television are aware that a lot of commentators aren't 'on site' but sitting perhaps a long way away in a studio seeing no more than the viewer is seeing.

Good 'off site' commentators will have done their homework by phoning the tournament site to find out about weather conditions, interesting things said by players, names of umpires, etc, but they are still vulnerable to an incident which they cannot see – the general rule in such cases is for the commentator not to lie by saying he/she is there, but also not admit he/she is not there!

There are sometimes radio rights for 'play-by-play commentary', and there is a media operation for radio reports and the written press.

The press room at tennis tournaments tends to be made up partly of reporters covering the event because it's local to their paper or station, and a selection of the 200 or so journalists who follow the tennis circus around the world. Many of those 200 are members of the International Tennis Writers Association (ITWA, see page 178), and many more are members of the three national tennis media associations that exist in America, Australia and Great Britain.

The biggest tournaments attract the media just because of their importance. Of the rest, the ones which are keener to attract media coverage offer financial incentives to journalists to attend their event – such incentives include free or discounted flights, free or discounted hotel rooms, and a full meal service in the press room.

Occasionally a situation arises where a newspaper can't afford to send its tennis correspondent to a big tournament because of the expense of a long flight but can send him/her to a smaller event closer to home where the organisers are offering a free hotel room. In such cases, the paper would rely on a freelance journalist already at the bigger event to file (send) stories, or use material filed by a news agency.

Players are obliged to attend a news conference after each match if they are requested by three or more journalists, and at Grand Slams they are obliged to do a one-on-one interview with the host television broadcaster. If they refuse they can be fined up to $5000. All other one-on-one requests are optional, though players are encouraged by the tour bodies to do a reasonable number of interviews to help promote tournaments and the sport.

Most interviews are given free, though when it comes to the biggest names, some charges are made for lengthy interviews or special photo shoots. All three tour bodies (ATP, WTA, ITF) employ communications managers who liase between players and the media at tournaments – these are generally people in their 20s or early 30s who love tennis and enjoy the travel, but few last more than about three years in the job because it is a very demanding and nomadic existence.

MARKETING OF TENNIS

Every tournament and tour has to make sure it is properly marketed along the lines outlined in 'Promotion' above, but there is a broader element to marketing: the marketing of the sport itself.

The ITF tackled this question at a seminar in Windsor, England, in November 2000, which came up with the following suggestions for priority action which are currently under discussion:

· *A uniform advertising campaign aimed at getting people to play tennis.*

· *A conversion chart that makes each country's ratings and handicap systems compatible (so a player from one country can work out how good a player from another is just by asking for their rating or handicap).*

· *A worldwide strategy for cross-promotion of tennis events, for example men's tournaments advertising Davis Cup and vice versa.*

· *An international schools internet project.*

· *Getting players in team tennis competitions (Davis Cup, Fed Cup, World Team Cup etc) to play in their national colours, like soccer teams do.*

It remains to be seen how many of these ideas actually come to fruition, and they are not without their risks.

At the 2000 Davis Cup final between Spain and Australia in Barcelona, there was a strong contingent in the crowd which was attracted to tennis for the first time, and for many of these people soccer was the sporting experience they had to draw on – yet their enthusiasm encroached on traditional tennis modes of behaviour, and many older tennis fans had their enjoyment compromised.

Clearly tennis's governing bodies have to get new people into tennis – as both players and spectators – but it will be a delicate balancing act to find ways of doing so without alienating the sport's traditional following.

Above: Brazilian fans frequently wear their national football colours to cheer on Gustavo Kuerten

1985

THE FIRST PROFESSIONAL TENNIS UMPIRES WERE APPOINTED THE YEAR THE HOLE IN THE EARTH'S PROTECTIVE OZONE LAYER WAS DISCOVERED, AND FAMINE STRUCK ETHIOPIA

Below: Hand-held television cameras – only for camera personnel with broad shoulders

Facing page: The media – all the four Grand Slam tournaments now have writing rooms in which the majority of newspaper reporters have televisions at their own desks by which they can follow the action on a number of courts (bottom); photographers sit courtside, and when there's a popular player on court the sound of the clicks of shutters as the player hits the ball can be louder than the sound of ball hitting strings

Facing pages:
(top) Line judging at the US Open,
(below) Line judges at the French
don 1920s wear for the 70th
anniversary of the Stade Roland
Garros in 1998

Above: A line judge at the Australian Open

These days all umpires officiating at satellites, tour events and the Slams are at least semi-professional. They are graded white, bronze, silver or gold according to their ability and experience under a system introduced in 1990 by the ITF, ATP and WTA.

All umpires in professional tournaments start as line judges, so anyone wanting to become an umpire must first contact the officiating section of their national tennis association (see appendix page 162).

By the time a line judge has become a chair umpire in the latter stages of a Grand Slam event, they will have gone through three umpiring 'schools' and have been further evaluated over many matches.

The structure works like this:

• *National tennis associations run Level 1 schools, which offer an introduction to officiating and train people to be line judges in professional tennis.*

As there are 7-10 line judges for every chair umpire, it is important for countries to have a good-sized pool of linespersons, especially if they have a tournament or two in their country. Line judges are always the responsibility of the national association, and almost all line judges are nationals of the country in which a tournament or cup tie is held.

• *The ITF runs 6-8 Level 2 schools each year. These are organised on a global basis, and those participants who pass emerge with a **white** badge, which allows them to take the chair in satellite events and above. This badge is recognised by the ITF, ATP and WTA.*

• *The ITF's and ATP's top officiating personnel team up to run 2-3 Level 3 schools each year. Those participants who pass emerge with a **bronze** badge. Virtually every umpire in the main draw singles of a Slam has at least their bronze badge.*

• *Promotion to **silver** and **gold** comes through evaluations – normally at the end of a year – by supervisors, referees, and senior umpires of how an umpire has handled their matches.*

OFFICIATING

There's an old adage in sport that a good referee or umpire is one that the spectator hardly notices. Well the antics of certain players, notably Ilie Nastase in the 1970s and John McEnroe in the 80s, elevated the tennis umpire almost to 'third player' status, but in the years since then the sport's governing bodies have made strenuous efforts to upgrade and professionalise the standard of officiating in all professional tournaments.

Although many countries have an umpires' association with a venerable history, for the first 15 years of 'open' tennis, many of the world's top athletes had their fate – certainly in close matches – in the hands of officials who had come into the game in the amateur era.

With the advent of new technology increasing the speed of the game, the discrepancy between players and officials was at times embarrassing, with many very worthy umpires just unable to keep up with the demands of a modern high-powered sport. In July 1985 the first two professional umpires, Richard Kaufman (USA) and Jeremy Shales (Great Britain), were hired by the Men's International Professional Tennis Council.

OVERRULING

THE QUESTION OF AN UMPIRE OVERRULING A LINE JUDGE'S CALL HAS ALWAYS BEEN A BIG ISSUE

THE RULE HAS UNDERGONE SOME CHANGES IN THE LAST 20 YEARS, BUT IN RECENT YEARS HAS REMAINED UNCHANGED

AN UMPIRE MAY ONLY OVERRULE IF HE/SHE IS INSTANTLY CONVINCED THAT THE LINE JUDGE HAS MADE A CLEAR ERROR

IF THE OVERRULE IS NOT INSTANT, THEN THE DECISION CANNOT BE OVERTURNED (UNLESS THERE HAS BEEN A PROCEDURAL ERROR, WHICH WOULD NEED THE TOURNAMENT REFEREE TO RULE ON)

THEREFORE WHEN PLAYERS ARGUE WITH AN UMPIRE ABOUT A CALL, THEY ARE DOING SO EITHER TO LET OFF STEAM OR IN THE HOPE THEY WILL INFLUENCE THE UMPIRE FOR FUTURE DECISIONS

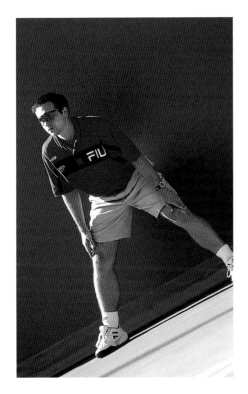

Promotion is not automatic, it depends on a certain amount of experience, and umpires have to have proved themselves over a number of events.

Worldwide there are currently around 600 white-badge umpires, 120 with bronze, 50 with silver, and 25 with gold. All those with gold and around half those with silver earn their living from umpiring. A gold or silver badge umpire would make around $1000-1500 in a tournament week, while full-time professional umpires currently make something either side of $50,000 a year.

The ITF hires around seven umpires on fixed contracts, the ATP about five, with the rest operating as self-employed freelance officials.

Some umpires move up to supervisor level, which means they have a more administrative role in the officiating of a tournament, and some become referees at tournaments or Davis Cup ties, which means they are the final arbiter of any disputes between players and umpires.

(Referees also have responsibility for the order of play, though frequently under strong guidance from the tournament director, especially if the tournament has signed a lucrative deal with a television company and has given it a say in which matches should go on which courts at which times.)

The main qualities an umpire needs are a sound knowledge of the Rules of Tennis, good concentration, communication skills (with both players and spectators), and a certain indefinable quality that gives the impression of being in control.

The rapport between players and umpires is much better than it was 25 years ago – mainly because of the professionalisation of officiating, and the fact that many umpires tour with players so are known as fellow members of the travelling 'circus' – but umpires still have to keep a certain distance so they remain impartial (and are seen to be).

The ITF and ATP have a code of conduct for officials, and they take action if that code is seriously breached, though such breaches only happen once or twice a year. Like players, umpires have good days and bad days, good runs and bad runs, and ultimately they will only survive if they're good enough.

WILD CARDS

NOTORIOUS CLASHES BETWEEN PLAYERS & OFFICIALS

EARL COCHELL v GARDNAR MULLOY
FOREST HILLS 1950

Cochell earned a lifetime's ban after not only arguing with the umpire and spectators over line calls, but also trying to climb the umpire's chair and grab the microphone to talk to the crowd.

He also played left-handed to show his disgust, and lauched a verbal assault on referee Ellsworth Davenport. His life ban was later rescinded but long after he was too old to compete.

PANCHO GONZALES v CHARLIE PASARELL
WIMBLEDON 1969

Gonzales, the feisty Californian by then 43, had just lost the first set 24-22, and in fading light wanted to come off court. The umpire Harold Duncan, under instruction from Wimbledon referee Captain Mike Gibson, told him to play on. Gonzales was furious, 'tanked' the second set 6-1 and came off in near darkness two sets down.

Under today's rules he would undoubtedly have received a warning for racket abuse and probably abuse of officials, but he came back next day to win the remaining three sets for a remarkable victory that is still the longest in Wimbledon's history. Gonzales won 22-24 1-6 16-14 6-3 11-9 in five hours 12 minutes.

ILIE NASTASE v PATRICK PROISY
BOURNEMOUTH 1974

Nastase was cruising through his quarter-final, leading 5-2 first set with two breaks, but Proisy came back to 5-4, and at 0-30 on the Nastase serve, the volatile Romanian picked a fight with the no-nonsense umpire Eric Auger. Auger asked Nastase to play on, Nastase kept arguing, and Auger eventually disqualified him.

The conversation between the two was noted for Nastase saying "You call me *Mr* Nastase", and since then all umpires have used a courtesy title when giving players a warning (eg. "Warning Mr McEnroe")!

Above: Gonzalez (left) remonstrates with umpire Harold Duncan about the fading light as Pararell looks on

Right: Nastase argues with Eric Auger (chair umpire) and the English army captain Mike Gibson (referee, with moustache left of Nastase) as Proisy prepares to reach the semi-finals after nine games

JOHN McENROE v
ILIE NASTASE
US OPEN 1979

After persistent stalling by Nastase that made McEnroe seem the good boy, umpire Frank Hammond first gave Nastase a point penalty, then a game penalty, and then disqualified the Romanian. However the crowd, which had been whipped up into expecting something dramatic by that morning's New York Post which headlined its preview to the match "Come and see the fight of the century", threw beer cans and other objects onto the court in protest.

Eventually the tournament director, the former American doubles specialist Bill Talbert, ordered the referee Mike Blanchard to reinstate Nastase and take over the chair-umpiring duties for the remainder of the match. McEnroe won in four sets.

JOHN McENROE v
TOM GULLIKSON
WIMBLEDON 1981

McEnroe's fame transcended the boundaries of tennis thanks in large part to his not infrequent tirades against umpires, and this match was thought to be the peak of them. Played on the old Court 1, McEnroe served down the middle and was shocked to see the line judge call "Fault".

He screamed at umpire Eddie James: "You can *not* be serious. That ball was on the line, chalk flew up, it was clearly in. How can you possibly call that out? How many have you missed?" – most of which now belongs to tennis folklore. McEnroe won the match, and the tournament.

JOHN McENROE v
MIKAEL PERNFORS
AUSTRALIAN OPEN 1990

Soon after the ATP Tour had introduced stricter rules which meant that a player's third offence meant disqualification (until then it was the fourth), much speculation reigned as to who the first victim would be. And it was hardly a shock when it proved to be McEnroe. He had looked so good in the first three rounds, dropping just 15 games in nine sets, but now in the fourth he looked altogether more fragile.

He earned a warning for staring intimidatingly at a lineswoman in the second set. He then threw down his racket which cracked, earning him a point penalty. McEnroe asked to speak to a supervisor, but the supervisor merely confirmed that if a racket is broken in anger the penalty is automatic and non-discretionary.

As the supervisor walked away, McEnroe used the f-word very loud, at which point umpire Gerry Armstrong disqualified him. McEnroe later claimed he had forgotten about the new rules.

JEFF TARANGO v
ALEXANDER MRONZ
WIMBLEDON 1995

Tarango, a student of philosophy, is one of the circuit's fiery and eccentric characters, and some believe his personality was always likely to clash with the laid-back French umpire Bruno Rebeuh.

The clash happened in a third round match on Court 13 at Wimbledon, when Tarango responded to some barracking from the crowd with an audible obscenity. Rebeuh gave him a warning, which Tarango disputed and called for the referee. When the supervisor confirmed the warning, Tarango called Rebeuh 'corrupt', causing Rebeuh to deduct a point penalty. Tarango then said "That's it, I'm not playing, no way" and walked off court. The matter further entered the realms of folklore when, on returning to the umpires' area after the match, Rebeuh was slapped in the face by Tarango's French wife Benedicte.

Above: Rules rule – a troubled McEnroe after the match against Pernfors trying to explain his actions to a packed press conference at Flinders Park

DROP *SHOTS!*

Fines are not bad for everyone. When a player gets fined for racket abuse or unsportsmanlike conduct in a Grand Slam, Davis Cup or Fed Cup match, the money goes into the ITF development department's coffers. In an average year, $90,000 goes from players' pockets into development as a result of their misdemeanours, and in an exceptional year it can be much higher.

When Jeff Tarango was disqualified at Wimbledon in 1995, he was fined his third round prize money, which put over $40,000 extra into development. ITF development director Dave Miley says: "When John McEnroe retired, we noticed a marked reduction in our income!"

Left: United front – Tarango and his wife Benedicte leave Wimbledon after both had an altercation with umpire Bruno Rebeuh

BALLPERSONS

Ballboys and ballgirls are a feature of every professional tournament these days. They are the servants of the players, and while – like officiating – it is another job done best if you don't notice it being done, ballpersons shouldn't be too anonymous because their clothing is increasingly being used as another advertising space for tournaments to increase their income.

There was a time when one only needed to speak of 'ballboys', but 'ballgirls' have been a feature of the circuit for several decades, and even Wimbledon, that bastion of tradition, introduced girls in 1977 (though the old army commander who trained the ballboys, Charles Lane, said he would have nothing to do with girls and left them to his deputy Wally Wonfor).

Ballpersons at Wimbledon (above) and the US Open (right)

These days 'ballkids' is heard a lot, which is appropriate for the European age range of 13-16, but in America state child labour requirements make the average age older – at the US Open most range from 18 to 23 years old – which perhaps explains why 'ballpersons' has become more or less the official term. The French call them 'ramasseurs' (meaning 'collectors'), which gets round the issue of age and largely of gender too.

For something that is an obligatory requirement at all professional events, there is a surprising absence of international coordination among people who train ballpersons. There are stipulations in the ATP and WTA tournament rule books about ballpersons (mostly referring to how many per court and the colour of their clothing), but apart from that, every tournament or cup tie seems to be on its own. As a result, it's perhaps somewhat remarkable that there is as much uniformity in ballperson systems as there is.

On the men's and women's tours, there are normally six ballpersons on a court: two each at the back behind each baseline, and two at the net (generally smaller in height than the baseline persons). The WTA stipulate six per court in all main draw matches, the ATP recommend six. Where there are only four, two patrol the net and one patrols each baseline.

At some tournaments the ballpersons at the net are always on opposite sides, which means that when the ball is hit into the net and the ballperson picking it up has to cross to the other side, the other net ballperson must cross empty handed to maintain the equilibrium. Balls are generally transferred between ballpersons by being rolled along the ground outside the sidelines of the court, the big exception being at the US Open where they are much older and are encouraged to use the skills they learn in baseball by throwing the ball overarm from one end of the court to the other.

Both WTA and ATP rules ban white or yellow clothing for ballpersons as this might affect a player's field of vision, but while the WTA advocates dark-coloured attire, the ATP recommends against this if ballpersons are likely to work in hot weather.

Ballpersons are normally taken from schools local to a tournament (though the original Wimbledon ballboys came from a nearby home for orphans). They are usually on court for between 15 and 45 minutes at a stretch (though the exact time may depend on local regulations regarding children at work), take three or four months to train, and be fairly fit with good concentration. They need to be able to roll a ball in a straight line, 'feed' it to a player so it arrives at hip height after one bounce, stand still during exciting rallies, and have a good understanding of tennis, notably a thorough understanding of the scoring system's impact on who serves from which end.

As the servant of the players, ballpersons end up performing all sorts of strange tasks. In the 1980s two ballgirls at Wimbledon had to hold towels in front of and behind the American Barbara Potter who having had back injuries insisted on changing her shirt after every set.

Many ballpersons have played a few balls during an injury time-out, because the uninjured player doesn't want to sit for three minutes without movement.

Ballpersons are often asked to remove insects or chase away unwanted birds. Recently ballpersons at women's tournaments have had to collect up the beads that fall out of the Williams sisters' hair (one ballgirl at the Eastbourne tournament collected 37 after a practice session!).

And at Wimbledon Wally Wonfor, who retired in 2001, never learned his ballkids names, preferring to give them numbers: "It's fairer," he said, "I don't develop any favouritism.

"One year I fired a kid because I didn't think he was good enough, and he turned out to be the son of the local school's head teacher. There you are, no favouritism!"

As well as throwing balls to players (Roland Garros, top), ballpersons have to be the players' servants during the changes of ends (Queen's Club, London, above)

DEVELOPMENT

These days it isn't enough for a sport just to regulate itself – in a competitive world, sports have to look to the future and make sure the conditions are right for continuation and growth.

In tennis, the majority of development is centred around the International Tennis Federation's development department, but there are also other initiatives, like the ATP's Smash Tennis and FunFests, plus there are occasional private initiatives by well-known players to increase interest and give opportunities to talented youngsters in places where there are few resources for tennis.

In 1981 the Davis Cup's first sponsorship deal with the Japanese electronics giant NEC enabled money to flow into development, and in 1984 the ITF founded a department specifically dealing with the issue. In 1986 the four Grand Slam events founded the Grand Slam Development Fund, and in 1990 the Compaq Grand Slam Cup was created with a specific mandate to give $2 million of its profits to development initiatives.

Though the cup has now disappeared to make way for the Tennis Masters Cup, the Slams still give $1.5m from the Masters Cup to the ITF for development.

With other sources of income, mainly a large chunk of the Davis Cup's profits, the ITF spends around $4.2m a year on development, which puts it roughly on a level with soccer's and track & field's world governing bodies Fifa and IAAF as the three sports doing most to work for a stable future for their sport.

Top right: Taking tennis to the town square of this city in Bhutan

Above: Moroccan No1 Hicham Arazi helps spread the word about tennis at a clinic in the Moroccan capital Rabat

Above Right: The Asian championships

Right: When you have no net, use a human as in this tennis clinic in Africa

The history of development work in tennis began in the 1970s, when the ITF president Philippe Chatrier ordered a fact-finding mission to study tennis in west Africa. Out of that the African Junior Championships were founded: players from just four nations took part in the first event in 1977, but by 2000 the event had grown to over 200 players from 35 nations.

The ITF's development work covers a range of initiatives:

· *Establishing circuits of junior tournaments in various parts of the world.*

· *Running three 'regional' residential centres for the best young players to be given top-level coaching (Pretoria, South Africa; Lautoka, Fiji; Inverarry, Florida).*

· *Running touring teams of players from less developed tennis nations or those with few tennis facilities.*

· *Offering travel grants for other players from countries with limited tennis resources.*

· *Offering grants for national associations to construct or refurbish tennis facilities.*

· *Administering a 'Schools Tennis Initiative' started in 1996 to introduce tennis to children; it currently reaches around 700,000 children in 80 countries.*

· *Funding eight development officers, each for a specific region of the world, who are the eyes and ears of the ITF in their region.*

· *Educating coaches in parts of the world where tennis has little tradition.*

· *Distributing equipment for use in national programmes.*

· *Producing publications and educational material (including one entitled 'Being a Better Tennis Parent'!).*

The overall aim is simple: to get more players and better players. But in some parts of the world there is very little to build on. For example in some parts of Africa, there are very few courts, and even if you can find a racket there are probably no strings – an ITF initiative to take tennis to a village in Burkino Faso several years ago opted for wooden bats instead of rackets, because the complexity of bringing strings and stringers was just too great.

While a football might last for several years, a tennis ball is worn out after several hours, and the absence of nets in some countries has led to some coaches using 'human nets', children from squads crouching in the middle of a mini-tennis court, all part of making the ITF's Schools Tennis Initiative more fun.

Among the players who have benefited from development help and have gone on to top-level professional tennis are Nicolas Lapentti (from Ecuador), Leander Paes (India), Gustavo Kuerten (Brazil), Byron and Wayne Black (Zimbabwe), Paradorn Srichaphan (Thailand), Karim Alami and Younes el Aynaoui (Morocco) among the men, and Cara Black (Zimbabwe) and the Madagascan Dally Randrianteffy in the women.

Kuerten, the only one of those to reach No1 in the rankings, spent eight weeks as a teenager playing tournaments in Europe three years running as a member of an ITF touring team.

To qualify for ITF development funding, players have to get noticed by their national associations which then apply for funding on their behalf.

Stars of the future – the 1993 ITF junior touring team; Gustavo Kuerten is second from the left in the front row, Nicolas Lapentti is second from left in back row, and Cara Black is third from left front row

Above: West African coaches workshop in Lomé

Left: ITF Schools Tennis Initiative in Morocco

TECHNOLOGY

Technology has exerted its influence on most aspects of modern life, and tennis is no exception. This section looks at how technology has affected rackets, balls and clothing, but perhaps the biggest technological advances have been those that have given us non-human line calling, instant serve speeds, and masses of statistics.

Speed guns... In just 10 years the radar 'gun' that measures the speed of serves has become a major feature on the professional tour, and there are now more tour-level tournaments that have them than don't. So how do they actually work?

The IBM system that's used at the four Slams uses a radar detector device that looks like a gun or long-lens camera and is positioned in the centre of the backboard behind each baseline. It uses a state-of-the-art digital signal processing system. Incorporated into the detector is a specific algorithm to recognise and pick up tennis ball speed information and filter out extraneous or erroneous signals (like a server's grunt). Because the speed of the ball decreases from the moment the ball leaves the strings, the system has to get the information it needs in less than 0.1 second from the time the racket hits the ball – in distance that's between 30 and 90 centimetres (1-3 feet).

The radar detector device is linked to a laptop, which itself is linked up with the courtside display board and various screens used by broadcasters, journalists and officials. A trained IBM statistician operates the system for each match – he or she has to have both tennis knowledge and technical expertise on the serve speed system.

Quick serve – the speed gun's display board is now a feature of all the major tennis arenas

For example the operator has to cancel the speed 'gun' after every serve and re-set it after every point, and also make sure that faults are not counted as part of a player's best or average service speed. Information & Display Systems (IDS), which operates the IBM service speed measuring equipment, says it has an accuracy of +/- 1 km/h (0.6mph), which ensures that a serve hit at one tournament can be fairly compared with a similar serve hit at another where the same measuring equipment is being used.

IDS Inc.
10275 Centurion Court
Jacksonville
Florida 32256
USA
Telephone: +1 904 645 8697
Fax: +1 904 645 8496
Website: www.ids-sports.com

The radar detector uses the "Doppler Principle", according to which if we transmit a known frequency and that frequency reflects off a moving object (in this case a tennis ball), the reflected frequency will change in proportion to its velocity. This change is measured, and the measurement is converted mathematically into the speed at which the ball travelled in the first 0.1 second after it was struck.

Do we need service speed guns? Well they're fun, and they're useful in measuring whether the game really is getting faster the way people often feel it is (interestingly, an experiment by an American tennis magazine several years ago showed Mark Philippoussis serving at up to 219 km/h (136mph) with a wooden racket).

The one danger is that they give the impression that a fast serve is a good serve, which is only a small part of the truth – a good serve is made up of several elements, including disguise, spin, placement, and variety, none of which get measured on anything like a radar system.

Statistics... Purists may dislike the increasing prevalence of statistics, but while one can clearly get too hung up on a set of numbers produced by a computer at the end of a match, they are being increasingly used. And after matches players are very interested in seeing the 'stats', so the people who matter certainly take an interest.

Some stats are easy to measure, like double faults and the number of break points converted. Others are harder, like winners and unforced errors. Trained tennis statisticians employed by IDS (see left) follow universal guidelines for what constitutes an error that was unforced and one which wasn't, in order to have some consistency – this means being a statistician requires more tennis knowledge than a speed gun operator. IDS defines an unforced error as "when a player fails to maintain a rally and is not under physical pressure as a result of the placement, power or spin of the opponent's stroke, excluding service return errors". But if a player is playing well, he or she can easily intimidate opponents into making errors they wouldn't normally make, so unforced error counts are somewhat arbitrary.

Even ace counts can be different from one statistician to another, especially if a statistician is seated in a part of the stadium that makes it hard to tell whether a winning serve caught the edge of the racket or not (if it did, it's not an ace).

What do statistics tell us? Often they're a statement of the obvious, and they should never be used to tell the story of a match on their own.

But many a player has lost a close match and emerged with a low conversion rate on break points (eg. they had 15 break points but only won two), and here the stats emphasise the mantra in tennis that it's often not the number of points you win but whether you win the important ones.

Winners and unforced errors should never be viewed separately but always together – if a player is going for their shots and their opponent is trying to weather the attack by playing a very consistent game, the aggressive player is likely to be well ahead in both winners and unforced errors, but by how much will determine whether they are being enterprising or reckless.

Electronic line calling... Many people wonder whether it is now only a matter of time before the human line judge is removed and the human umpire's authority to overrule decisions reduced. With some other sports resorting to electronics and television-based adjudications, surely tennis can't be far behind!

Well it's not that simple, and in many ways tennis is far ahead. It has had the 'electronic eye' for two decades, the system known as 'Cyclops' that was introduced at Wimbledon in 1980. Cyclops shines a beam of light over the first 20 centimetres (8in) beyond the service line, and if the ball lands in it, a loud beep is heard and the serve is a fault. If it can be done for the serve, surely it can be done for other calls?

The human netcord judge is largely redundant now, having been replaced by a sensor known as a 'Trembler' device that is finely tuned to spot if the ball brushes the net after the serve; if it does it sends a signal to a little control panel in the umpire's hand.

QUIET PLEASE!
"I don't know if I'd want to trust the line calls to a machine. It can still make mistakes."
ROGER FEDERER
Swiss tennis player, quoted in 2001 in 'Tennis' magazine

But the netcord judge's demise is also partly a matter of safety as he/she is in a very vulnerable position. The matter of line judging is more complex.

A number of systems have been developed for technology to take over line-calling, using either electrical/magnetic signals, or laser-based equipment. Only two, Accu-Call and TEL, have been used in professional tournaments. Accu-Call is made by a Norwegian company. It relies on electric circuits embedded in the court, and was tried out at the Stockholm Open in 2000. TEL ('Tennis Electronic Lines') was used once in a Slam. Its system places a series of magnetic fields about 3cm (1 $\frac{1}{4}$ in) below the surface of the court.

DROP *SHOTS!*
IT IS ROCKET SCIENCE!

In August 2000 the first-ever conference of scientists working on issues which impact on tennis took place in England. And the fashionable phrase "It's not rocket science" was turned on its head!

Rabi Mehta, a scientist with the American space agency Nasa in California (yes, a rocket scientist), admitted he had always been baffled by the motion through the air of a tennis ball. So he and Jani Macari Pallis from Cislunar Aerospace (another rocket scientist) tried to figure out what happens with the fluff when a ball flies through the air.

The results would make interesting reading for players at all levels of the game. They ranged from the fact that the 'seam' on a tennis ball does nothing to affect its flight through the air (unlike balls used in cricket and baseball) to the fact that the more used a ball is, the quicker it flies through the air, implying a big server should use a more worn ball for first serves and a fluffier one for second serves.

Details of the conference (called 'TST') are available from the ITF (see page 162).

Left: Greg Rusedski, who holds the record for the fastest serve ever measured in an official tournament at 149 miles per hour (239.78 km/h)

1978

THE YEAR THE ITF INTRODUCED
WORLD RANKINGS FOR JUNIORS
WAS THE YEAR THE FIRST
'TEST-TUBE BABY' LOUISE
BROWN WAS BORN, AND THERE
WERE THREE POPES – PAUL VI
DIED, JOHN PAUL I WAS
MYSTERIOUSLY FOUND DEAD IN
HIS SLEEP AFTER JUST 33 DAYS,
AND JOHN PAUL II BECAME THE
FIRST POPE FROM POLAND

The players then play with balls impregnated with tiny metal particles – so tiny you really don't know they're there – and different signals are then sent to a console in the umpire's chair about whether the ball landed in or out. The signals are generally a loud beep for 'out', and a soft beep only audible to the umpire for 'in'. TEL's managing director Brian Williams claimed an accuracy rate within 6 millimetres or quarter of an inch.

The Australian Open installed the magnetic fields under Court 2 for the 1993 tournament, but thanks to bad glueing of the Rebound Ace surface, the court started to peel and couldn't be used for several days. It was finally used on the first Saturday for the third round match between Manuela Maleeva-Fragnière and Ginger Helgeson, but with Maleeva leading 5-2 in the first set, it was agreed to turn the system off, and it was never used again.

The reason was a lack of confidence among the players, but there was more to it than that. When asked at their post-match news conferences at that Australian Open, many players said they would be sad to see the human element of line-judging disappear, and many lamented the passing of good arguments as perfected by John McEnroe (who had retired two months earlier).

In addition, the accuracy of the TEL system revealed that there was a potential for optical illusions in which some balls are seen to be in by the human eye but then prove to be out when viewed on a camera. In other words, the TEL system may have been too accurate for humans playing a match to have confidence in it!

For the time being, humans are still to be used, and the old maxim that 'life isn't always fair' will continue to play a part in tennis line calling.

Most players accept a few bad calls – at least they do after the match, in the heat of the moment their powers of reason aren't always as strong, as Andy Roddick showed when an overrule went against him at 4-5 in the fifth set of his 2001 US Open semi-final against Lleyton Hewitt and he became so incensed he called the umpire Jorge Dias "an absolute moron".

Money in tennis – a bottle of champagne with the Wimbledon logo on it

Money in tennis – tickets which can frequently sell on the black market for many times their face value

'Cyclops'
Telephone: +356 871766

TEL
E-mail:
teleurope@compuserve.com

Accu-Call
Telephone: +47 2 228 4322

MONEY

Tennis these days is a multi-billion dollar industry. This is because the sport is not just popular but also offers tremendous advertising and marketing opportunities for big business. That of course means the fortunes of top-level professional tennis are subject to fluctuations in national and global economies, and it's clear that the recession hitting the developed world in the second half of 2001 - coupled with the possible adverse economic impact of the aftermath of the attacks on New York and Washington on 11 September – means tennis is currently having to cut back more than expand.

At any time it's impossible to work out the sport's total turnover, because it reaches into so many different spheres of economic activity, but the following facts make interesting reading:

· *More than $100 million in prize money is available on the ATP and WTA tours, the Grand Slams and the Davis and Fed Cups. The ATP puts its total prize money at $58m while the WTA Tour says "over $50m". Players can augment their share of that through racket and clothing contracts, and sponsorship deals.*

· *The highest earners in the game are Pete Sampras in men's tennis who had earned $41,490,190 by 23 July 2001, and Steffi Graf in women's with $21,895,277. But that is just prize money – any player who has earned $10 million or more is likely to have made at least three times more in contracts, sponsorship and endorsements.*

· *At lesser-known tournaments, top players whose presence will help the image of the tournament are frequently given an appearance fee or guarantee. The appearance fee is a set payment which a player gets in addition to prize money if he/she turns up and plays (even in the event of a first round defeat). A guarantee is a minimum payment that is made if a player loses early, so if a player is offered a $30,000 guarantee which is equivalent to the quarter-final prize money and then loses before the quarter-finals, they get the $30,000, but if they reach the semi-finals or beyond they get just their prize money.*

Place in the sun – the New York economy profits greatly in direct and indirect revenue from the US Open

Charities chairmen – Tim Henman (below middle) turned his passion for golf into a vehicle for raising money during his year as chairman, while Guy Forget (bottom) was one of the early figureheads for the ATP's charity initiatives

• Major tennis tournaments can have a significant impact on local economies. A study of the economic impact of the 2000 US Open on the metropolitan region of New York found that the tournament generated just under $420 million in direct revenue for the area, more than any other annual sports or entertainment event in any city in the USA.

This represents 3 per cent of the total economic impact of tourism for New York in 2000, and the number of full-time (or equivalent) jobs created either directly or indirectly from the staging of the event was 11,437.

NOT ALL TAKE TAKE TAKE

It can sometimes seem as if top tennis players are always cashing big cheques, but there are many instances where they do give a lot back.

The ATP has its own charities programme run by a committee which it asks a leading player to chair for a year.

ATP CHARITIES CHAIRMEN

1991 Stefan Edberg
1992 Pete Sampras
1993 Guy Forget
1994 Michael Chang
1995 Andrei Medvedev
1996 Jim Courier
1997 Todd Woodbridge & Mark Woodforde
1998 Gustavo Kuerten
1999 Goran Ivanisevic
2000 Tim Henman
2001 Jan-Michael Gambill

But many of the top players also have charity initiatives of their own.

One of the top charity fund-raisers is Andre Agassi. Since the creation of the Andre Agassi Charitable Foundation in 1994, more than $14 million has been raised to benefit for at-risk organisations in the Las Vegas area where Agassi lives.

The cornerstone of Agassi's fund-raising is his annual Grand Slam for Children, which involves a concert, auctions, and a VIP dinner. Some of the top names in popular music perform free of charge at the concert including Elton John and Stevie Wonder, and the event in 2001 raised more than $4 million. In August 2001 Agassi also opened up a school in Las Vegas for underprivileged children.

Patrick Rafter founded his Cherish the Children Foundation in 1999, and organises celebrity tennis and golf days to raise money for it. One of the foundation's first recipients was a programme called Youth Off The Streets aimed at helping homeless and drug-addicted children.

Because of his brother suffering from cerebral palsy, Gustavo Kuerten raises over $100,000 a year through his own donations and those of his sponsors for an association for parents and friends of handicapped children.

PRIZE MONEY AT THE FOUR SLAMS IN 2001

The singles draws all have 128 players, therefore there are seven rounds.
The doubles draws all have 64 pairs, therefore six rounds (hence no fourth round prize money).
The prize money for doubles is per pair, not per individual competitor.

AUSTRALIAN OPEN

	MEN'S SINGLES	MEN'S DOUBLES	WOMEN'S SINGLES	WOMEN'S DOUBLES
WINNER	830,500	345,400	830,500	345,400
Runner-up	415,250	172,700	415,250	172,700
Semi-finalists	207,900	85,800	207,900	85,800
Quarter-finalists	106,150	42,900	106,150	42,900
Fourth Round Losers	56,760	x	56,760	x
Third Round Losers	32,450	24,200	32,450	24,200
Second Round Losers	19,800	13,200	19,800	13,200
First Round Losers	12,790	7,425	12,790	7,425

All in Australian dollars: exchange rate is roughly US $1 = Aus $2

FRENCH OPEN

	MEN'S SINGLES	MEN'S DOUBLES	WOMEN'S SINGLES	WOMEN'S DOUBLES
WINNER	4,538,000	1,646,000	4,312,000	1,522,500
Runner-up	2,269,000	823,000	2,156,000	761,250
Semi-finalists	1,134,500	409,500	1,078,000	348,000
Quarter-finalists	600,000	208,500	570,000	177,200
Fourth Round Losers	321,000	x	289,000	x
Third Round Losers	186,000	118,500	167,500	100,800
Second Round Losers	112,500	59,000	101,300	48,800
First Round Losers	67,500	40,250	60,800	33,200

All in French francs: exchange rate is roughly US $1 = FF 7.5

WIMBLEDON

	MEN'S SINGLES	MEN'S DOUBLES	WOMEN'S SINGLES	WOMEN'S DOUBLES
WINNER	500,000	205,000	462,500	189,620
Runner-up	250,000	102,500	231,250	94,810
Semi-finalists	125,000	52,500	112,500	47,250
Quarter-finalists	65,000	27,500	56,875	23,840
Fourth Round Losers	35,000	x	29,750	x
Third Round Losers	20,250	14,500	16,200	12,300
Second Round Losers	12,250	7,900	9,800	6,320
First Round Losers	7,500	4,650	6,000	3,720

All in British pounds: exchange rate is roughly US $1 = GBP 1.4

US OPEN

	MEN'S SINGLES	MEN'S DOUBLES	WOMEN'S SINGLES	WOMEN'S DOUBLES
WINNER	850,000	350,000	850,000	350,000
Runner-up	425,000	175,000	425,000	175,000
Semi-finalists	225,000	90,000	225,000	90,000
Quarter-finalists	115,000	45,000	115,000	45,000
Fourth Round Losers	56,000	x	56,000	x
Third Round Losers	35,000	22,500	35,000	22,500
Second Round Losers	20,000	15,000	20,000	15,000
First Round Losers	10,500	9,500	10,500	9,500

All in US dollars

Goran Ivanisevic has played exhibition matches to raise money for children in Croatia affected by the war with Serbia in the early 1990s.

With cancer claiming the lives of two of Tim Henman's relatives in recent years, the British No1 has put a lot of his efforts into two cancer charities, Sargent Cancer for Children and Sparks (Sport Aiding Medical Research for Kids).

Tom, Tim and Jerry –
Tim Henman pictured with friends
and cartoon characters at his
Kids at Heart day which he holds
every October for charity

In 2000 he agreed to give $140 for every ace he served, and with 537 aces he served up more than $85,000. And in 2001 he pledged $700 per match he won, raising over $30,000. He holds a Kids at Heart golf charity day every year.

Arantxa Sanchez Vicario also has a Sanchez-Vicario Foundation in Spain which gives money towards research into cancer in children.

Shocked by the poverty and sickness she saw when playing a tournament in Asia, Martina Hingis agreed to take on the role of ambassador for the World Health Organisation. Two years ago she visited Colombia, and currently raises money for work towards the eradication of polio.

A number of other players are involved in charity programmes to boost the number of other players playing tennis. Venus and Serena Williams donate money to schemes encouraging underprivileged girls to play tennis, the Richard Krajicek Foundation gives money for building playgrounds and sports facilities in deprived areas and introduces a number of children to tennis, and former Venezuelan player Nicolas Pereira has set up his own foundation to send kids from poor areas to school and set up a tennis school.

Cynics may claim such generosity is all part of minimising a player's tax liability, and no doubt these players' accountants do advise on the most appropriate amounts to give. But there is no doubt that thousands of disadvantaged people have experienced breaks and benefits thanks to the charity initiatives of countless players, of whom those mentioned here are just a few.

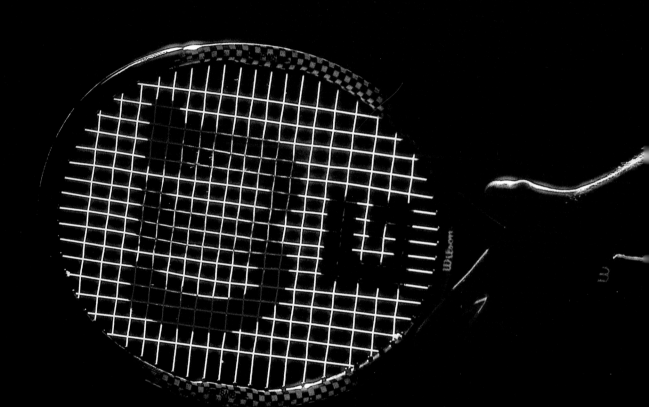

5. TENNIS EQUIPMENT

Though an essentially simple game, there is a lot of equipment involved in tennis, much of which forms the products of multi-million dollar industries. Insufficient records are kept to know how many balls are sold every year, the racket companies guard their sales figures very carefully, and the absence of a global tennis industries federation makes the guesswork even harder.

Sales of tennis balls ought to be a good indication of how much tennis is played, but no-one has accurate data. The best estimate of global sales of tennis balls is approximately 25 million dozen (300 million) premium quality balls per year, but that does not include the millions of lower-priced balls specifically designed for coaches, and balls sold for fun tennis.

RACKETS

From the birth of lawn tennis in the 1870s up to the 1970s, tennis rackets were made from wood and strung mostly with sheep's gut (literally twisted sheep's intestine), but much has changed in recent years. And some of those changes are being held responsible for jeopardising the popular appeal of tennis by making the professional game too fast.

On the other hand, modern equipment has generally improved the enjoyment of the millions of leisure-time players who play tennis for fun.

FRAMES

From the 1920s frame technology started blending different types of wood, and the last wooden rackets used at the highest level of tennis in the early 1980s had carbon fibre linked into the wood strata through the use of epoxy resin.

In the 1960s the first aluminium frames came in, but it was only with Howard Head's first racket with an 'oversize' head in the mid-1970s that racket technology was really revolutionised.

The demise of wood was rapid, with Wimbledon in 1981 providing the last Grand Slam singles final in which both players (Borg and McEnroe) used a wooden frame.

Above: 'State of the art' rackets from 100 years ago

Right: Arthur Ashe winning Wimbledon in 1975 with Howard Head's first 'oversize' racket

1924

THE USSR'S REVOLUTIONARY LEADER LENIN DIED, THE FIRST WINTER OLYMPICS TOOK PLACE, MOHANDAS GHANDI WENT ON HUNGER STRIKE IN INDIA, AND A TOP-QUALITY TENNIS RACKET COST $12

The generic word used to describe modern rackets is 'graphite', but 'composite' would be more accurate because they are essentially a composite construction made mainly from carbon fibre, reinforced with graphite and kevlar, and increasingly titanium. The latest rackets are an offshoot of the aerospace industry, in that the exotic materials that most rackets are made from today (carbon fibre, ceramic fibres, boron etc) are generally acknowledged to be products which resulted from the huge research and development effort that went into the aerospace industry in the 1960s as a result of space programmes.

A comparison between state-of-the-art wooden rackets in 1973 and state-of-the-art carbon fibre composites in 1998 showed the modern rackets to be much lighter, noticeably longer, to have a much bigger head size, and to have about twice the vibration frequency. On weight, the composites were 210-280g compared with 370-425g (7-10oz compared with 13-15oz); on length they were 68-73cm compared with 66-68cm (27-27in, 26-27in) and the head size was 580-870cm^2 compared with 420-450cm^2 (90-135in^2, 65-70in^2).

The fact that composite rackets never warp and seldom break – in marked contrast to wood – has led to a decrease in global sales of premium rackets from around 15 million in 1980 to little more than 7m in 1999. But the fact that wood is biodegradable while the composite substances are not means there may one day be an issue involving the disposal of rackets.

The composite rackets have given players at all levels of tennis two major advantages: a bigger sweet spot and a more efficient power:weight ratio.

The bigger sweet spot has given club players a better chance of making optimum contact with the ball as they don't have to middle it the way they used to with the small sweet spots of wooden and aluminium rackets.

Chart showing the development of the racket.
(Gianni Clerici, The Ultimate Tennis Book)

It has given higher-level players the chance to take speculative swings at balls coming towards them with great power, knowing they have a bigger sweet spot with which to hit a decent shot back.

The power:weight ratio has meant the weight of the racket has got lighter while the power of the ball coming off it has become greater, and improvements in the way composite materials are used in racket manufacture, among them the use of sophisticated mixtures of graphite and titanium fibres, are increasing this trend.

For leisure players it allows them an improvement in the quality of their tennis, but some fans are worried that it's making men's tennis too quick to be watchable, especially on grass, although recent Wimbledons suggest men's grasscourt tennis is hardly suffering a drop in popularity.

The lighter rackets have also changed tennis technique, notably making it more viable to hit wristy shots, with a resultant change in the grips and strokes that are taught.

Above: Andre Agassi was one of the first to use a racket with titanium, made by Head

Left: Firing bullets – Jimmy Connors with the Wilson T2000 aluminium racket he used for most of his career

Centre: Patrick Rafter with a midsize racket from Prince

TALKING POINT

THE SPEED OF THE GAME

One of the big talking points in tennis over recent years has been whether modern rackets have become so powerful they have speeded up the game to the point of destroying it as a spectacle. The debate is hardly new.

Consider this:

• Spencer Gore, who in 1877 won the first ever Wimbledon, told an interviewer that the serve was too dominant because 376 games out of 601 had gone with serve (62.5%).

• In an interview in 1920 Bill Tilden said the dominance of the serve was so great that the second serve would soon be eliminated.

• In 1932 the big-hitting Ellsworth Vines won Wimbledon with an ace which his opponent Bunny Austin claimed was so fast he didn't know whether it had passed his forehand or backhand side.

• The last amateur Wimbledon final in 1967 between John Newcombe and Wilhelm Bungert had virtually no rallies because both men had powerful serves.

There is no doubt the modern rackets do give more power. According to scientific analysis, a modern graphite racket has about 28.5% more power in a rally and 7.4% on a serve.

These figures come from a calculation in which the Apparent Coefficient of Restitution (the speed of the ball after impact divided by the speed of the ball before impact multiplied by 100%) was worked out for a wooden and a graphite racket, and in the case of the 28.5% figure, it assumes a ball reaching the racket at 25 metres per second (82 feet per second).

This means the opponent has less time to react (about 15% less time facing a serve with a composite racket than facing the same serve delivered with a wooden racket). But the modern racket has a bigger sweet spot, so the returner doesn't have to hit the ball quite as precisely in the middle of the racket as was the case with wooden or aluminium rackets.

Connors and Agassi both had brilliant returns of serve, but their different eras means it's impossible to say who was better

For example, Jimmy Connors and Andre Agassi are recognised as arguably the greatest returners of serve in the history of tennis, but who was better?

It's impossible to judge, because Connors faced less powerful servers but had a much smaller sweet spot on his Wilson T2000 racket, while Agassi has a much bigger sweet spot but faces much faster serves.

So have rackets contributed to the game getting faster? Yes, but there are a whole load of other factors too. The size and weight of the ball has an impact on speed. And what of human beings? – today's top professionals are much fitter than their counterparts from 30 and more years ago. They are trained intensively from an early age and have nutritional advisers alongside technical coaches.

And here's another point: male tennis players are generally taller and more powerful than they were in the past. But is that because of racket technology, or would that have happened anyway?

Does this prove anything? That modern players are taller and heavier, yes. But does it explain the increased speed of the game? Not really.

HEIGHTS & WEIGHTS OF SELECTED MALE TENNIS CHAMPIONS FROM THE PAST & PRESENT

	YEAR OF FIRST GS TITLE	HEIGHT	HEIGHT	WEIGHT	WEIGHT
Henri Cochet	1926	1.67m	5' 6"	66kg	145lbs
Bill Johnston	1915	1.67m	5' 6"	55kg	121lbs
Ken Rosewall	1953	1.70m	5' 7"	61kg	135lbs
Bobby Riggs	1939	1.73m	5' 8"	not known	
Rod Laver	1960	1.74m	5' 8"	66kg	145lbs
Jimmy Connors	1973	1.78m	5' 10"	70kg	155lbs
Norman Brookes	1907	1.80m	5' 11"	68kg	150lbs
Andre Agassi	1992	1.80m	5' 11"	77kg	170lbs
Frank Sedgman	1949	1.80m	5' 11"	77kg	170lbs
John McEnroe	1979	1.80m	5' 11"	75kg	164lbs
Björn Borg	1974	1.80m	5' 11"	73kg	160lbs
Vitas Gerulaitis	1977	1.83m	6' 0"	70kg	155lbs
Arthur Ashe	1968	1.85m	6' 1"	69kg	151lbs
Donald Budge	1937	1.85m	6' 1"	73kg	160lbs
Fred Perry	1933	1.85m	6' 1"	78kg	171lbs
Pete Sampras	1990	1.85m	6' 1"	77kg	170lbs
Ellsworth Vines	1931	1.88m	6' 2"	65kg	143lbs
Bill Tilden	1920	1.90m	6' 3"	70kg	155lbs
Gustavo Kuerten	1997	1.91m	6' 3"	80kg	178lbs
Marat Safin	2000	1.93m	6' 4"	88kg	195lbs
Richard Krajicek	1996	1.96m	6' 5"	88kg	195lbs

Source: Andrew Coe: ITF/TST

Is the increased speed of the game a problem? The technology exists to make tennis on clay faster and tennis on grass slower, but is this desirable? – isn't it part of the fun to have different players doing well on different surfaces?

Every tournament strives for playing conditions that give all players a chance – after all, it's hardly in Wimbledon's interest for the baseliners to feel they haven't a chance, nor in Roland Garros' interest for the attackers to feel it's only worth turning up for the first round losers' prize money.

That means we are seeing aces and rallies on all surfaces, and they do seem to be getting faster, but it doesn't mean there aren't grasscourt, claycourt and indoor specialists. Maybe we're blaming technology because technology can't answer back!

Above: Composite rackets are much tougher than wooden ones, normally

GRIP SIZES

Grip sizes in imperial & metric measurements

1	4$\frac{1}{8}$"	10.5cm
2	4$\frac{1}{4}$"	10.8cm
3	4$\frac{3}{8}$"	11.1cm
4	4$\frac{1}{2}$"	11.4cm
5	4$\frac{5}{8}$"	11.7cm

A general guide to working out a player's optimum grip size is to measure in inches the distance between the tip of the third finger and the second lifeline (as shown)

Above: If a professional has a logo on their strings, it normally means they are paid to use that racket

Tennis rackets today generally cost a lot more than the old wooden rackets used to sell for, but for that they last longer and don't go out of shape. In America in the 1920s, a top-quality Wilson, Wright & Ditson or Spalding wooden racket cost around $12, which with increases in the retail price index would today mean around $110.

With the top-grade rackets today costing up to $300, there has been a considerable price increase to pay for the technology that goes into modern rackets.

The leading brands of tennis racket are: (in alphabetical order) Babolat, Donnay, Dunlop, Fischer, Head, Penn, Prince, Pro-Kennex, Slazenger, Wilson, Yonex (see page 174).

STRINGS & STRINGING

Rackets are coloured and branded to sell, but needless to say the greatest racket will only work if it has been properly strung, and strings too have been vastly improved in recent years as a result of technological advances.

Until the 1940s, all rackets were strung with sheep's gut, but then the first synthetic strings began to be made of nylon, and these days there are a number of synthetics, which can broadly be divided into nylon, polyester, kevlar and other substances. Nylons account for most synthetic stringing because they offer resilience and power, polyesters are the next most popular for offering control and durability, and kevlar has lost popularity in recent years and now may account for just five per cent of the market.

Though a modern racket strung with synthetic will offer a much better deal for the player than a wood racket with gut, gut is still thought of as being the string which offers the maximum 'response' to the player. Until 20 years ago, gut was very fragile and notoriously vulnerable to breaking when wet, but advances in coating have made gut strings more durable.

There are essentially two ways of stringing a racket: using two strings or one. For many years stringers had to use two strings, because between 11 and 12.2 metres of string (37-40 feet) is needed for one racket, and the size of a sheep's intestine meant it was hard to find anything more than about 8m (26ft).

But since the advent of synthetic strings, and the development of cow's gut (cows have bigger intestines than sheep), it's now possible to string a racket with one string.

If you look at a stringing job and see only two knots on the inside of the frame, it means its been strung with one string. Using one string is also quicker, but many people are not convinced that using one string gives the best performance.

There are some players who like using two different strings because it gives them their own preferred 'feel'. For example Andre Agassi uses synthetics for his vertical (or main) strings and gut for his horizontals (or crosses), which obviously requires two strings. And the Japanese racket maker Yonex insist on two strings to ensure the longevity of their rackets – a damaged racket brought back to them will not have its guarantee respected if it is found to have been strung with one string.

The traditional wisdom has been that the tighter the strings the more 'feel' a player has, and the slacker the strings the more power. This is true in terms of the measured performance of rackets strung with different tensions.

However, recent research has suggested it may not be quite that simple, and that players are best having the tension that makes them feel best when they hit the ball.

Periodic experiments with exotic stringing techniques have led to one or two bizarre concoctions, the most notorious of which was the knotted 'spaghetti stringing' in the 1970s. It generated so much topspin that it had to be banned because it threatened to wreck the sport – a simple topspin shot with a spaghetti strung racket was virtually unplayable for the opponent. The legacy of 'spaghetti stringing' was that the ITF subsequently drew up rules on the dimensions allowed in a racket and stringing.

The leading brands of string are: (for gut) Babolat, Bow Brand, Clip, Pacific, Technifibre; (for synthetics) Babolat, Gamma, Gosen, Prince, Toa, Wilson, Yonex (see page 174).

Left: The two-handed backhand
is so common that rackets have
to have a long enough grip for the
width of two hands

Below: Stefan Edberg replaces the
overgrip during a change of ends

GRIPS

If the string bed is the racket's interface with
the ball, the grip is the player's interface with the
racket, and a comfortable grip is vitally important
to a properly functioning racket, despite the fact
that the frame gets all the attention from the
marketing executives.

Grips have traditionally been made from leather,
though most new rackets are now automatically
fitted with grips made from polyurethane.

Many players at all levels use a thin overgrip that
is wound onto the main polyurethane grip and
is renewed every couple of sets or matches –
professional players frequently change overgrips
at changes of ends (try doing that in less than
90 seconds, and see how difficult it is!). Overgrips
are particularly good for players with sweaty
hands, as too much sweat can shorten the lifespan
of the leather or polyurethane grip considerably,
and anyway it's often nice to start a new set or
match with a new clean grip.

Grips have traditionally been measured in
inches, and the measurement is taken from the
circumference of the grip once the base leather
or polyurethane grip has been put on (ie. without
any overgrip).

The most common grip size is $4^3/_8$, meaning it
is $4^3/_8$ inches (11.1cm) around the base grip.

Despite increasing metrification, grip sizes
haven't gone into centimetres, but manufacturers
now tend to use new grip sizes 1-5 (see table on
facing page).

A grip has to be the right size for the player's
hand or there can be problems in the forearm
and elbow tendons, and a lack of confidence when
hitting the ball. While every hand is different, a
general guide is to take a measurement from the
tip of the ring finger (third finger on the playing
hand) to the second 'lifeline' on the palm of the
hand. If that doesn't feel comfortable, experiment!

For those players for whom grip size 5 is still
too small, there are 'grip enlargers' which are
essentially heat-shrink tubing that can be put under
the base grip to make the grip circumference an
eighth of an inch wider, or one grip size larger.

DROP SHOTS!

All official tennis balls were
made white until the late 1960s.
Then the first experiments
were made with yellow balls, as
they were thought to be more
visible to television viewers.
Though they were soon on sale
in shops, it wasn't until 1972
that the International Lawn
Tennis Federation allowed yellow
balls to be used in its sanctioned
tournaments, which included
the Grand Slam events.

Wimbledon was the last major
tournament to play with white
balls in 1985, the now ubiquitous
yellow being introduced in 1986.

BALLS

A standard ball weighs just under 60 grammes (2 ounces), of which about 11g ($^1/_3$ oz) is made up of cloth and about 47g (1$^2/_3$ oz) of rubber and a bit of glue. Most of the rubber comes from east Asian countries, notably Malaysia.

Under the Rules of Tennis (see page 134), a ball has to be uniform in colour (white or yellow), and the seams have to be stitchless. It must weigh between 56 and 59.4g (1.975-2.095 oz), and have a diameter between 6.541 and 6.858 centimetres (2.575-2.700 inches). There are also pressurised balls where the internal pressure is greater than the external pressure – these are allowed for tournaments at altitude (more than 1219 metres, or 4000 feet, above sea level).

The ITF is currently seeking opinions on whether a bigger ball – 6-8 per cent bigger – would help slow down the pace of the game. It has also just allowed the use of three different types of balls designed for fast, medium and slow paced courts – the bigger the ball, the more appropriate it is for a slower surface (see The Rules of Tennis page 134).

Sales of tennis balls are an important indicator as to the health of the sport, because the relatively short lifespan of a ball means that if balls aren't being bought, tennis isn't being played. Andrew Coe, who until June 2001 was the ITF's technical director, estimates the number of premium-quality balls sold each year at 23-25 million dozen, or around 300 million balls.

Compared with inflation, the price of balls came down during the 20th century. In 1921 the Wilson 'official' top-grade ball was advertised in America at $6 per dozen; allowing for increases in the retail price index, that should make a dozen balls around $54 today, but in America they cost around $12 – that's 80 per cent less than in the 1920s.

America is by far the cheapest place to buy tennis balls, but even the European prices are cheaper than 100 years ago.

The French and US Opens are two of the tournaments that have their own names on their balls, even though neither manufactures its own

A dozen Slazenger tennis balls in England cost 13 shillings or 65 pence in 1906; allowing for inflation, this would make a dozen 32 British pounds, but the Slazenger Wimbledon ball currently costs around 26 pounds per dozen – that's 19 per cent cheaper than in 1906.

The leading ball manufacturers (in alphabetical order) are: Dunlop, Penn, Pro-Kennex, Slazenger, Tretorn, Wilson, (see page174).

SHOES

In a sport that developed on grass, the major requirement of lawn tennis footwear was that it gave maximum grip without wrecking the grass.

This meant that for years tennis shoes were made with canvas tops and rubber soles. But since the second world war, the growth of the sport opened up business opportunities for the shoe manufacturers, and the advances in technology have made today's shoes unrecognisable from those worn 60 years ago.

Today's top tennis shoes are made of leather and polyurethane – leather as a breathable fabric for the upper, polyurethane for the sole because of its ability to be durable but also lightweight.

Different soles for different surfaces – there is an array of varying footwear in tennis to go with the array of different conditions underfoot

That's why today's tennis shoes look much bulkier than those worn two generations ago, but are in many cases lighter.

The polyurethane soles also allow for different profiles to be made for different foot types and different surfaces. While club players using a grass court will by and large use a multi-purpose tennis shoes, the professionals and other high-level players use special grasscourt shoes with pimpled soles. The soles for indoor play are generally flatter, and the main difference between the profile for hard and clay courts are that on clay a player needs to slide, while on hard courts the emphasis is on maximum grip.

Almost all tennis shoes are manufactured in Asia these days, and all the leading manufacturers have come in for criticism for using cheap labour in degrading working conditions. Many have responded by paying minimum wages, though campaign groups point out that minimum wages in many Asian countries aren't high enough to guarantee an income that people can live off.

Nike came in for major criticism among American students in 2000 for paying poor wages to sweatshop workers in Asia, but while the criticisms are widely felt to be justified, Nike is only the worst because it probably sells more shoes than its competitors.

Few of the other companies have escaped criticism, including Reebok even though it has taken the progressive step of forming an in-house human rights department at his headquarters in Massachussetts.

The names which manufacture tennis footwear are generally the same as those associated with tennis clothing. Among the top brands are: Adidas, Asics, Diadora, Fila, Lotto, Nike, Reebok and Sergio Tacchini (see page 174).

RACKET, CLOTHING & SHOES SPONSORS

Every August, the American magazine 'Tennis Week' publishes a
list of the top 45 men and women players together with the racket they use,
and the company that provides their clothing and shoes.

MEN

NAME	RANK	COUNTRY	RACKET	CLOTHING	SHOES
Gustavo Kuerten	1	BRA	Head i. Prestige MP	Diadora	Diadora
Andre Agassi	2	USA	Head i. Radical OS	Nike	Nike
Marat Safin	3	RUS	Dunlop 200g MuscleWeave	Adidas	Adidas
Lleyton Hewitt	4	AUS	Yonex Super RD Tour 90	Nike	Nike
Juan Carlos Ferrero	5	ESP	Prince Triple Threat Graphite MidPlus	Sergio Tacchini	Sergio Tacchini
Patrick Rafter	6	AUS	Prince Triple Threat Warrior Midsize	Reebok	Reebok
Yevgeny Kafelnikov	7	RUS	Fischer Pro No1	Nike	Nike
Sebastien Grosjean	8	FRA	Head i. Prestige MP	Reebok	Reebok
Tim Henman	9	GBR	Dunlop 200g Muscle Weave	Adidas	Adidas
Alex Corretja	10	ESP	Babolat Pure Drive Plus	Lacoste	Asics*
Pete Sampras	11	USA	Wilson Pro Staff Original 6.0	Nike	Nike
Arnaud Clement	12	FRA	Head i. Prestige MP	Lacoste	Lacoste
Roger Federer	13	SUI	Wilson Pro Staff 6.0 85"	Nike	Nike
Thomas Johansson	14	SWE	Dunlop 200g Muscle Weave	Adidas	Adidas
Tommy Haas	15	GER	Dunlop Muscle Weave 200G	Nike	Nike
Carlos Moya	16	ESP	Babolat Pure Drive	Nike	Nike
Goran Ivanisevic	17	CRO	Head i. Prestige Mid	Sergio Tacchini	Sergio Tacchini
Jan-Michael Gambill	18	USA	Prince Triple Threat Hornet Oversize	Adidas	Adidas
Thomas Enqvist	19	SWE	Head i. Prestige MP	Asics	Asics
Andrei Pavel	20	ROM	Fischer Pro Tour	Nike	Nike
Fabrice Santoro	21	FRA	Head i. Prestige MP XL	Lacoste	Lacoste
Dominik Hrbaty	22	SVK	Fischer Pro Extreme	Nike	Nike
Nicolas Kiefer	23	GER	Wilson Hyper Pro Staff 5.0 Stretch	Adidas	Adidas
Magnus Norman	24	SWE	Wilson Hyper Pro Staff 6.1	Nike	Nike
Albert Portas	25	ESP	Babolat Pure Drive	Adidas	Adidas
Nicolas Lapentti	26	ECU	Babolat Pure Drive	Adidas	Adidas
Hicham Arazi	27	MAR	Head i. Prestige Mid	Sergio Tacchini	Sergio Tacchini
Guillermo Canas	28	ARG	Wilson Pro Staff 5.0 Stretch	Ellesse	Ellesse
Greg Rusedski	29	GBR	Donnay Rusedski Pro	Donnay	Adidas*
Andy Roddick	30	USA	Babolat Pure Drive Plus	Reebok	Reebok
Nicolas Escude	31	FRA	Babolat Pure Drive Plus	Sergio Tacchini	Asics*
Guillermo Coria	32	ARG	Prince Triple Threat Graphite MidPlus	Adidas	Adidas
Sjeng Schalken	33	NED	Dunlop 200g Muscle Weave	Nike	Nike
Wayne Ferreira	34	RSA	Dunlop Muscle Weave 200G	Fila	Fila
Todd Martin	35	USA	Wilson Hyper Hammer 5.2	Wilson	Wilson
Bohdan Ulihrach	36	CZE	Fischer Pro No1 98	Adidas*	Adidas*
Mark Philippoussis	37	AUS	Dunlop 200g Muscle Weave	Fila	Fila
Alberto Martin	38	ESP	Babolat Pure Drive Plus	Reebok*	Reebok*
Tommy Robredo	39	ESP	Prince Triple Threat Graphite MidPlus	Nike*	Nike*
Albert Costa	40	ESP	Prince Triple Threat Graphite MidPlus	Nike	Nike
Jiri Novak	41	CZE	Völkl C10 Pro	Alea	Nike*
Xavier Malisse	42	BEL	Prince Triple Threat Rebel MidPlus	Adidas	Adidas
Andreas Vinciguerra	43	SWE	Wilson Hyper Pro Staff 6.1 ST	Asics	Asics
Galo Blanco	44	ESP	Prince	Lotto	Lotto
Franco Squillari	45	ARG	Head Ti. Fire Pro Edition	Le Coq Sportif	Nike*

WOMEN

NAME	RANK	COUNTRY	RACKET	CLOTHING	SHOES
Martina Hingis	1	SUI	Yonex Ultimum RQ Ti-1700 98	Adidas	Adidas
Lindsay Davenport	2	USA	Wilson Hyper Hammer 5.2	Nike	Nike
Jennifer Capriati	3	USA	Prince Triple Threat Rebel Midsize	Fila	Fila
Venus Williams	4	USA	Wilson Hyper Hammer 4.3	Reebok	Reebok
Kim Clijsters	5	BEL	Babolat Pure Drive	Nike	Nike
Justine Henin	6	BEL	Wilson Hyper Hammer 5.2	Le Coq Sportif	Le Coq Sportif
Amelie Mauresmo	7	FRA	Dunlop 200	Nike	Nike
Serena Williams	8	USA	Wilson Hyper Hammer 6.3	Puma	Puma
Nathalie Tauziat	9	FRA	Kinetic 20g Reach	Nike	Nike
Monica Seles	9	USA	Yonex Ultimum RQ TI 200 Long	Yonex	Yonex
Nathalie Tauziat	10	FRA	Kinetic 20g Reach	Lacoste	Lacoste
Serena Williams	11	USA	Wilson Hyper Hammer 6.3	Puma	Puma
Elena Dementieva	12	RUS	Prince Triple Threat Graphite Oversize	Nike*	Nike*
Amanda Coetzer	13	RSA	Wilson Hyper Hammer 5.2	Nike	Nike
Magdalena Maleeva	14	BUL	Yonex Ultimum RD Ti-50	Yonex	Yonex
Meghann Shaugnessy	15	USA	Head Ti.Fire Pro Edition	Adidas	Adidas
Jelena Dokic	16	AUS	Head Ti.S2	Fila	Fila
Silvia Farina Elia	17	ITA	Wilson Hyper Hammer 6.3	Sergio Tacchini	Sergio Tacchini
Arantxa Sanchez-Vicario	18	ESP	Yonex Ultimum RQ TI-1700 Long	Reebok	Reebok
Sandrine Testud	19	FRA	Wilson Hyper Pro Staff 6.1	Lacoste	Lacoste
Anna Kournikova	20	RUS	Yonex Ultimum RQ Ti-1500	Adidas	Adidas
Conchita Martinez	21	ESP	Wilson Hyper Hammer 5.2	Kappa	Kappa
Anke Huber	22	GER	Yonex SRQ-500	Essence	Puma*
Barbara Schett	23	AUT	Head i.S 6	Adidas	Adidas
Iroda Tulyaganova	24	UZB	Babolat Pure Control	Adidas*	Adidas*
Magui Serna	25	ESP	Wilson Hyper Hammer 5.3	Nike	Nike
Henrieta Nagyova	26	SVK	Yonex Pro RD-70	Nike	Nike*
Paola Suarez	27	ARG	Prince Precision Chang Titanium MidPlus	Sergio Tacchini	Sergio Tacchini
Elena Likhovsteva	28	RUS	Wilson Hyper Hammer 5.2	Diadora	Diadora
Chanda Rubin	29	USA	Head i.S 6	Adidas	Adidas
Amy Frazier	30	USA	Prince	Adidas	Adidas
Angeles Montolio	31	ESP	Pure Drive Plus	Nike*	Nike*
Tamarine Tanasugarn	32	THA	Prince Triple Threat Graphite MidPlus	Prince	Prince
Anne Kremer	33	LUX	Babolat Pure Control Plus	Asics	Asics
Lisa Raymond	34	USA	Prince Triple Threat Graphite Midsize	Prince	Prince
Cristina Torrens Valero	35	ESP	Prince	Adidas	Adidas
Patty Schnyder	36	SUI	Head Ti.S2	Adidas	Adidas
Francesca Schiavone	37	ITA	Fischer Pro No1	Nike*	Nike*
Lina Krasnoroutskaya	38	RUS	Dunlop	Reebok	Reebok
Nadia Petrova	39	RUS	Prince Triple Threat Hornet Midsize	Prince	Prince
Ai Sugiyama	40	JPN	Prince Triple Threat Warrior Midsize	Nike	Nike
Tatiana Panova	41	RUS	Prince	Diadora	Diadora
Denisa Chladkova	42	CZE	Völkl C10 Pro	Ellesse	Ellesse
Marlene Weingartner	43	GER	Babolat VS Control	Nike*	Nike*
Rita Grande	44	ITA	Yonex Ultimum RD Ti-50	Ellesse	Yonex
Jana Kandarr	45	GER	Babolat	Sergio Tacchini	Sergio Tacchini
Daja Bedanova	45	CZE	Babolat VS Drive	Nike	Nike

This table from August 2001 is reproduced thanks to 'Tennis Week' and www.tennisweek.com (©copyright tennisweek.com).

* means a player wears these shoes or this clothing but not under contract.

THE YEAR TED TINLING CAUSED
UPROAR AT WIMBLEDON WITH
HIS DESIGN FOR GUSSY
MORAN'S LACE PANTIES WAS
THE YEAR OF THE FIRST ORGAN
TRANSPLANT AND THE
START OF JOSEPH MCCARTHY'S
ANTI-COMMUNIST WITCH HUNT
IN THE USA

*Right: Jack Crawford modelling
1930s off-court wear – an overcoat*

*Below: Bunny Austin, pictured both
on a Player's cigarettes card and
at Wimbledon, was the first man to
wear shorts on the centre court*

CLOTHING

The history of tennis clothing goes back almost to the start of tennis itself. When lawn tennis was first popularised in the 1870s, there was no set attire, but it soon developed. The tendency towards white came in the 1880s though was by no means universal, and women were encouraged to wear black shoes to avoid grass stains showing.

In Great Britain well-brought-up ladies were not supposed to sweat, and certainly not show any naked flesh other than hands and faces, so dresses went nearly to the ground, sleeves to the wrist, and hats were worn on court.

The first indications of function and comfort challenging establishment style came from America, and the first non-British Wimbledon champion, May Sutton in 1905, did her bit to move tennis clothing forward, not least in causing a stir by rolling up her sleeves.

After the first world war hats disappeared, and then the era of Suzanne Lenglen brought some French panache to tenniswear and increased the function and comfort by several steps. She broke the established practice of women wearing corsets, she became known in 1920 for the 'Lenglen bandeau' (a length of coloured silk chiffon wrapped several times round her head), and in 1923 for a silk dress.

All this time the men were dressed in long white trousers and long-sleeved shirts. In the early 1930s Bunny Austin became the first man at Wimbledon to wear shorts, while his sister Joan Lycett became the first woman to play on the centre court without stockings. Fred Perry helped popularise the short-sleeved polo-style shirt when he dominated tennis in the mid-30s.

*Gussy Moran caused a storm when
she wore a pair of lace panties at
Wimbledon designed by Ted Tinling*

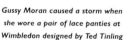

In some countries tennis is still nicknamed 'the white sport' for its tradition of white clothing, but few people realise that Wimbledon's rule about white only dates from 1948. In 1949, one of its umpires Ted Tinling tried to inject some fun into the austere post-war tennis fashions by designing some panties for Gertrude 'Gussy' Moran which had half an inch (1.3cm) of lace trim.

With the 84-year-old dowager queen Mary due to attend the women's doubles final which Moran had reached, the All England Club went into a minor panic. As it happened the queen didn't show because of hot weather, but the damage was done and Tinling fell out with Wimbledon for 20 years.

1936

FRED PERRY'S GREATEST YEAR, AND THE LAST YEAR GREAT BRITAIN WON THE DAVIS CUP, SAW SPORT GET SERIOUSLY INVOLVED WITH POLITICS. JESSE OWENS WAS THE STAR OF THE BERLIN OLYMPICS AND HIS FOUR GOLD MEDALS ANGERED GERMAN DICTATOR ADOLF HITLER WHO STORMED OUT OF THE STADIUM. THAT YEAR HITLER ALSO SENT GERMAN TROOPS INTO THE RHINELAND

In 1972, with Tinling now the official couturier to the newly founded and burgeoning Women's Tennis Association, Wimbledon changed its 'all white' rule to 'predominantly white', allowing for some colour.

By then, coloured clothing had taken root elsewhere, notably in the latter years of the professional circuit before 'open' tennis arrived in 1968, and on the indoor circuit. Yet it seemed the men who benefited more from colour than the women.

In the 1980s, while the women abandoned dresses in favour of the shirt-and-skirt look, the men enjoyed some creative designs, notably the predominantly white shirts worn by Ivan Lendl and Stefan Edberg at the height of their careers.

And in the late 1980s Andre Agassi broke onto the scene, initially in shorts that looked like cut-off jeans, and later in lycra cycle shorts in a range of striking luminous colours. The 1990s saw the partial return of the women's tennis dress, and a return to white, though with navy or black shorts thought of as conservative everywhere except Wimbledon.

Before the tracksuit –
Fred Perry (top centre) in cricket sweater and flannels, G P Hughes (left) wearing a white blazer over his tennis clothes, and (above) Gottfried von Cramm and Henne Henkel sporting striped blazers at Wimbledon

Cuts and colours – Ivan Lendl's Salvador Dali shirt from Adidas in the mid-1980s (middle), Stefan Edberg's first Wimbledon title in 1988 came in this colourful creation from Adidas (top right), Björn Borg's pinstripe shirt from Fila in the 1970s (above right), and (above) the late 1990s fashion for crop tops, worn here by Arantxa Sanchez Vicario (Reebok)

Tennis clothing these days is big business. In the 1970s Björn Borg became the first professional to sign a big-money clothing contract with the Italian company Fila. The pin-stripe shirt in which he won all his 11 Grand Slam titles was so distinctive that Fila has yet to find anything as successful and has even brought back some pin-stripe designs since the mid-1990s.

The big company to emerge in the 1980s was Nike, which now has more top 20 players under contract than any other company. When it bought Pete Sampras out of his contract with Sergio Tacchini in 1994, he was reported to have been paid $20 million over three years to wear Nike's clothing. Though it won't confirm figures Nike is believed to pay Andre Agassi considerably more.

Nike is also the only company that refuses to let its players have logos for other companies on its tenniswear so as to emphasise the Nike brand, but it says it pays its players a compensation fee for this.

Above: Venus Williams is reported to have a $40 million contract with Reebok, believed to be the biggest single endorsement deal in women's tennis

Most tennis shirts, shorts and skirts are still made predominantly from cotton, but with cotton responsible for so many of the world's pesticides, there may soon be strong demand for organic cotton.

Of the tennis clothing manufacturers, Nike is showing greatest interest in incorporating organic cotton into its clothing, though world production is still too small for any company to switch completely to organic.

Because all the clothing companies consider sales information confidential, it is impossible to say who is the market leader in tennis clothing, but it is widely believed to be Nike, with Adidas and Reebok competing for second place.

Other major players include Diadora, Fila, Sergio Tacchini, Asics, Lacoste, Prince and Wilson (see pages 84 and 85 for other names).

The manufacture of tennis clothing has been an area of major technological development, in which textile researchers have constantly striven for the best combination of comfort and absorption of sweat, especially given that during a tennis match a shirt has to soak up a lot of perspiration.

Above: Sergio Tacchini's logo displayed prominently on Gabriela Sabatini's skirt

Left: Anna Kournikova is under contract with Adidas who have difficulty finding anything that looks bad on her

The latest synthetic innovation tried at some of the top tournaments in 2001 is 'Tyvek', a material that looks and feels like paper but is obviously many times stronger. It was used by Roger Federer and Carlos Moya at Wimbledon and Andre Agassi at the US Open, but only in warm-up tops, and it remains to be seen whether it will become usable for tennis shirts.

As well as shirts, tops, shorts, skirts, socks, and both parts of what used to be known as track suits, the last 20 years have seen major growth in accessories such as caps, headwear and wrist bands. The wrist bands are essentially to absorb sweat, but are also used to emphasise a logo.

Below: Martina Navratilova designed her own tennis wear from 1989 to 1991

Above right: Anne White in her full-length body suit that she only wore once at Wimbledon

Right: Andre Agassi's striking look from Nike in the late 1980s – the shirt was deliberately cut shorter at the front than the back so his navel would be seen on the follow-through after a forehand

Headbands were originally worn to keep players' hair out of their eyes and soak up sweat from the forehead, but they have largely given way to tie-your-own bandanas and pirate-style headscarves.

Again, the manufacturers have not been slow to put their logos where they can. For example when Andre Agassi had his flowing locks cut off at the start of 1995, he wore a pirate-style head-dress at the Australian Open, but shortly afterwards Nike gave him a head-dress with the Nike 'swoosh' logo at the front.

White has survived as tennis's principal colour, not so much for traditional reasons, but because it reflects light and is therefore more comfortable than darker colours in hot weather. It is also very good at not showing much sweat, and some players who have played in bolder colours in hot weather have not looked pretty in the latter stages of matches!

1989

ANDRE AGASSI'S LIVELY CLOTHING WAS WORN AS THE BERLIN WALL AND SOVIET INFLUENCE IN EASTERN EUROPE COLLAPSED AND STUDENTS WERE MASSACRED BY CHINESE GOVERNMENT FORCES IN BEIJING'S TIANENMEN SQUARE

6. SEMI-PROFESSIONAL & LEISURE TENNIS

Much of this book has concentrated on tennis as an international professional spectacle, yet there are numerous people who play the game to a lesser but highly creditable level.

There are a number of national, regional and global circuits that are neither fully professional nor strictly amateur. And for many people the appeal of tennis is merely a a way of having exercise and fun with friends.

For people wanting to play tennis, the first port of call is going to be a local club or sports centre, or perhaps their national tennis association. But there are still some things that apply to players in any country – this chapter pulls together the general principles relevant to the leisure player, and begins by looking at the main semi-professional circuits which represent the highest level of the game outside the global professional tours.

1980

THE FIRST WHEELCHAIR US OPEN TOOK PLACE THE YEAR JOHN LENNON WAS ASSASSINATED AND THE INTERNATIONAL TELEVISION NEWS CHANNEL CNN WAS ESTABLISHED

WHEELCHAIR TENNIS TOUR

There are various forms of tennis designed for people with disabilities, but the one circuit that is global and partly professional is the NEC Wheelchair Tennis Tour.

Tennis played by people in wheelchairs really dates from 1976 when a Californian Brad Parks, who was wheelchair bound following a ski-ing accident at age 18, organised it into a sport in its own right. The rules are the same as for able-bodied tennis, with the exception that the ball is allowed to bounce twice before a player has to hit it back (see page 145).

The first US Open wheelchair event took place in 1980 though it didn't have prize money until 1991. By 1981 there was a Wheelchair Tennis Players Association (WTPA), and the growth of the sport was so rapid that the International Wheelchair Tennis Federation (IWTF) was set up in 1988 by eight countries.

In the following 10 years more than 50 others joined, and it is estimated that some form of organised wheelchair tennis is played in at least 70 countries.

Wheelchair doubles as played on the grass of Wimbledon in 2001

Brad Parks, the effective founder of wheelchair tennis

In 1992 the global Wheelchair Tennis Tour was started with sponsorship from the Davis Cup's then sponsor NEC. In 1998 the IWTF was fully integrated into the International Tennis Federation (ITF), making wheelchair tennis the first sport for disabled people to be run by the sport's overall world governing body. Wheelchair tennis is now run by the ITF's Wheelchair Tennis Committee, with the remnants of the IWTF now acting as an advisory body to this committee under the name IWTA (Association).

The 2001 NEC Wheelchair Tennis Tour had 118 events in 32 countries on three surfaces: clay, hard and indoor carpet. The two Super Series events – the British Open in July and the US Open in October – are the pinnacle of the year, except in Olympic years when the Paralympic tennis event is the highlight.

The competitors on the tour are a mixture of amateur and professional, with the pros chasing total prize money exceeding $500,000.

The tour also has its own stars, with the two wheelchair world champions crowned alongside the full world champions in an annual dinner held in Paris during Roland Garros. The 1999 world champions Stephen Welch from the USA and Australian Daniela di Toro are among the most charismatic figures in wheelchair tennis. The 2001 champions were Australian David Hall and Esther Vergeer from the Netherlands.

Some of the top wheelchair players are sometimes asked to play a demonstration match at full able-bodied tour events, and frequently leave spectators who are watching for the first time gasping with admiration at the speed, variety and athleticism of wheelchair tennis.

TENNIS FOR OTHER DISABILITIES

Wheelchair tennis is currently the only form of tennis for disabled people coordinated at international level. Among the other forms, tennis for the deaf looks to be the closest to organising itself into a global circuit. There are already a number of tennis tournaments for the deaf, some of them 'open' though the prize money is nominal.

QUIET PLEASE!

*"I was always a believer in stamping on
my opponent if I got him down,
at Wimbledon or anywhere else.
I never wanted to give him the chance to get up"*

FRED PERRY

Hall of Fame page 125

There are tournaments in America for single-leg and single-arm amputees, there are some in Australia for the visually impaired, and some national associations run tennis for people with learning difficulties, though there are numerous problems in finding a practical definition of 'learning difficulty' that can be used to determine who is eligible for a tournament. There is also the question of allowing people with minor disabilities to compete in mainstream tennis, and a number of national tennis associations have staff working to break down barriers which currently prevent people with minor disabilities from playing the game.

For details about wheelchair tennis, contact the ITF (see page 162), or for other forms of tennis for handicapped people try your national association (also page 162).

VETERANS' TOURNAMENTS

Much as many thirtysomethings will not like to hear this, in tennis you are a veteran at 35. At least that is the age at which you can play international veterans' tournaments, and while you can play as long as you like, the highest age group considered is 85 and over for men and 75 and over for women. Between 35 and 85 there are age divisions every five years, though in some countries some divisions are missed out (for example in Great Britain after 35 and over the next category is 45 and over, not 40).

For many spectators, veterans' tournaments mean the competitive exhibition tournaments involving the great players of yesteryear. These do exist and receive a lot of publicity. The ATP runs a seniors tour, Jimmy Connors runs his own 'Champions' circuit, and all four Slams run invitation tournaments for players over 35, some matches of which end up on the show courts. Yet there is a fully structured veterans tour run by the International Tennis Federation which determines the best in the world in each official 'Vets' age group.

Obviously players can play in a lower age group if they feel sufficiently confident and competitive, but they cannot play in an older age group until they reach that age.

In 2000 there were 144 international veterans events on the international circuit supervised by the ITF. Though it is a global circuit, Europe and North America predominate, with only a few events in Central America, Asia/Oceania and Africa.

The world championships are held in two stagings at different times of the year: one for the 35-50 age divisions and one for the divisions for players aged 55 and over.

According to the ITF, veterans' tennis is now bigger than any other group of tennis competitions worldwide. Though the quality of tennis is generally considered to be better among the ITF veterans' tournaments compared with the exhibition events involving former great players, very few of the big names of tennis show longevity by playing through the age groups at a high level. This is probably because they have achieved all they want to in their peak years and find little motivation to stay competitive.

Notable exceptions are Roger Taylor, Gardnar Mulloy, and Judy Tegart Dalton. Taylor, three times a semi-finalist at Wimbledon, has played on the veterans' circuit since he retired from top-level tennis in the late 1970s. Mulloy, who won five Grand Slam doubles titles in the late 1940s, has won US national veterans championships in singles and doubles in every age division, has had a veterans cup named after him, and continues to play world championships in his late 80s. And Dalton, who won eight Grand Slam doubles titles and was Wimbledon singles finalist in 1968, won back-to-back women's over-60 world championship titles in 1997-98.

JUNIOR TOURNAMENTS

Junior tournaments are organised on a variety of levels, ranging from the local club or public courts to the junior events at the four Grand Slams. Local junior tournaments therefore also have a variety of players, ranging from youngsters who just want to check out how good they are, to those aspiring to greatness who view the local junior tournament as the initial rung of a ladder that leads to the great arenas of tennis.

Martina Hingis (left) lost her final junior match to Meilen Tu in the 1994 US Open girls singles final

ITF WORLD JUNIOR CHAMPIONS SINCE 1978

BOYS

Boys who finished at the top of the junior world rankings in the year in question.

1978 **Ivan Lendl** TCH	
1979 **Raul Viver** ECU	
1980 **Thierry Tulasne** FRA	
1981 **Pat Cash** AUS	
1982 **Guy Forget** FRA	
1983 **Stefan Edberg** SWE	
1984 **Mark Kratzmann** AUS	
1985 **Claudio Pistolesi** ITA	
1986 **Javier Sanchez** ESP	
1987 **Jason Stoltenberg** AUS	
1988 **Nicolas Pereira** VEN	
1989 **Nicklas Kulti** SWE	
1990 **Andrea Gaudenzi** ITA	
1991 **Thomas Enqvist** SWE	
1992 **Brian Dunn** USA	
1993 **Marcelo Rios** CHI	
1994 **Federico Browne** ARG	
1995 **Mariano Zabaleta** ARG	
1996 **Sebastien Grosjean** FRA	
1997 **Arnaud di Pasquale** FRA	
1998 **Roger Federer** SUI	
1999 **Kristian Pless** DEN	
2000 **Andy Roddick** USA	
2001 **Gilles Muller** LUX	

Marcelo Rios – world No1 junior in 1993, world No1 in 1998

Unfortunately, junior tournaments are not just an interesting showcase for young talent, but also increasingly a very sad showcase for highly ambitious parents, many of whom seem to see nothing wrong in making a spectacle of themselves courtside during their offspring's matches and humiliating them afterwards if they've lost.

ASPIRING TO GREATNESS

The worldwide junior circuit run by the ITF began in 1977 and is for the world's best juniors aged between 12 and 18 (players have to be 12 to compete, and can go on in juniors until the end of the year in which they have their 18th birthday).

The tournaments are graduated in level from the Grand Slams at the top through five levels, below which are national and local events. The ITF junior programme also includes regional championships (for groups of countries) and international team competitions for juniors.

Up to the end of 2001, the top level of junior tournaments, known as Group A, involved nine events: the four Grand Slam junior tournaments plus the Coffee Bowl in Costa Rica (January), the Banana Bowl in São Paulo (March), the Italian Open in Milan (May), the 'Super Japan' in Osaka (October), and the Orange Bowl in Miami (December).

However, from 2002 the four Slams will form a tier of their own. There is no prize money at these tournaments, though players may have some income from a sponsor that is dependent on them reaching a certain round at major tournaments.

The junior rankings, introduced in 1978, work in a similar way to the rankings on the adult men's and women's tours, with points gained for wins in internationally sanctioned junior tournaments, and more points to be gained in the later rounds.

Partly because of the need to allow youngsters the chance to keep up some level of education, and partly because of the cost of travelling internationally, juniors can take their best six results to make up their ranking compared to the much higher numbers on the adult tours.

There are rankings in singles and doubles, and the top-ranked player at the end of the year is considered the world junior champion and is honoured at the ITF's plush champions dinner in Paris during the following year's French Open.

There are numerous top-level players who have done well in juniors and gone on to major success on the full circuits. Ivan Lendl and Hana Mandlikova were the first world junior champions in 1978, Pat Cash topped the junior rankings in 1981, Stefan Edberg became the first and so far only player to win the junior Grand Slam when he was world junior champion in 1983, and more recent junior No1s to make the grade include Gabriela Sabatini, Thomas Enqvist, Marcelo Rios, Martina Hingis, Sebastien Grosjean and Roger Federer.

The world first took notice of Hingis when she won the French Open girls' singles aged 12 in 1993, making her still the youngest-ever Grand Slam junior champion.

But there are also plenty of cases where a player doing well in juniors has not fulfilled their potential at full tour level, and plenty of players who did little or nothing in juniors but have gone on to great things. For example, Brian Dunn, Cristina Tessi, Zdenka Malkova and Nino Louarssabichvili have all been world junior champions, but few tennis fans will have heard of them. On the other hand, Andre Agassi, Pete Sampras, Yevgeny Kafelnikov, Monica Seles, Steffi Graf and Arantxa Sanchez-Vicario all did very little in juniors yet all reached the full No1 ranking.

The likelihood of anyone emulating Stefan Edberg's junior Grand Slam is small, not just because of the high level of competition on the junior circuit, but because the need to protect youngsters from a full global circuit means very few of the world's top juniors play all four Slams.

Martina Hingis aged 12 at Roland Garros in 1993 after becoming the youngest-ever winner of a junior Grand Slam title

It's hard breaking into the junior circuits, but for those who show promise there can be financial assistance. National associations often have money available to support juniors, and the ITF offers travel grants and runs touring teams for the most promising youngsters from traditionally poorer countries.

The ITF is the only organisation that runs an international junior circuit, though some regional tennis associations run circuits for specific age groups. For example, the European and South American associations ETA and Cosat run circuits for under 16, under 14 and under 12 age groups (age on 1 January), but the ITF is the only body running an international under 18 circuit. In some countries there are a few junior tournaments at national level organised outside the auspices of the recognised national tennis association (page 162).

JUST FOR FUN

The fact that there are many highly ambitious players at junior tournaments should not put off those youngsters who either just want a bit of competition or who want to check out how good they are compared to their age group. If you want to play in a tournament but don't know where the nearest one is, your national association will have a list of events (see page 162).

A Note of Caution – It's part of being a youngster to have dreams, and the world would be a dull place without a child hitting a tennis ball in the street or a public park and dreaming of being on the centre court. But to turn those dreams into reality can be heartbreakingly difficult.

Professional tennis is a fiercely competitive world, and a look at the players who have 'made it' reveals a very high percentage whose parents were either tennis coaches or members of tennis clubs, who started at age 4-6 and who were having three tennis lessons a week by the age of eight. It doesn't mean those who aren't from that background can't make it, and it certainly doesn't mean that tennis can't be fun if you don't become a professional. But unless a youngster has started by 10 and has regular exposure to good quality coaching, experience shows they will have to be a genuinely exceptional talent to make it into the world's top 100.

HOW DOES SOMEONE START PLAYING TENNIS?

The times when tennis spawns most new recruits are when a major tournament has either come to town or been well featured on television. Just after the four Slams, the streets, gardens and public courts of towns in Australia, France, Britain and America have people who have dug out an old racket from a garage or attic, and are busy finding out that what they've seen the top professionals do isn't quite as easy as it looks.

The ATP's FanFests, in which people could hit balls against painted walls, and the now ubiquitous netted radar guns for measuring the speed of serves, have got people holding a racket and hitting a ball, sometimes for the first time, often for the first time in a while. And that can lead to people wanting to play.

For those starting absolutely from the beginning, the obvious essentials are rackets and balls. Once you've found a court to use, the next most important thing is shoes. Because tennis requires sudden movements from side to side and front to back, and lots of little steps in a short space of time, the most important item of clothing is a pair of tennis shoes, and bad shoes can lead to all sorts of injuries.

The technology has improved to a stage where reasonable tennis shoes are available for reasonable prices. Either go for a pair of shoes specifically made for tennis, or for a pair of cross-trainers that are well supported around the heel.

Because tennis involves a number of multi-directional movements that often involve sudden changes in direction, it's vital that players are properly warmed up before they go on court to reduce the risk of muscle strains, ligament sprains and damage to joints. Awareness of the need for pre-activity warm-up and stretching exercises has grown during the last two decades, but stretching cold muscles is ineffective and may be more damaging than not stretching at all. (*The Book of Tennis* offers a programme of stretching exercises on page 98.)

Anna Kournikova at 12 – she has still to scale the same heights she did as a junior

Two eight-year-olds play on a short tennis court, half the length of a full court with a lower net

Qualified physiotherapists recommend gentle mobility and warm-up exercises – for example several minutes' steady cycling on an exercise bike, a few minutes' of easy jogging, or perhaps a brisk 10-minute walk to the tennis club – as a good start to raise the body's temperature and get the muscles warmed up. This should be followed by a controlled stretching routine involving all muscle groups plus those muscles used specifically in tennis.

As part of their warm-up, many players from amateur club players to top-level professionals play a half-court game for the first few minutes, which involves both players hitting the ball from just behind the service line, and gradually moving back to use the full court until they are fully warmed up. Players can also be at risk of injury if they sit out after having played one game and don't stretch before playing again – they don't realise they've cooled down, and when they go back on court that's when Achilles tendons can snap!

PUBLIC COURTS

For people who want to play but who aren't members of a club, there are normally courts available for public hire.

These generally fall into three categories:

• **Public parks** – *courts maintained by the local civic authorities which members of the public can use, either free or for a fee payable to a civic official.*

• **Clubs** – *some clubs try to maximise income from their courts by hiring them out to non-members at times when members seldom want to play.*

Coaching good technique at an early age is a key to youngsters fulfilling their potential

1 9 8 3

STEFAN EDBERG COMPLETED THE FIRST JUNIOR GRAND SLAM JUST AFTER SALLY RIDE HAD BECOME THE FIRST AMERICAN WOMAN IN SPACE

• **Tennis centres** – *sports centres which may be specifically or mainly for tennis but frequently include other facilities like squash courts, and increasingly fitness rooms and swimming pools. Members of the public can normally hire out courts, though in some of these a registration or membership fee might be necessary.*

In some inner cities in North America, there are practice walls with a line painted at the height of the net to be found in public recreation playgrounds. These are usually free to use on a first-come-first-served basis, though they sometimes share the same playing area as a basketball hoop or a street hockey space.

CLUBS

The simple tennis club has gone through many forms and many eras. When lawn tennis took off in the 1870s, it needed land, lawns and gardeners, and that combination was normally only found in large houses and private clubs frequented by rich people. (Wimbledon had started as a croquet club in 1870, so the shift to making grass fit for tennis was a relatively easy one.)

Until the second world war, grass and clay were the predominant surfaces, both of which require considerable maintenance, but the advent of all-weather maintenance-free concrete courts opened up the possibility of clubs with fewer overheads, which helped reduce the elite image of tennis somewhat. Ironically, the perceived need for indoor courts is making tennis more economically elite again, because the cost of the building, the courts, heating, lighting and administration is much higher than at a club where players can just turn up if they have a key to the club gates.

Clubs take many forms. Some are run by a committee of lay people; some are private commercial initiatives where the customers form themselves into a club for the purpose of playing interclub matches; some are clubs run by the regular users of civic sporting facilities; and an increasing model aimed at families is the multi-sports club that has tennis courts alongside other facilites, normally squash and badminton courts, a high technology fitness room, a swimming pool, restaurant, shops and a play area for young children.

It is different from country to country, region to region, and town to town, but in general the cheaper the club is to join, the more it will be run by voluntary work (or be heavily subsidised by a local government or sponsor).

Unfortunately, tennis clubs in many countries still suffer from an elitist image. That is partly due to the remnants of tennis's image as a 'white sport' practised by rich people in affluent clubs. Yet there is also the question of economics of land, time required and equipment.

A tennis court is between 750 and 800 square metres in area (8000-8600 square feet) 800m² is championship size, but most club courts have shorter run-backs and side areas and are therefore somewhat smaller. A match can have a maximum of four players, that is 360-400m² per player in singles or 180-200m² in doubles (4000ft² singles, 2000ft² doubles).

Tennis players need rackets and normally at least three balls, plus a time commitment for matches of at least an hour and a half per session.

By contrast, in soccer 22 players fill around 6500m² (70,000ft²) of space, making 295m² (3,175ft²) per player. As just one ball and a couple of goalposts are needed between all 22, and no equivalent of rackets, and a maximum of an hour and three quarters is required, it is easy to see why soccer is less elitist than tennis.

At the other end of the scale, the average golf course is around 160,000m² (1,722,240ft²), which means that even with an average of six players on every hole you need 1481m² (15,940ft²) per player. Add the need for a bag of clubs which costs more to put together than the club tennis player's kit bag, plus about four hours for a round which generally only the more affluent have time for, and it is clear why tennis is much less elitist than golf.

ADULT TOURNAMENTS

For adults who play tennis to a reasonable level and would like to test themselves against other players of similar standard, most national tennis associations run a programme of adult tournaments.

Sun, sea and tennis – Jonathan Markson's tennis camp on the Algarve coast of southern Portugal

In about 20 countries these are based on a national system of standard classification or ratings, which allow players to know their level of play and compete in events right for them. Many events offer some prize money.

Ratings are not the same as rankings, as more than one person can have the same rating, but only one can have a given ranking. Unfortunately most ratings systems are nation-specific, but the ITF is currently looking into an international classification system to help promote a 'common language' among players from different countries.

For details of adult tournaments in your country, contact your national tennis association (see page 162).

TENNIS HOLIDAYS

One of the best ways to improve quickly – no matter what level you're starting from – is to go on a tennis holiday. There are literally thousands of camps around the world, some of them connected with big corporations like the Nike Amherst camp in Massachussetts, or the Evert Academy in Florida, others run by enterprising individuals like Jonathan Markson, a Scottish player who has camps in England, Spain and Portugal.

Most of these camps really do offer coaching for everyone from beginners to a reasonably high level, plus the chance to meet like-minded people in the 'après tennis' sessions in the evenings. Bookings are generally made in week-long slots.

If we were to list all the tennis holidays in a book like this, it would run to hundreds of pages. If you want to look into going on a tennis holiday, ask your national association for a list of places and companies that offer tennis holidays.

Whatever clothes you wear, make sure you have decent tennis shoes!

The best websites for starting to look for tennis holidays are:
www.tennis.com
www.tennisresortsonline.com

SPECIAL FEATURE

WARMING UP FOR TENNIS

Tennis is for fitness – yet you have to be reasonably fit to play tennis regardless of your level. In this special feature, we suggest a programme of stretching exercises so you are warmed up for tennis when you play (or use them after tennis as a cool-down routine), and then offer various approaches for increased well-being, fitness and – should you need it – rehabilitation.

A word of warning – Before starting any stretching or fitness exercises, if you have any doubts about your health and/or fitness, first consult your general physician and/or any specialist you might be under the care of.

The following are stretches that are useful for all the muscle groups and those that are commonly used in tennis. The stretches can be done indoors or out without the need for special equipment.

Note that the words 'gently' and 'slowly' appear a lot – that's because these exercises should be done gently and slowly, and without straining, as that is when damage can happen! And don't go straight into them – do a bit of warming up first just to get the heart rate and body temperature up.

It's important to remember the following when doing these stretching exercises:

· *Do not use drastic force to limber up.*

· *Do not hold your breath during a stretch.*

· *Stretch slowly and always under control.*

· *The feeling of a good stretch is what is important, not how far you can stretch.*

· *Let your body adjust gradually to regular stretching.*

· *Don't bounce when you stretch.*

· *Find a place that is comfortable and allows you to stretch and relax at the same time.*

· *Do not lock your knees when stretching.*

For more detailed information, get hold of 'Tennis Medicine for Tennis Coaches', published by the ITF in 2001 and available from the ITF (see page 162).

figure 1   *figure 2*

❶ CALF

This calf stretch will help your walking and running. It will give flexibility and energy to the legs.

To stretch your calf, stand a little way from a solid support and lean on it with your forearms, your head resting on your hands.

Bend one leg and place your foot on the ground in front of you with the other leg straight behind. Slowly move your hips forward, keeping your lower back flat. Be sure to keep the heel of the straight leg on the ground, with toes pointed straight ahead or slightly turned in as you hold the stretch. Hold an easy stretch for 30 seconds. Do not bounce. Then stretch the other leg.

❷ SHOULDERS & NECK

Extend your arms to your sides. Rotate your arms in small circles, increasing their size during the course of 25 repetitions. Repeat in opposite direction. This stretch is excellent for your shoulders and neck.

❸ TRICEPS & TOP OF SHOULDERS

This is a simple stretch for the triceps and top of your shoulders. With arms overhead (figure 1), hold the elbow of one arm with the hand of the other arm (figure 2). Gently pull the elbow behind your head, creating a stretch. Do it slowly. Hold for 15 seconds, and repeat with the other arm.

figure 1

figure 2

❹ NECK

(a) Sit on the floor and cross your legs so your hips don't move. Place the back of your right hand onto your left cheek. Turn the neck as far right as possible (figure 1). When you cannot go any further, force the chin – gently but firmly – a bit further (figure 2). Then release slowly and carefully.

Start with three stretches to the left then three to the right. Increase the number weekly until you reach 10. Hold each stretch for 10 seconds. This stretch can also be done seated with your back to the wall. This way is particularly useful for people with restricted movement.

figure 1

figure 2

(b) *Same as Neck exercise 4a, except instead of your head turning to the right or left, you take your right hand and place it over the left part of the head (figure 1) and pull gently down until you reach a comfortable stretch position (figure 2).*

(c) *Sit on the floor and cross your legs so your hips don't move. Drop your head as if you are trying to touch your shoulder with your right ear. Hold for 10 seconds. Repeat three times, building up each week until you reach 10. Repeat on the other shoulder.*

❺ ARMS, SHOULDERS & UPPER BACK

Interlace your fingers above your head. Now with your palms facing upward, push your arms slightly back and up. Feel the stretch in the arms, shoulders, and upper back. Hold for 15 seconds. Excellent for slumping shoulders.

❻ SHOULDERS & ARMS

This stretch is for the front of the shoulders and arms. You need a doorway, chain-linked fence or wall. Face the fence and hold onto it (or press against it) with your left hand at shoulder level (figure 1). Hold for 10 seconds. Stretch your arm and shoulder at various angles. Each angle will stretch the arm and shoulder differently. Do the same with the other arm.

❼ SIDE MUSCLES

This stretch is excellent for stretching the muscles along your sides, from your arm to your hip and abdominal muscles Stand with your feet about shoulder-width apart and toes pointed straight ahead. Lean to your left side with your left hand sliding down your left side. Repeat stretch leaning to right side. Do 25 sets.

❽ GROIN

Put the soles of your feet together and hold onto your toes. Gently pull yourself forward, bending from the hips, until you feel a good stretch in your groin. You may also feel a stretch in the back. Hold for 40 seconds. Do not make the initial movement of stretch from the head and shoulders but move from the hips. Try to get your elbows on the outside of your legs so the stretch position has stability and balance.

❾ FRONT OF HIP

To stretch the muscles in the front of the hip, move one leg forward until the knee of the forward leg is directly over the ankle. Your other knee should be resting on the floor. Now, without changing the position of the knee on the floor or the forward foot, lower the front of your hip downward to create an easy stretch. Hold for 30 seconds.

Repeat with the other leg. You should feel this stretch in the front of the hip and possibly in the hamstrings and groin. This is an excellent exercise for the lower back.

❿ LOWER BACK

The squat stretches the front part of the lower legs, the knees, back, ankles, Achilles tendons and groin. From a standing position squat down with your feet flat and toes pointed out at approximately 15 degree angles.

Your heels should be 10-30 centimetres (4-12 inches) apart, depending on how flexible you are. Keep your knees outside of your shoulders. Knees should be directly above your big toes in this squat position. Hold for 30 seconds.

⓫ FOREARM & WRIST

Start on all fours. Support yourself on your hands and knees. Your thumbs should be pointed to the outside with your fingers pointed toward your knees. Keep palms flat as you lean back to stretch the front part of your forearms. Hold an easy stretch for 20 seconds. Relax, then stretch again. Repeat 10 times.

⓭ BACK, HIPS, GROIN & HAMSTRINGS

The spinal twist is good for the upper and lower back, the side of hips and rib cage. It is also beneficial for internal organs and will help keep your waistline trim. It helps your ability to turn to the side or look behind you without having to turn your entire body.

Sit with your right leg straight. Bend your left leg, cross your left foot over and rest it on the outside of your right knee. Then bend your right elbow and rest it on the outside of your upper left thigh, just above the knee. During the stretch use the elbow to keep this leg stationary with controlled pressure to the inside.

Now with your left hand resting behind you, slowly turn your head to look over your left shoulder, and at the same time rotate your upper body toward your left hand and arm. As you turn your upper body, think of turning your hips in the same direction (though your hips won't move because your right elbow is keeping the left leg stationary).

This should give you a stretch in your lower back and side of hip. Hold for 15 seconds. Do both sides.

figure 1

figure 2

figure 3

⓮ LOWER BACK & TOP OF HIP

Lying on your back, bring your knees up together and rest your feet on the floor. Interlace your fingers behind your head and rest your arms on the floor (figure 1).

Now lift the left leg over the right leg (figure 2).

From here, use the left leg to pull the right leg towards the floor (figure 3) until you feel a good stretch along the side of the hip or in the lower back. Stretch and be relaxed. Keep the upper back, back of the head, shoulders and elbows flat on the floor. Hold for 30 seconds.

Repeat this stretch for the other side, crossing the right leg over the left and pulling down to the right.

⓯ QUADRICEPS & KNEES

To stretch the quad and knee, hold the top of your right foot with your right hand and gently pull your heel toward your buttocks (with your free hand holding onto a post if you need to). This stretch is also good for knee rehabilitation and with problem knees. Hold for 30 seconds for each leg.

figure 1

figure 2

⓰ ACHILLES TENDONS

Start as in figure 1. Bring the toes of one foot almost even or parallel to the knee of the other leg. Let the heel of the bent leg come off the ground about half an inch, (figure 2). Lower the heel towards the ground while pushing forward on your thigh (just above the knee) with your chest and shoulder.

The idea is not to get the heel flat but to use the forward pressure from your shoulder on your thigh to give an easy stretch to the Achilles tendon. To stretch the Achilles tendon adequately requires only a slight stretch. Hold for 15 seconds. Repeat with the other leg.

figure 1

figure 2

⓬ HAMSTRINGS

To stretch the hamstrings, straighten the right leg with the sole of your left foot slightly touching the inside of the right thigh. You are now in the straight-leg, bent knee position (figure 1).

Slowly bend forward from the hips towards the foot of the straight leg (figure 2) until you create the slightest feeling of stretch. Hold this for 20 seconds.

After the stretch feeling has diminished, bend a bit more forward from the hips. Hold this development stretch for 25 seconds. Then switch sides and stretch the left leg in the same way.

OTHER APPROACHES

In recent decades there has been a growing awareness that physical well-being for a specific purpose – like playing tennis – is strongly linked with general physical, mental and emotional well-being. Those who are generally fit and healthy, who eat and sleep well and look after themselves (though without getting health-obsessed), are more likely to avoid illness and injury, and recover more quickly when an injury does strike.

There are so many different approaches to general well-being that to include even half of them would turn The Book of Tennis *into a manual of modern living.*
But here is a small selection of approaches to health, fitness and rehabilitation which have helped tennis players at all levels of the game.

⑰ LEGS, FEET & ANKLES

Rotate your ankle clockwise and anti-clockwise through a complete range of motion with slight resistance provided by your hand (figure 1). Rotary motion of the ankle helps to gently stretch out tight ligaments. Repeat 10-20 times in each direction.

Do this to both ankles and feel if there is any difference between the ankles in terms of tightness and range of motion. Sometimes an ankle that has been sprained will feel a bit weaker and tighter. This difference may go unnoticed if you don't work each ankle separately and compare.

Remove your shoes if you're wearing them. With your thumbs, massage up and down the longitudinal arch of your foot (figure 2). Use circular motions with a good amount of pressure to loosen tissues. Do both feet.

figure 1

figure 2

YOGA

Yoga comes from a Hindu discipline aimed at training the consciousness for a state of perfect spiritual insight and tranquillity. It is also a system of exercises practised as part of this discipline to promote balance of body and mind. Yoga has many forms, and is simultaneously used for self-diagnosis, healing, prevention and maintenance. The exercises are done slowly and often overlap with the stretching exercises pictured in the previous pages.

Breathing is a central part of yoga, as it looks to promote a balance between mind and body. The differences between the different styles of yoga centre mainly on emphasis, such as focusing on alignment of the body, coordination of breathing and movement, and holding postures. For those interested in serious workouts, there are two branches of yoga that are designed with this in mind: Ashtanga and Bikram.

There are many yoga websites. Try **www.yogaclass.com** *as a place to start.*

PILATES

A number of tennis players have used the programme of exercises developed in Germany in the 1920s by Joseph Hubertus Pilates. Martina Navratilova and Pat Cash credit Pilates for their relative longevity, and Mark Philippoussis used it in 2001 after a third knee operation.

The Pilates system works the body as a whole, offering various routines of exercises made up from a bank of over 500 exercises. They include breathing with movement (similar to yoga), body mechanics, balance, coordination, position of the body, posture, strength and flexibility. Numerous exercises can be done with no more than a resistance band (or towel), a chair, and ideally a mat. A wide range of equipment is available both for advanced training and/or rehabilitation, and can be used at home.

For rehabilitation, Pilates can help with structural back problems, hips, knees, neck, trauma, severe silicosis, joint injuries, and sciatica pain. There are now many ways to learn Pilates, ranging from private instructors and classes at studios, to home training with books and videos.

www.pilates.co.uk
www.bodymind.net

TAE BO

A fitness regime based on Tae Kwon Do and Thai boxing, Tae Bo is a blend of martial arts, dance, stretching and boxing combined with music. It can be done in the home, a hotel room or in a structured class. Practitioners say a Tae Bo workout gives a feeling of power, confidence, increased agility and general fitness, and can be one of the highest calorie-burning workouts devised.

Martial arts champion Billy Blanks has spread the word of Tae Bo through his World Training Center at 14708 Ventura Blvd, Sherman Oaks, California 91403, USA.
Telephone: +1818 325 –0335
Fax: +1 818 325 0368
www.billyblanks.com

RESISTANCE BANDS

Resistance rubber bands first became popular within hospitals looking for rehabilitation equipment for people who had suffered anything from road accidents to a sports injury, and they have found their way into tennis.

There is a range of bands with different resistance levels, normally colour-coded to differentiate between the levels of resistance. Routines with bands are aimed at improving muscular strength and endurance, and increase the range of motion and flexibility. Because they are lightweight and flexible, they are easy to take anywhere and inexpensive.

Pat Rafter used a resistance band following the shoulder surgery he had in November 1999.

Leading brands are Dyna-Bands, and Therabands.

More details from:
www.bodyandsoul.org
www.simplefitnesssolutions.com

CARDIOVASCULAR BLADES

Cardiovascular blades are relatively new on the fitness scene. The principle is to use inertia to generate up to 270 muscle contractions per minute – training with the blades, you push and pull on them, accelerating the blades and creating a force.

The greater the force, the greater the resistance that is needed by the body to counteract it. There are different size cardiovascular blades, but all are portable.

The blades help in boosting muscular endurance and strength, improved balance, coordination and posture. The attraction for tennis players is that the blades are reported to increase quickness and agility, and assist pre- and post-operative rehabilitation.

More details from:
E-mail: moreinfo@bodyblade.com
Telephone: +1 800 772 5233
Website: www.bodyblade.com

EXERCISE BALLS

Exercising with inflatable exercise balls is promoted to assist in improving balance and coordination. It can also help improve cardiovascular and postural endurance, encourage mobility and promote stability. The balls are made from heavy-duty vinyl and the fact that they can be deflated when not in use makes them portable. They can be used in Pilates and yoga regimes with resistance bands for additional exercises. Generally available from sports shops, internet sites, and some medical equipment retailers.

www.gymball.com or **www.qfac.com**

INVERSION THERAPY

Inversion therapy – hanging upside down – has been around for centuries, but in the last 20+ years, A-framed machines for home or gym use have become available.

Based on methods used by many hospitals to reduce pressure on spinal columns and increase blood circulation, inversion tables allow you to hang, putting your spine into traction and decompression. They can stretch, strengthen, and rejuvenate muscles, and help alleviate sciatica pain caused by pressure onto a nerve root.

For inversion therapy equipment :
www.mastercare.se
www.teeterhangups.com

DEEP VEIN THROMBOSIS

Also known as 'economy class syndrome' DVT is when potentially lethal blood clots can form during long flights, even in young and fit people. American doubles player Debbie Graham had to be resuscitated after a blood clot lodged in her lungs flying home to California from Wimbledon in 1995.

To prevent DVT, walk around the plane regularly as this stimulates blood circulation, and wear flight socks to support the veins. You could also try an Airogym cushion which is designed to keep blood-flow active (available from most pharmacies and health shops), and as long as you don't have any medical reason not to, taking an aspirin can sometimes help as it thins the blood.

Other well-established areas relevant to tennis worth knowing about include:

Acupressure – (Chinese and Japanese) treatment of symptoms by applying pressure with the fingers to specific pressure points on the body [shiatsu is one form of acupressure].

Acupuncture – A procedure used in or adapted from Chinese medical practice in which specific body areas are pierced with fine needles for therapeutic purposes or to relieve pain or produce regional anaesthesia.

Aromatherapy – The use of selected fragrant substances in oils and inhalants in an effort to affect mood and promote health.

Kinesiology – The study of the anatomy, physiology, and mechanics of body movement and treatment of muscular imbalance or derangement.

Massage – The rubbing or kneading of parts of the body especially to aid circulation, relax the muscles, or provide sensual stimulation. Many different forms. Can also be combined with aromatherapy and reflexology.

Nutrition (including vitamins and minerals) – The science or study that deals with food and nourishment.

Orthopaedic pillows, mattresses and chairs – Products designed to help give you support and put you in the right position for sleeping, or sitting.

Osteopathy – A system of medicine based on the theory that disturbances in the musculoskeletal system affect other bodily parts, causing many disorders that can be corrected by various manipulative techniques in conjunction with conventional medical, surgical, pharmacological, and other therapeutic procedures.

Physiotherapy – The treatment of physical dysfunction by the use of therapeutic exercise and the application of treatments including – ultra-sound, traction, exercises for rehabilitation – intended to restore or facilitate normal function or development.

Reflexology – A method of massage that relieves nervous tension through the application of finger pressure, especially to the feet.

Supports and braces – Products for protecting necks, backs, elbows, knees, ankles during injury, or as part of a rehabilitation program following surgery.

7. SO YOU WANT TO WORK IN TENNIS?

A lot of tennis fans would love to work in tennis, and a lot of players would like to stay with the global circuit when they finish playing. There is good news for both – there are normally many job opportunities in this world-wide 'industry'.

If there's a general rule, it's that a love of tennis is not enough by itself – you have to have an appropriate skill for working in any industry. But if you have a skill that is needed in the tennis world, you could become one of those lucky people who earn their living being a part of their passion. For those who really want to work in tennis, either short-term or over many years, there are masses of different jobs, some for just a few days, others permanent employment.

Here is a brief outline of the kind of jobs that are available – we have not offered any indications about the kind of money you can earn, as these can vary considerably from one country to another.

Above: Cyberjobs – the internet is a now a useful place to find jobs in tennis

Right: The growth of the internet has led some tournaments to have their own radio stations

MANAGERIAL, ADMINISTRATIVE & SECRETARIAL

In many ways working in tennis is no different from working in another walk of life. A freight forwarding company needs administrative and secretarial staff to back up the main aim of attracting customers and making sure their goods are transported quickly and safely.

In tennis, the customers just happen to be players (if the job is at a club or sports complex) or spectators (if the job is at a tournament), but the same principle applies: they have to be kept happy or they might not come back.

The same goes for managerial jobs like sales and marketing. A knowledge of the game is useful, a passion for it might help, but the most important thing is a knowledge of sales, marketing or whatever. If you can't sell tennis or market it to the right public, you will fail regardless of your knowledge or love of the game.

If you want to work for a tournament or sports club, the best thing is to write directly to them explaining what motivates you to want to work for them and enclosing your CV/resume (see page 182 for tournament addresses, see your phone book for the nearest sports clubs). If you want to work for your national tennis association, write to it with your CV/resume (see page 162).

PLAYER MANAGEMENT

One area which does require a certain amount of tennis knowledge and attracts a lot of tennis fans and former players is player management, but again the qualification has to be the ability to do business deals to maximise the player's income.

It is also a job which has at times been known to involve concessions to a top player's ego, often at the expense of the manager, but if you build up a good relationship with a player, the managing role could last well beyond his/her playing days. The role of the player management companies is explained in chapter 4 (page 54) and the addresses of the top management companies are on page 177.

QUIET PLEASE!

"Sure I know where the press room is –
I just look for where they throw the dog meat"

MARTINA NAVRATILOVA
Hall of Fame page 124

JOURNALISM & PR

For many tennis fans, the first exposure they have to tennis is by watching it on the television, so if they don't want to emulate the player, they could well want to emulate the commentator. The people who become television and radio commentators, or reporters, newspaper correspondents and columnists, can generally be divided into two categories: journalists who have moved into tennis after proving themselves in news and/or general sports reporting, and ex-players who retire in their late 20s or early 30s and wish to stay in the sport.

In America there are very few pure journalists left in broadcasting. Almost all networks prefer commentators who have played the game at a high level – the best current examples are John McEnroe, Cliff Drysdale and Fred Stolle.

There are signs that this trend is becoming more universal, though there are still a number of specialist journalists who never played at a high level but have held onto their place in the tennis commentary box by being good broadcasters and reading the game well. And there are the occasional figures who carve their own niche in tennis, like Bud Collins, the correspondent of the Boston Globe who also worked for NBC television and became known for his garish multi-coloured trousers. Other ex-players to be regularly seen in the commentary box include Pat Cash, Vijay Amritraj and Martina Navratilova.

The majority of newspaper reporters are journalists who have moved into tennis, rather than tennis fans or ex-players who have moved into journalism. The nature of journalism is such that those who get the stories will often be able to make money, regardless of their training and qualifications, so there's always a chance for a keen tennis fan with a nose for a good story to become a journalist. But in reality, it is generally the professionally qualified expert who has the ability to step back and judge the significance of a story.

Above: The global tennis circuit attracts a number of top-quality photographers, but there is a lot of equipment that has to be carried around to justify the courtside seat

Left: John McEnroe in his new role as one of the most respected television commentators in tennis

Any tennis fan wanting to become a tennis reporter should probably first try to get established in general journalism and leave tennis reporting as an ambition for the future.

An example of a job which does lend itself to tennis fans with good interpersonal skills is a tour communications manager. The ATP, WTA Tour and ITF all have about half a dozen people who are responsible for liaison between players and the media, and these are known as communications managers. It seems a glamorous job because there is personal contact with the top players, but the hours are long, the work hard (because it is almost always supplemented with additional writing duties for internal tour publications), and it takes a very understanding person to handle a globally known star when he/she has just lost a match and has to face the media.

At top-level claycourt
tournaments groundstaff are
needed to sweep the court and
the lines between sets,
though the two-minute break
introduced in 2000 has made it
less of a rushed job

Most communications managers are in their
20s or 30s, speak at least one other language than
English, and last around three years – they tend to
either get burned out after that because of all the
travelling and working long days at tournaments,
or have gained good experience and contacts to
move up further in the industry of tennis. If you're
interested, the ATP, WTA Tour and ITF addresses
are in chapter 2, and send letters with CV/resume
to the Head of Communications.

There is a lot of public relations work in tennis,
but much of it is done by companies with a proven
record in the general and sporting PR fields, for
example Bell Pottinger at Wimbledon. If you are
interested in tennis PR, the best bet is to contact
tournaments (see page 182) and ask which PR
companies work for them. Then contact the PR
firm, expressing your interest in tennis, and ask
whether there might be any job vacancies.

WORKING FOR NATIONAL
ASSOCIATIONS

National associations require staffs of secretaries,
office managers, and sales, marketing and PR
personnel. To some extent working for a national
tennis association is no different than working for
a company, with the need to justify initiatives
by results and work within tight income limits
(only the associations in the four Grand Slam
countries have the luxury of a large amount of
guaranteed income from their tournaments).
But there are some jobs specific to national
associations, such as coaching coordinators,
results processors, and liaison between head
office and local associations.

If you're interested in working for your
national tennis association, write to it with your
CV/resume (see page 162).

As part of the national structure of tennis,
most national tennis associations are linked to
branches of local associations. In the US and
Germany there are the state associations, in
Great Britain there is the county network, and
this pattern is followed in most countries
These local associations also offer jobs, and some
work closely with their national association.

QUIET PLEASE!

"The serve was invented so that the net could play"

BILL COSBY
American comedian

COACHING

There's an old saying: "Those who can, do. Those who can't, teach!" And indeed the ranks of coaches the world over are populated with players who set their hearts on becoming world class players but turned to coaching when their results didn't quite match their playing dreams.

Having said that, there are plenty of coaches who can read the game much better than they could ever play it, and one of the greatest coaches in the history of tennis, the Australian Harry Hopman (page 120) was a very average player who never hit the heights on court the way he did off it.

Not so long ago, there were certain countries where a moderately proficient player who had an ability to teach could make a living as a coach. These days there are few coaching jobs which can be done without a minimum qualification, and these qualifications are almost always created and administered through the national tennis association, often with a graduated qualification which the coach achieves one step at a time. This has made it hard for the impromptu or untrained coach to make a living, but it has had the advantage of making tennis coaching a quantified and qualified profession, with fees rising according to the level of qualifications achieved by the coach.

There are, of course, different types of coaches, who themselves might have different aspirations. At club level there is the coach who is totally happy just trying to make people play tennis better. Then there is the coach who is hoping to discover a potential champion. For the latter, there can be the heartbreak associated with a local coach discovering a real talent, nurturing the youngster to the point where he/she gets noticed by a wider public, and then has to watch as the youngster is snatched away by a bigger tennis academy or national association training squad which then takes the credit when the player proves to be good.

Coaching at the top level is often a matter of whether a player feels comfortable with their coach and is having good enough results to keep the arrangement (see page 52).

There is also work for coaches at holiday destinations coaching holidaymakers. For a list of tennis holiday websites see page 97.

A job which requires no formal qualification except a reliable gauge of your standard of play is being a hitting partner. If a professional tournament comes to your town, let the tournament practice desk have your business card or some other record of your contact details, together with an indication of your standard of play – you could get a call from a player who is either travelling without a coach or whose coach doesn't play to a high enough standard to offer decent practice. Payment is variable, but on a few rare occasions it does lead to a more permanent coaching arrangement with the player.

If you're good enough to coach, the chances are you don't need any further advice from *The Book Of Tennis*, but if you think you have a strong tennis perception which might lead you to be a much better coach than your playing ability would suggest, give your national association a ring and find out about coaching courses.

Walking wounded – qualified physiotherapists who enjoy travel can find work on a temporary or permanent basis with the men's and women's tours; with only three minutes allowed to treat an injury in the middle of a match, they have to be fast!

1961

MANOLO SANTANA WON SPAIN'S FIRST GRAND SLAM SINGLES TITLE IN PARIS THE YEAR THE BERLIN WALL WENT UP, SOUTH AFRICA WAS DECLARED A REPUBLIC, CUBAN EXILES INVADED THE BAY OF PIGS, YURI GAGARIN BECAME THE FIRST MAN IN SPACE, AND THE CONTRACEPTIVE PILL FIRST WENT ON SALE

1991

ECSTATIC SCENES IN LYON
ACCOMPANIED FRANCE'S FIRST
DAVIS CUP TRIUMPH FOR
59 YEARS, JUST AS THE ONCE
POWERFUL SOVIET UNION WAS
PREPARING TO BE DISBANDED
AFTER 74 YEARS, SOUTH AFRICA
HAD REPEALED ITS APARTHEID
LAWS, AND A USA-BACKED
COALITION HAD SUPPORTED
KUWAIT IN A THREE-MONTH WAR
AGAINST IRAQ

Examples of coaches who have worked at the top of the game without having any formal tennis background are a few parents like Richard Williams (for Serena and Venus Williams) and Jimmy Evert (for Chris Evert), fitness or biomechanics coaches who have 'grown into' tennis (like the Australian Gavin Hopper who worked with Amanda Coetzer, Monica Seles and Mark Philippoussis, or Brad Langevad with Greg Rusedski), and the occasional individual like Henri Dumont, a psychologist who was Cedric Pioline's coach when Pioline reached the 1993 US Open final.

For a range of coaching jobs visit:
www.tennisjobs.com

At the larger events, providing on-site information is part of the tournament's service to fans; people doing this job need to be able to absorb lots of information very quickly and have good interpersonal skills

LOGISTICS & FACILITIES

Another option is facilities management, or the logistics of organising a tournament (like getting in stands to increase the capacity of a court). The logistics are normally left to specialist equipment and catering companies, but many tennis fans and ex-players have indulged their passion for the sport by running a tennis facility. Again, technical know-how and business acumen are more important qualifications than an understanding of tennis, but in running a tennis club, centre or other facility, the knowledge of what tennis players want can be very useful.

Such jobs are likely to come about through your own contacts with tennis centres, so if you play at a club or indoor tennis complex, ask to chat to the manager about possible jobs.

If you can coach, a combined coaching/facilities management job is a good plus, if for no other reason than it could could save the facility having to employ two different people.

HOLIDAY JOBS

For the fan who would love to work in tennis but not to the extent of changing careers or giving up an existing job, there are a number of temporary jobs on the international tennis circuits which can be done in a holiday.

The best opportunities arise for those who live near a one or two week-long tournament on the men's or women's tours, or a Davis Cup tie that comes to your area.

Most tournaments are run with a small year round staff, supplemented by a number of people who come in a week or two before the tournament and whose contract ends after the last player has left town. These can be stewards, rubbish collectors, scoreboard operators, waiters, and some additional ground staff.

One of the most popular jobs is being a driver of the official courtesy cars, but it's such a good job many tournaments don't pay their drivers. Instead they try to give them a big-name player to take to the airport or a restaurant at least once, so they can say to their friends or grandchildren "I drove Gustavo Kuerten" or whoever.

The one area that tends not to be staffed with casual workers is security, which is now very much a domain for the professionally trained personnel of specialist security companies.

If you fancy a holiday job at your local tournament, write to the tournament director well in advance of the event (ideally about six months), say what you're willing to do, and ask if there are any openings. For Tournament Directors, see page 182.

8. THE TENNIS YEAR 2001

The year 2001 came to an end with many people wondering whether the world would ever be the same again. Just 38 hours after the final Grand Slam of the year ended in Lleyton Hewitt's first major title at the US Open, international terrorism struck New York and Washington in the form of four hijacked passenger aeroplanes being used as explosive weapons to attack the World Trade Center and the Pentagon, killing over three thousand people and leaving the world in a state of tension as views polarised on how best to deal with international terrorism.

The impact on tennis will be hard to gauge, though it is likely to go well beyond the changed Manhattan skyline that is such a feature of the view from Row Z of the Arthur Ashe Stadium at Flushing Meadows. The US Open just finished had been one of the most relaxed in terms of security checks for many years – that is unlikely to happen again.

All four Slams have had to tighten their security since the attack on Monica Seles in Hamburg in 1993, and they will probably have to make it even stricter. It'll be hard for tournaments like the Australian Open, which has prided itself on being one of the friendliest tournaments on the circuit, to keep that reputation when security staff have to keep a bigger eye open for possible disruption than has been necessary to date.

Above: Lleyton Hewitt celebrates his first Grand Slam triumph

Right: Venus Williams en route to her second Wimbledon title

Above: Martina Hingis sported a new-style tennis shirt with one long sleeve and one short sleeve

Right: Jennifer Capriati holds aloft the Daphne Akhurst trophy at the Australian Open

The atrocities in America also had a minor impact on the No1 ranking in women's tennis. After winning her first Grand Slam title at the Australian Open, Jennifer Capriati headed the women's standings on 2001 results alone, but Martina Hingis spent the majority of the year at No1 in the 52-week rankings despite going a second successive year and 11 majors without a Grand Slam singles title. Had Capriati not chosen to miss the Princess Cup in Tokyo after the attacks on New York and Washington, she would probably have taken over the top spot in September.

But her moment of triumph was not long delayed. On 15 October, after Hingis had injured her ankle in the Filderstadt semi-final two days earlier, Capriati finally ascended to the No1 ranking, completing her remarkable comeback story. Venus Williams probably deserves the title of best Grand Slam player of the year after beating Capriati at the US Open, but she opted out of so many tour-level events that she jeopardised her chances of becoming the actual world No1. The year-end No1 was Lindsay Davenport who didn't even reach a Slam final, an achievement which prompted the WTA Tour to give more ranking points for the four majors in 2002. But even Davenport's late run of form in October couldn't stop 2001 being Capriati's year.

Capriati's Australian and French Open successes crowned a comeback that warmed the hearts of more than just the tennis community. The pre-teen prodigy, who seemed to have the tennis world at her fingertips at 14 but who went off the rails and ended up in trouble with the police, finally did justice to her immense talent, and also had the humility to highlight her achievements in Melbourne and Paris when her defeat by Justine Henin in the Wimbledon semi-finals removed the chance of a pure Grand Slam. But Capriati wasn't the only comeback kid.

*"I think Pete Sampras has really reached his peak.
The only thing he doesn't do is cook"*

MICHAEL CHANG
American tennis player

Andre Agassi once again confounded those who had written him off mid-way through 2000 by winning the Australian Open and the first two Masters Series tournaments of the year in Indian Wells and Miami. Agassi's form slipped in the second half of the year, but he was still making headlines in October when he and Steffi Graf married just days before the birth of their son Jaden Gil Graf-Agassi. With 29 Grand Slam singles titles between Jaden's parents, there has probably never been a baby with a greater tennis genetic inheritance!

And another comeback kid was Goran Ivanisevic, who needed a wildcard to enter Wimbledon because his ranking was down at 125 but thanked the All England Club by beating the top two British players Greg Rusedski and Tim Henman, and then winning the title against Pat Rafter on an ecstatic 'People's Monday'.

*Above: Goran Ivanisevic celebrates
his unlikely Wimbledon title*

*Middle: Gustavo Kuerten proving
himself the king of clay in Paris*

*Left: Andre Agassi's Australian
success means he has now won
more Australian Open titles than
any other Slam*

As well as Hewitt's breakthrough at the US Open, the 20-year-old South Australian steered his country to the Davis Cup final against France, though that proved one of his few setbacks of the year. Hewitt's loss on the opening day to Nicolas Escude set the visitors on the way to a dramatic fifth-rubber victory, also won by Escude who was the outstanding Davis Cup player of the year. And that after Australia had gone to the lengths of installing a temporary grasscourt at the Rod Laver Arena to maximise home advantage.

Although Hewitt's breathtaking run of form in the last three months of the year saw him pip Gustavo Kuerten to win the Tennis Masters Cup and finish the year as the youngest No1 ever, arguably his greatest achievement was winning three matches for which there were no ranking points at stake. The three rubbers he won on clay in Florianopolis to beat Brazil in the Davis Cup quarter-finals were an accomplishment of astonishing maturity, which included taking the decisive fourth rubber against Kuerten in front of the Brazilian's adoring home town crowd.

Kuerten dominated most of the year but – plagued by a groin strain – his form slumped in October and November, and he couldn't finish the year at the top despite topping the 52-week rankings for all but 12 weeks of the year. And he will find it tough going in 2002, as there were major strides made by two of Hewitt's contemporaries. Juan-Carlos Ferrero finished the year fifth after looking set to dominate the claycourt season – he won Rome and reached the final in Hamburg, but then was outclassed by Kuerten in the semi-finals of Roland Garros. And Roger Federer won his first title, was a star for Switzerland in the Davis Cup for two rounds, and ended Pete Sampras's run of 31 straight victories at Wimbledon. Marat Safin had a poor 2001 but still topped the 52-week rankings for four weeks in February and three in April thanks to the seven titles he won in 2000.

*Above: Andy Roddick became
the year's rising star after being
world junior champion in 2000*

Above: Dinara Safina (left) with her doubles partner Anna Bastrikova

Right: Kaia Kanepi's win at Roland Garros put Estonia on the tennis map

Andy Roddick, the 2000 world junior champion, made a very impressive transition to the full tour, winning three titles by mid-August and breaking into the world's top 15. And Belgium can look forward to a golden era with Kim Clijsters and Justine Henin both reaching Grand Slam finals – if Henin can stay fit, she could usher the single-handed topspin backhand back into popularity on the women's circuit.

There were no obviously outstanding juniors who looked poised to follow in Roddick's footsteps, but the tiny east European state of Estonia won its first Grand Slam title when Kaia Kanepi took the French Open girls title with a devastating display of power based around a mighty forehand. And the tennis family spread its net even further when Angelique Widjaja of Indonesia took the Wimbledon girls' title, and then became the first player since Henin to win her debut WTA Tour event when she won the title in Bali in September.

Perhaps the star of the junior Slams was Dinara Safina, the younger sister of Marat Safin, but she will need to develop greater variety in her game if she is to emulate her brother's achievements.

Off court, the game lost Jaroslav Drobny, the champion of France 1951-52 and Wimbledon 1954, who died in September. And the seven-times Australian Champion Nancye Wynne Bolton died in November.

The ITF general assembly in Cancun, Mexico, approved a handful of rule changes, the most prominent of which could see different tennis balls being used for different surfaces, and Davis Cup and Fed Cup players wearing their national colours, all within two or three years.

The match of the year? In terms of atmosphere and emotion probably the Wimbledon final between Ivanisevic and Rafter. In terms of history, the US Open women's final in which Venus and Serena Williams became the first sisters to contest a Grand Slam final since Lilian and Maud Watson played the first Wimbledon final in 1884, but like most of the matches between the Williams sisters it proved anticlimactic.

In terms of sustained high quality play, the match of the year had to be the US Open quarter-final between Pete Sampras and Andre Agassi, which Sampras won 6-7 7-6 7-6 7-6, with neither player losing serve in the entire match. Most people who saw it said it was hard to remember a match of better quality, and when the two players shook hands at the net Agassi said to Sampras: "Go win the whole thing."

Unfortunately for Sampras the win, plus others over Rafter and Safin, left him drained for the final and he finished the year without adding to his record total of 13 Grand Slam singles titles.

Above: Angelique Widjaja

Right: Venus Williams celebrates back-to-back Wimbledon titles

THE BOOK OF TENNIS HALL OF FAME

Any sport with a modern history going back nearly 150 years will have thousands of people who deserve a place in the sport's annals. Many of the great names of tennis are now being recognised in halls of fame, the biggest of which is the International Tennis Hall of Fame in Newport, Rhode Island (see below).

There are also various national halls of fame, notably the Australian one which receives two new inductees each year on Australia Day, the country's national day (26 January) which always falls during the Australian Open.

The Book of Tennis here presents its own Hall of Fame, bringing together the most prominent personalities in the history of tennis.

The criteria we have used for inclusion is that a player has to have won at least two Grand Slam singles titles (since the abolition of the challenge rounds) or 10 Grand Slam doubles titles. However, as strict criteria don't cover every player and non-player who can rightly claim to be a major personality in the history of tennis, a few people are included on the basis of some other overriding reason.

The Hall of Fame Key:

b = born

d = died

*GS = singles titles at Grand Slam events
(not calendar year Grand Slams)*

dbls = doubles titles at Grand Slam events

DC = played in Davis Cup in year nation won cup

*FC = played in Fed Cup (or its predecessor Federation Cup)
in year nation won cup*

*Grand Slam tournaments appear in the order
they take place in the year:*

Aus = Australian Open

RG = Roland Garros or French Open

Wim = Wimbledon

US = US Open

All years are 19.. unless stated otherwise

International Tennis
Hall of Fame (right)
The Newport Casino
194 Bellevue Avenue
Newport RI 02840
USA
Telephone: +1 401 849 3990
Fax: +1 401 849 8780
Website: www.tennisfame.com

AGASSI, ANDRE
(1970 -)
Andre Kirk Agassi
b. Las Vegas, Nevada

*7 GS Titles: Aus 1995. 2000. 01 /
RG 1999 / Wim 1992 / US 1994. 99.
2 DC Titles: 1990. 92.*

*Also Olympic singles gold medal 96.
Most charismatic player of his
generation, only second man after
Laver to win all four GS singles titles
in a career, ranked No1 for 77 weeks.
Holds record with Tilden of 16
straight wins in DC. Son of boxer who
represented Iran in 52 Olympics.
Married Steffi Graf in 2001.*

ASHE, ARTHUR
(1943 - 93)
Arthur Robert Ashe
b. Richmond, Virginia
d. New York

*3 GS Titles: Aus 1970 / Wim 1975 /
US 1968.
7 DC Titles: 1963. 68. 69. 70. 71.
72. 78.*

*First black man to win a Grand Slam
tournament, also a leading figure
in the creation of the Association of
Tennis Professionals in 73 (president
74-79), and US non-playing Davis
Cup captain 81-85. Heart attack in
1980 ended playing career, died from
Aids-related illness having contracted
HIV from transplant during heart
surgery.*

AUSTIN, TRACY
(1962 -)
Tracy Ann Austin
b. Los Angeles, California

*2 GS Titles: US 1979. 81.
2 FC Titles: 1979. 81.*

*Youngest US Open winner at
16 yrs 271 days, and first brother-
sister winners of Wimbledon mixed
doubles with brother John in 80.
Turned pro at 14, but her injury-
induced retirement at 21 made her
notable as a high-profile case of
'teenage burnout'.*

BECKER, BORIS
(1967 -)
Boris Franz Becker
b. Leimen, Germany

*6 GS Titles: Aus 1991. 96 /
Wim 1985. 86. 89. US 1989.
2 DC Titles: 1988. 89.*

*Charismatic German who
launched golden age of German
tennis by winning Wimbledon aged
17 in 1985 and leading country to
first DC triumph. Topped ATP world
rankings for two periods totalling
12 weeks.*

BETZ, PAULINE
(1919 -)
Pauline May Betz
Later Addie
b. Dayton, Ohio

5 GS Titles: Wim 1946 / US 1942.
43. 44. 46.

A dominant figure in the 40s, would almost certainly have won more titles if not for initially the second world war and then the friction between amateur and professional circuits – despite not being professional she was refused permission to defend her Wim title in 47 because of discussing pro contracts. Later Pauline Addie.

BINGLEY, BLANCHE
(1863 - 1946)
Blanche Bingley
Later Hillyard
b. Greenford, England
d. Pulborough, England

6 GS Titles: Wim 1886. 89. 94. 97. 99. 1900.

Known for the longevity of her career, won her 6th title at 36 and made her final appearance at Wimbledon aged 49. 5 of 6 titles won as Blanche Hillyard after marrying Cmdr George Hillyard, secretary of Wim 1907-24.

BJURSTEDT, MOLLA
(1884 - 1959)
Anna Margrethe Bjurstedt
Later Mallory
b. Oslo, Norway
d. Stockholm, Sweden

8 GS Titles: US 1915. 16. 17. 18. 20. 21. 22. 26.

Norwegian who became American after marriage to New Yorker Franklin Mallory in 1919, she was the greatest American until Wills Moody, but seldom played well outside USA, and lost only other GS final at Wimbledon to Lenglen in 1922. The only player to beat Lenglen after the first world war. Won a bronze medal for Norway at 1912 Olympics.

BORG, BJÖRN
(1956 -)
Björn Rune Borg
b. Södertäljie, Sweden

11 GS Titles: RG 1974. 75. 78. 79. 80. 81 / Wim 1976. 77. 78. 79. 80.
1 DC Title: 1975.

Spent 109 weeks as top-ranked player in dominating world tennis in late 1970s. Achieved rare feat of winning French and Wimbledon in same year three times despite lacking a natural grasscourt game. Never won US Open despite reaching four finals, and only once went to Australia as 18-year-old. Led Sweden to first DC title single-handedly in 1975. With long blond hair he attracted a massive teenage female following and became a high-profile personality despite being quietly spoken.

BOROTRA, JEAN
(1898 - 1994)
Jean Robert Borotra
b. Arbonne, France
d. Biarritz, France

4 GS Titles: +13 dbls: Aus 1928 / RG 1931 / Wim 1924. 26.
6 DC Titles: 1927. 28. 29. 30. 31. 32.

One of the four French 'Musketeers' (and the last to die), he helped France to the DC success that caused Stade Roland Garros to be built. Known for his beret, he played last DC tie aged 49, and played competitions into his 80s. Served as minister for sport in French 'Vichy' government 1940-42 until arrested by German authorities.

BROMWICH, JOHN
(1918 - 99)
John Edward Bromwich
b. Sydney, Australia
d. Geelong Vic, Australia

2 GS Titles +17 dbls: Aus 1939. 50.
2 DC Titles: 1939. 50.

One of the great doubles players, who won 10 of his 13 GS men's doubles titles with Adrian Quist (Aus 39-40, 46-50, Wim 50, US 39), and the pair won 20 of 21 DC doubles rubbers. Unorthodox playing style characterised by two-handed forehand and one-handed backhand.

BROOKES, NORMAN
(1877 - 1968)
Norman Everard Brookes
b. Melbourne, Australia
d. Melbourne, Australia

3 GS Titles: Aus 1911 / Wim 1907. 14.
6 DC Titles: 1907. 08. 09. 11. 14. 19.

The first great Australian player, the first left-hander to win Wimbledon, and the first overseas player to win Wimbledon. His achievements for Australian tennis, including spending 28 years as president of Lawn Tennis Association of Australia, are reflected in Australian Open men's singles trophy bearing his name. Became Sir Norman Brookes in 1939.

BROUGH, LOUISE
(1923 -)
Althea Louise Brough
Later Clapp
b. Oklahoma City, Oklahoma

6 GS Titles +29 dbls: Aus 1950 / Wim 1948. 49. 50. 55 / US 1947.

Arguably the outstanding woman player of the immediate post-war era, her serve-and-volley style took her to three of the four major singles titles, and she won singles, doubles and mixed titles at Wimbledon in 48 and 50. Won 20 of her 21 women's doubles titles with Margaret Osborne, losing just 8 matches in 15 years, making them one of the most successful partnerships ever.

Jean Borotra, the bounding Basque pictured at Wimbledon sporting the beret he always wore on court

Above centre: Björn Borg

Facing page top: Andre Agassi

Facing page below: Boris Becker

MEMORABLE MATCHES
Jimmy Connors v Arthur Ashe Wimbledon Final 1975

This had all the makings of a grudge contest off-court, as it took place against a background of Connors suing the ATP and its president (Ashe) over contractual matters, but on-court Connors came into the match as both defending champion and in seemingly irresistible form to face a man just five days off his 32nd birthday. Yet it turned into one of the most tactically astute displays on a major stage.

Ashe abandoned his normally forcing style of play to float the ball at the big-hitting Connors – as he said later: 'He feeds on speed, so I gave him junk.'

The tactic, allied to Ashe's superb use of the away-swinging slice serve to Connors' two-handed backhand, frustrated Connors for 2 sets, but when the champion won the third a comeback seemed inevitable. Yet Ashe refused to alter his game plan, kept the soft balls coming at Connors, and won 6-1 6-1 5-7 6-4.

Above centre: Jennifer Capriati

BROWNE, MARY
(1891 - 1971)
Mary Kendall Browne
Later Smith
b. Santa Monica, California
d. Laguna Hills, California

3 GS Titles: US 1912. 13. 14.

Dominated the US championships before first world war, winning singles, doubles and mixed three years running. After 1914 disappeared from tennis circuit to concentrate on golf, but returned in 21 to win three more GS doubles titles. Turned professional after last GS title (Wim dbls 26) to play series of exhibition matches against Lenglen, but Lenglen won all 40. Golf achievements include reaching final of US amateur championships in 24. Also a distinguished portrait painter. Later Mary Smith.

BRUGNON, 'TOTO'
(1895 - 1978)
Jacques Brugnon
b. Paris, France
b. Paris, France

10 GS dbls Titles
4 DC Titles: 1927. 30. 31. 32

The doubles specialist among the four French 'Musketeers', he played with both Cochet and Borotra, winning 5 GS titles with each. 3 of 4 DC final wins partnering Cochet. Reached 4th round at Wim in 49 aged 54 with Borotra (himself aged 50).

BUDGE, DONALD
(1915 - 2000)
John Donald Budge
b. Oakland, California
d. New York

6 GS Titles: Aus 1938 / RG 1938 / Wim 1937. 38 / US 1937. 38.
2 DC Titles: 1937. 38.

Dominant player before second world war, based around sharp returns and rolled backhand. First man to win all four major titles in same year, thereby giving rise to phrase 'Grand Slam'. Won singles, doubles and mixed at Wim 37 & 38. Would almost certainly have won more had he not turned pro after golden year in 1938. Competed professionally till age 55.

BUENO, MARIA
(1939 -)
Maria Esther Andion Bueno
b. São Paulo, Brazil

7 GS titles +12 dbls: Wim 1956. 60. 64 / US 1959. 63. 64. 66.

One of the most elegant champions who used her guile and court craft to beat more powerful players. Enjoyed rivalry at top of women's game with Margaret Smith Court. Achieved a calendar year doubles GS in 1960 with Christine Truman (Aus) and Darlene Hard (RG/Wim/US), among 5 Wim titles and 4 US. Last US title came with old rival Court.

CAPRIATI, JENNIFER
(1976 -)
Jennifer Capriati
b. New York

2 GS Titles: Aus 2001. RG 2001.
2 FC Titles: 1990. 2000.

Teenage prodigy who became known as high-profile example of teenage burnout but made remarkable recovery to win 2 GS titles in 2001 and briefly top the rankings. Last player to make pro debut before 14th birthday, reached last four at RG at 14 to become youngest GS semi-finalist, and won Olympic gold in 92. Left tennis circuit for two years after drugs and shoplifting offences, but made slow comeback culminating in 2001 successes. WTA Tour's age eligibility rules tightened in 95 largely as a result of Capriati's fall from grace.

CASALS, ROSIE
(1948 -)
Rosemary Casals
b. San Francisco, California

12 GS dbls Titles

Charismatic player, daughter of immigrants from El Salvador, never won a Grand Slam singles event but was twice US Open finalist, and one of the greatest doubles players of her era, winning 12 Grand Slam titles (9 women's, 3 mixed) including seven with Billie-Jean King. One of the nine players to walk away from official events in 1970 and join Gladys Heldman's breakaway Virginia Slims circuit.

CHATRIER, PHILIPPE
(1928 - 2000)
Philippe Chatrier
b. Creteil, France
d. Paris, France

Though a French junior champion (45) and DC player (48-50) and captain (69-72), his place in tennis history stems from being president of ITF 77-91 and French federation 72-92. Credited with three major achievements: restoring organisation and prestige of French Open (including Roland Garros stadium), initiating ITF development programme to boost tennis in third world, and getting tennis reinstated as olympic sport (88).

COCHET, HENRI
(1901 - 87)
Henri Jean Cochet
b. Villeurbane
d. Paris, France

7 GS Titles: RG 1926. 28. 30. 32 / Wim 1927. 29 / US 1928.
6 DC Titles: 1927. 28. 29. 30. 31. 32.

One of four French 'Musketeers' and one of the greatest touch players and volleyers in tennis. Won 5 French titles but first in 22 came before overseas players could compete. Played singles in all France's DC triumphs. Won Wim in 27 after being two sets down in quarter-finals, semi-finals and final; he was 1-5 down in third set against Tilden in semis, and saved six match points against Borotra in final after being 2-5 down in third set. Turned professional in 33 but reinstated as amateur after second world war.

CONNOLLY, MAUREEN
(1934 - 69)
Maureen Catherine Connolly
Later Brinker
b. San Diego, California
d. Dallas, Texas

9 GS Titles: Aus 1953 / RG 1953. 54 /
Wim 1952. 53. 54 / US 1951. 52. 53.

First woman to complete a pure
GS in 53 at age 18, would almost
certainly have won more but for a
horseriding accident just before
54 US which ended career. Known as
'Little Mo' she won the US title at
16, lost just four matches after that,
and never lost in 3 visits to
Wimbledon. Later Maureen Brinker,
died of cancer aged 34.

CONNORS, JIMMY
(1952 -)
James Scott Connors
b. East St Louis, Illinois

8 GS Titles: Aus 1974 /
Wim 1972. 82 /
US 1974. 76. 78. 82. 83.

The most dominant player after
Laver and one of the best returners
in history of tennis, he spent 268
weeks at top of world rankings
and took power play to a new level.
Might have won a calendar year
GS in 74 if RG had not barred him
for not being member of ATP.
Tremendous longevity saw him reach
US semi-finals in 91 at 39. Total of
109 singles titles a record in open
era unlikely to be beaten. Played just
three years in DC, never winning.

COOPER, ASHLEY
(1936 -)
b. Melbourne, Australia

4 GS Titles: Aus 1957. 58. /
Wim 1958 / US 1958.
2 DC Titles: 1957. 58.

One of the many players in 1950s
who might have had a period of
major domination had the
professional circuit not lured them
away from the top events. Fell just
two matches short of calendar year
GS in 58, losing to Sven Davidson in
RG semi-final. Played DC just twice,
winning challenge rounds (finals)
both times. Turned pro after 58.

COOPER, CHARLOTTE
(1870 - 1966)
Charlotte Reinagle Cooper
Later Sterry
b. Ealing, England
d. Helensburgh, Scotland

5 GS Titles: Wim 1895. 96. 98.
1901. 08.

Won first 3 Wim titles as Cooper,
her last 2 as Charlotte Sterry.
Oldest Wim singles winner in 1908
at 37 yrs 282 days. First woman to
win olympic title in 1900 with singles
and mixed doubles gold medals.

COURIER, JIM
(1970 -)
James Spencer Courier
b. Sandford, Florida

4 GS Titles: Aus 1992. 93 /
RG 1991. 92.
2 DC Titles: 1992. 95.

Powerfully-built baseliner who
looked set to dominate men's tennis
when he first topped world rankings
in Feb 92, but could never assert
himself and career tailed off from
late 93. Reached all four GS singles
finals. Topped rankings for 58 weeks.
USA lost just 1 of 14 DC ties when
Courier on team.

COURT, MARGARET
(1942 -)
Margaret Jean Smith
Later Court
b. Albury, NSW, Australia

24 GS Titles +38 dbls: Aus 1960. 61.
62. 63. 64. 65. 66. 69. 70. 71. 73 /
RG 1962. 64. 69. 70. 73 / Wim 1963.
65. 70 / US 1962. 65. 69. 70. 73.
4 FC Titles: 1964. 65. 68. 71.

Second woman after Connolly to
achieve a calendar year GS in 70.
Total of 62 GS titles a record unlikely
ever to be beaten. Also won mixed
dbls GS with Ken Fletcher in 63.
Powerfully built player with big serve
and superb volleys, she took
athleticism in women's tennis to new
levels. Born Smith, married Barry
Court in 67; she is now a priest.

CRAWFORD, JACK
(1908 - 91)
John Herbert Crawford
b. Albury, NSW, Australia
d. Cessnock, NSW, Australia

6 GS Titles + 10 dbls: Aus 1931. 32.
33. 35 / RG 1935 / Wim 1933.

Dashing Australian of 1930s whose
long-sleeved attire and square-
headed racket was a throw-back to
the pre-war era. Never played US
championships. One of the few great
Australians not to win DC, he came
closest in 36 but lost live fifth rubber
of final to Fred Perry in straight sets.

Don Budge in his Grand Slam
winning year of 1938

Far left: Jimmy Connors

Above left: Margaret Court

A Player's cigarettes card of
Jack Crawford from the 1930s

Lindsay Davenport

DAVENPORT, LINDSAY
(1976 -)
Lindsay Ann Davenport
b. Palos Verdes, California

3 GS Titles: Aus 2000 / Wim 1999 /
US 1998.
3 FC Titles: 1996. 99. 2000.

Tall American who conquered
early weight problems to become
tremendous athlete and one of the
best strokemakers in history of tennis.
Ended 2001 at No1 and continues to
win many of the leading prizes.
Made breakthrough winning Olympic
singles gold in 96. Likeable player
who seems unaffected by success.

DAVID, HERMAN
(1905 - 74)
Herman Francis David
b. London, England
d. London, England

Administrator who earned his
place in history of tennis for being
chairman of the All England Club
(Wimbledon) in 1967, when his
committee's decision to admit
contract professionals to 1968
championships broke the deadlock
between amateur and professional
worlds and allowed the 'open' era to
begin. Died shortly after refusing to
accommodate 79 ATP members who
refused to play Wimbledon in 1973
over the ILTF's ban on Nikki Pilic
playing ILTF-sanctioned events.

DÉCUGIS, MAX
(1882 - 1978)
Maxime Omer Décugis
b. Paris, France
d. Biot, France

First great French player and
most successful tennis Olympian.
Won 4 gold medals, 1 silver, 1 bronze
between 1900 and 20, including
mixed gold with Suzanne Lenglen
in 20. Won 8 singles titles at closed
French championships. He and André
Gobert first French champions at
Wim in 1911 doubles. Distant relative
of Arnaud Décugis, coach and
husband of 90s pro Julie Halard
Décugis.

Stefan Edberg pictured in
1983, the year he won the junior
Grand Slam

DELL, DONALD
(1938 -)
Donald Lundy Dell
b. Savannah, Georgia

Former player who became lawyer
and later one of the most influential
off-court figures in tennis. First sports
attorney to represent tennis players
on professional basis, but his
ProServ company (now called SFX)
was eclipsed in size by Mark
McCormack's IMG. Influential figure
in foundation of Association of Tennis
Professionals and move to make
tennis 'open'. Played DC for USA
61-63 but didn't play in victorious
63 final, and captained winning team
in 68 & 69.

DOD, LOTTIE
(1871 - 1960)
Charlotte Dod
b. Bebington, England
d. Sway, England

5 GS Titles: Wim 1887. 88. 91.
92. 93.

Youngest ever GS champion at
15 yrs 285 days. Unbeaten in all five
years played at Wim, only lost five
official matches in six-year tennis
career. Retired at 21 to pursue other
sports, playing field hockey for
England, winning the British women's
golf championship, and winning a
silver medal in archery at the 1908
London Olympics.

DOHERTY, LAURIE
(1875 - 1919)
Hugh Laurence Doherty
b. Wimbledon, England
d. Broadstairs, England

6 GS Titles +10 dbls: Wim 1902. 03.
04. 05. 06 / US 1903.
4 DC Titles: 1903. 04. 05. 06.

The younger of the two Doherty
brothers who dominated Wimbledon
at the start of the 20th century,
both in singles and doubles. In 1903
became first overseas player to win
US championships. Also Olympic gold
medallist 1900 in singles and doubles
(with brother Reggie).

Unbeaten in 12 DC rubbers, 7 singles,
5 doubles (all with Reggie). Unusually
aggressive player for his era, quick
around the court and made much of
smash and volley.

DOHERTY, REGGIE
(1872 - 1910)
Reginald Frank Doherty
b. Wimbledon, England
d. London, England

4 GS Titles +10 dbls: Wim 1897. 98.
99. 1900.
4 DC Titles: 1903. 04. 05. 06.

The elder and more solid of the
two brothers, he won Wimbledon four
years running and reached US final
in 1902 losing to Bill Larned. Lost just
once in 8 DC rubbers, to Larned in
1903. Often suffered from ill health,
and lost 1901 Wim final to A W Gore
after doctor had forbidden him to
play.

DOUGLASS, DOROTHEA
see Lambert Chambers

DROBNY, JAROSLAV
(1921 - 2001)
b. Prague, (then) Czechoslovakia
d. London, England

3 GS Titles: RG 1951. 52 / Wim 1954.

Likeable left-hander, sentimental
favourite when winning Wimbledon
at 11th attempt as 32-year-old in 54,
as by then a political refugee with
Egyptian citizenship applying for
British citizenship. Won silver medal
with Czechoslovak ice hockey team
at 48 Olympics, but fled a year later.
Welcomed back to Prague by Czech
Tennis Association just before 75th
birthday for Czech Republic's first DC
semi-final in 96.

DU PONT, MARGARET
see Osborne

EDBERG, STEFAN
(1966 -)
Stefan Bengt Edberg
b. Västervik, Sweden

6 GS Titles: Aus 1985. 87 /
Wim 1988. 90 / US 1991. 92.
4 DC Titles: 1984. 85. 87. 94.

Reserved Swede who charmed
crowds with serve-and-volleying style
of play. Topped rankings for 72 weeks.
Peaked in 91 US final dropping just
6 games to Jim Courier. Lost sole
RG final in 98 after leading 17-year-
old Michael Chang 2-1 in sets.
Loyal servant to Sweden's DC cause.

EMERSON, ROY
(1936 -)
Roy Stanley Emerson
b. Blackbutt Qld, Australia

12 GS Titles: Aus 1961. 63. 64. 65.
66. 67 / RG 1963. 67 /
Wim 1964. 65 / US 1961. 64.
8 DC Titles: 1959. 60. 61. 62. 64. 65.
66. 67.

The outstanding player of the
mid-60s, though clearly benefited
from absence of Hoad, Rosewall and
Laver on professional circuit.
Immensely quick around the court,
he completed set of GS titles with
1st Wim title in 64. Total of 12
GS titles stood as record among men
until Sampras beat it at Wim 2000.
Played 9 successive DC finals,
winning 8.

EVERT, CHRIS
(1954 -)
Christine Marie Evert
Later Lloyd
b. Fort Lauderdale, Florida

18 GS Titles: Aus 1982. 84 /
RG 1974. 75. 79. 80. 83. 85. 86 /
Wim 1974. 76. 81 / US 1975. 76. 77.
78. 80. 82.
7 FC Titles: 1977. 78. 79. 80. 81.
82. 86.

Phenominally consistent icon with
unflappable temperament.
Though not a natural athlete, she
made the most of her accuracy,
consistency and tactical awareness to
win 157 titles and spend 262 weeks
at the top of the rankings. Won some
titles as Chris Evert-Lloyd after
marrying British player John Lloyd;
later married skier Andy Mill
(now separated) though never used
his name. Credited with ushering
in era of the two-handed backhand
in women's tennis.

FRASER, NEALE
(1933 -)
Neale Andrew Fraser
b. Melbourne, Australia

3 GS Titles +16 dbls: Wim 1960 /
US 1959. 61.
4 DC Titles: 1959. 60. 61. 62.

Powerful, left-hander who served
Australia as player, captain and
sports ambassador. One of a great
generation of Australian doubles
players. Won 11 GS doubles titles
covering four majors, 7 titles with
Roy Emerson. Australian DC non-
playing captain for 24 years, winning
4 times (73, 77, 83, 86) and losing
2 finals.

FRY, SHIRLEY
(1927 -)
Shirley June Fry
Later Irvin
b. Akron, Ohio

4 GS titles +13 dbls: Aus 1957 /
RG 1951 / Wim 1956 / US 1956.

Third player (after Hart & Connolly)
to win all 4 GS titles, thought of
as best in world in 56. Formidable
doubles player, she and Hart won
11 titles in early 50s – they lost just
4 games in entire Wim dbls in 53,
winning final 2 rounds 6-0 6-0.
Played Wightman Cup for 6 years.

GIBSON, ALTHEA
(1927 -)
Althea Gibson
Later Darben
b. Silver, South Carolina

5 GS Titles: RG 1956 /
Wim 1957. 58 / US 1957. 58.

The first black top-level tennis
player, she might have won more had
racial restrictions not hampered
her ability to compete. Not allowed
to compete at US championships
until aged 23, won first GS title at 28.
Powerful serve and great reach made
her the top player for two years.
Turned professional after 58.
Competed briefly on women's LPGA
golf tour, winning one tournament.

GODFREE, KITTY
see McKane

GONZALES, PANCHO
(1928 - 95)
Richard Alonzo Gonzales
b. Los Angeles, California
d. Las Vegas, Nevada

2 GS Titles: US 1948. 49.

Despite winning just 2 GS titles,
generally thought of as one of the
greats of the sport. Turned
professional after 49, so best years
spent away from top events, but still
made RG semi-finals in 68 aged 40.
He and Charlie Pasarell hold record
for longest match at Wim from 69:
312 minutes, 112 games. World
professional singles champion 54-62.
Naturally talented, claimed never to
have had a tennis lesson.

GOOLAGONG, EVONNE
(1951 -)
Evonne Fay Goolagong
Later Cawley
b. Barellan, NSW, Australia

7 GS Titles: Aus 1974. 75. 76. 78 /
RG 1971 / Wim 1971. 80.
3 FC Titles: 1971. 73. 74.

One of the most fluent and
elegant players tennis has seen, her
RG and Wim titles aged 19 in 71
marked the end of Margaret Court's
period of domination. 3 times
beaten finalist at Wim and US in 70s,
she became first mother since
Dorothea Lambert Chambers in
1914 to win Wim in 80. Partly of
Australian aboriginal parentage,
became icon for aboriginal
community. Married Roger Cawley
in 75 and played under name Cawley
until retirement in 82.

GORE, WENTWORTH
(1868 -1928)
Arthur William Gore
b. Lyndhurst, England
d. London, England

3 GS Titles: Wim 1901. 08. 09.
1 DC Title: 1912.

Wim champion of remarkable
longevity, played first in 1888 and
every Wim held till 1927 (35 times).
Only player to have won Wim singles
aged over 40, oldest singles finalist
at 44 (in 1912). Won olympic singles
and doubles gold at 1908 games.
Captained Great Britain in first
DC in 1900, won without playing in
final in 1912. Game based entirely
round powerful forehand, used quick
footwork to avoid weak backhand.

*Chris Evert pictured en route to
her first Wimbledon title in 1974*

Left: Roy Emerson

*Althea Gibson, the first black
Grand Slam singles champion*

GORE, SPENCER
(1850 - 1906)
Spencer William Gore
b. Wimbledon, England
d. Ramsgate, England

1 GS Title: Wim 1877.

First GS champion, though valued rackets and cricket much more than tennis, which he described as 'monotonous'. Won 5 matches to take first title, and made great use of volley. Lost 1878 final to Frank Hadow who worked out how to lob the in-rushing Gore.

GRAF, STEFFI
(1969 -)
Stefanie Maria Graf
b. Brühl, Germany

22 GS Titles: Aus 1988. 89. 90. 94 / RG 87. 88. 93. 95. 96. 99 / Wim 1988. 89. 91. 92. 93. 95. 96 / US 1988. 89. 93. 95. 96. 2 FC Titles: 1987. 92.

Total of 22 GS singles titles makes her second behind Margaret Court with 24. Spent 377 weeks at top of women's rankings, a record for man or woman. Also won Olympic gold in 88 to gild calendar year Grand Slam. Benefited from stabbing of great rival and then No1 Monica Seles in Apr 93. Superb athlete who took fitness and footwork to new levels (many said she could have been a top class 800 metres runner), though suffered serious knee and back problems late in career. Reserved person who didn't enjoy off-court promotional work. Married Andre Agassi in 2001 and gave birth to their son Jaden.

HARD, DARLENE
(1936 -)
Darlene Ruth Hard
b. Los Angeles, California

3 GS Titles +18 dbls: RG 1960 / US 1960. 61. 1 FC Title: 1963.

One of the leading doubles players of her generation, would have had higher place in tennis history had she won two Wim singles finals in 57 (lost to Althea Gibson) and 60 (lost to Maria Bueno). Won final US dbls title in 69 in semi-retirement with Françoise Durr.

Steffi Graf celebrates her 22nd and final Grand Slam title in Paris in 1999

Above right: Lew Hoad

Martina Hingis first became world No1 at age 16 and has spent more than four years at the top of the rankings

HART, DORIS
(1925 -)
Doris Jane Hart
b. St Louis, Missouri

6 GS Titles +29 dbls: Aus 1949 / RG 1950. 52 / Wim 1951 / US 1954. 55.

Her 35 GS titles is a remarkable achievement, even more so given restricted use of right leg following childhood illness. Lost 11 GS singles finals, 3 in Maureen Connolly's GS winning year 53. Superb doubles player, winning 14 women's dbls GS titles and 15 mixed, the latter with Frank Sedgman and Vic Seixas. Subtle and graceful player despite restricted movement.

HEWITT, BOB
(1940 -)
Robert Anthony John Hewitt
b. Sydney, Australia

15 GS dbls Titles 1 DC Title: 1974.

Superb doubles player with great longevity: GS titles spanned 17 years. Volatile Australian, won 4 titles with Fred Stolle. Then as naturalised South African formed partnership with Frew McMillan for 5 more titles; pair went 39 matches unbeaten in 67. Member of 'victorious' South African Davis Cup team in 74 which won final by default after India refused to play in apartheid South Africa.

HILLYARD, BLANCHE
see Bingley

HINGIS, MARTINA
(1980 -)
b. Kosice, (then) Czechoslovakia

5 GS Titles: Aus 1997. 98. 99 / Wim 1997 / US 1997.

Phenomenal teenager named after Navratilova who holds several 'youngest-ever' records, including GS junior champion (RG 93 age 12), world No1, & Wim dbls champion. Natural player who seems able to play any shot, but her slight though durable body means she has difficulty resisting power of taller players. Excellent doubles player, only fourth woman to complete calendar year doubles GS in 98; won Aus singles and doubles three years running.

HOAD, LEW
(1945 - 94)
Lewis Alan Hoad
b. Glebe NSW, Australia
d. Fuengirola, Spain

4 GS Titles: Aus 1956 / RG 1956 / Wim 1956. 57. 3 DC Titles: 1953. 55. 56.

Recognised as one of the all-time greats, having come within one match of pure GS in 56 and proving himself on professional circuit despite back problems. Lost to doubles partner and contemporary Ken Rosewall in 56 US Open final to miss GS. Turned professional after crushing Ashley Cooper in 57 Wim final. Retired to Spain where he ran Lew Hoad tennis ranch. Died of leukaemia.

HOPMAN, HARRY
(1906 - 85)
Harold Christian Hopman
b. Sydney NSW, Australia
d. Largo, Florida

Greatest captain in DC history, winning cup 16 times in 23 attempts between 1939 and 1967. Operating during split era of amateur and professional circuits, Hopman brought in a string of great names, including Sedgman, McGregor, Hoad, Rosewall, Cooper, Fraser, Stolle, Rose, Hartwig, Emerson, Laver, Newcombe, and Roche. As player won six Aus dbls titles, 2 men's with Jack Crawford, 4 mixed with wife Nell Hall. Hopman Cup named after him.

HUNT, LAMAR
(1932 -)
Lamar Hunt
b. Eldorado, Arkansas

One of tennis' leading off-court figures, he helped increase player earnings, establish a global circuit and add to the commercialisation of the sport through his World Championship Tennis (WCT), a rival to the newly 'open' international circuit in the early 1970s. Born into a prominent Texan oil family, he made his name in American football, but moved into tennis with WCT, which reached its peak in 1972.

JACOBS, HELEN
(1908 - 97)
Helen Hull Jacobs
b. Globe, Arizona
d. Long Island, New York

4 GS Titles: Wim 1936 / US 1932. 33. 35.

Would have won more titles but for getting the worse of a long-standing rivalry with fellow-Californian Helen Wills. Reached 14 GS finals without ever going to Australia but won just four, and only beat Wills once in a GS final (US 33). Great athlete and tactician whose success came despite a notoriously weak forehand which she tended to slice. Played in more Wightman Cup ties than anyone except Chris Evert.

JOHNSTON, BILL
(1894 -1946)
William M Johnston
b. San Francisco, California
d. San Francisco, California

3 GS Titles: Wim 1923 / US 1915. 19. 7 DC Titles: 1920. 21. 22. 23. 24. 25. 26.

Known as 'Little Bill' compared with 'Big Bill' Tilden, lost to Tilden in 5 successive US finals 20-24. Attacking style characterised by superb volleys and lethal topspin forehand. Missed 17 and 18 US events because of war service.

JONES, ANN
(1938 -)
Adrianne Shirley Haydon
Later Jones
b. Birmingham, England

3 GS Titles: RG 1961. 66 / Wim 1969.

First left-hander to win Wim women's singles, beating Billie-Jean King in 69 final using aluminium racket. Won first RG title as Ann Haydon. Originally a tabletennis player reaching five World finals as a teenager, she became a classic tennis strokemaker. Later became British FC captain, WTA administrator and television commentator.

KAFELNIKOV, YEVGENY
(1974 -)
b. Sochi, Russia

2 GS Titles: Aus 1999 / RG 1996.

Most successful player from Russia, noted in his homeland more for Olympic gold medal in 2000 than for GS triumphs. Versatile and energetic player who won titles on all four recognised surfaces, and became 16th player to top men's rankings. Steered Russia almost single-handed to two DC finals (94 & 95), and won 3 GS dbls titles at time when few top singles players competed in doubles.

KING, BILLIE-JEAN
(1943 -)
Billie-Jean Moffitt
Later King
b. Long Beach, California

12 GS Titles +27 dbls: Aus 1968 / RG 1972 / Wim 1966. 67. 68. 72. 73. 75 / US 1967. 71. 72. 74. 7 FC Titles: 1963. 66. 67. 76. 77. 78. 79.

One of the greatest woman players ever, certainly the greatest stateswoman of the sport. Holds record 20 Wim titles, including all three in 67 and 73. Total 39 GS titles second only to Margaret Court's 62. Superb on-court performances based on serve-volley game mirrored by off-court willingness to take on establishment. One of breakaway nine players who began Women's Tennis Association, she won best-attended match ever against Bobby Riggs in Houston in 73. Later WTA president and US FC captain.

KODES, JAN
(1946 -)
Jan Kodes
b. Prague, (then) Czechoslovakia

3 GS Titles: RG 1970. 71 / Wim 1973. 1 DC Title: 1980.

One of the first top-level players to emerge from then Soviet bloc countries. Known for winning Wim during boycott year, but had already won RG twice, and was US finalist twice (71, 73). Later president of Czech Tennis Association.

KRAMER, JACK
(1921 -)
John Albert Kramer
b. Las Vegas, Nevada

3 GS Titles: Wim 1947 / US 1946. 47. 2 DC Titles: 1946. 47.

One of the leading statesmen of the sport, whose paltry GS haul reflects split amateur-professional era rather than his unquestioned domination of the years after second world war. Turned pro after winning Wim, and in 6-year career played 123 matches against Pancho Gonzales, winning 96. Became leading promoter in 1950s running his own tour, and leading activist in campaign to make tennis 'open'. Was first executive president of ATP 72-75.

Billie-Jean King combined the qualities of a great champion with immense presence as a 'tennis stateswoman'

Left: Yevgeny Kafelnikov en route to winning the gold medal at the Sydney Olympics

Jack Kramer, who probably did more to professionalise tennis than any other individual

MEMORABLE MATCHES
Rod Laver v Ken Rosewall WCT Final Dallas 1972

This match probably did more to sell tennis to commercial television than any other in the early years of 'open' tennis – and introduced TV to how the sport's scoring system can play havoc with the schedules!

Although the top players were back playing the Slams and other traditional events, the big money was in the commercial WCT circuit, and the winner of the finals not only picked up $50,000 – five times more than the Wimbledon champion – but a diamond ring, a car, and a gold cup.

It's hard to think of a 37-year-old at the top of the men's game today, but that's what made Rosewall great, and his ability to read his opponents and attack their weaknesses was the bedrock of his longevity. The 33-year-old Laver won the first set, but Rosewall stormed back to take the second and third, and led 3-1 in the fourth. Laver then took some of the pace off his serve to make it harder for Rosewall to counterpunch, and won the fourth set on a tiebreak.

Rosewall led 4-1 in the fifth, and had a match point at 5-4, but once it got to the tiebreak most people felt he would run out of strength. But somehow he found more reserves, and reeled off four points on the run to overturn a 3-5 deficit in the tiebreak and win 4-6 6-0 6-3 6-7 7-6 in three hours 34 minutes. NBC television stayed with the match despite having other programmes scheduled, and posted viewing figures of around 22 million, a record at the time.

Above right: Rod Laver

Above left: Gustavo Kuerten

KRIEK, JOHAN
(1958 -)
Johan Kriek
b. Pongola, South Africa

2 GS Titles: Aus 1981. 82.

Gutsy South African who played most of his career under US nationality because of international disadvantages of being citizen of apartheid South Africa. Not generally considered one of the greats because his two Grand Slam titles came during 'dark ages' of Aus when depleted fields somewhat devalued the title. Stocky counterpuncher who who 14 titles in 10-year pro career.

KUERTEN, GUSTAVO
(1976 -)
b. Florianopolis, Brazil

3 GS Titles: RG 1997. 2000. 01.

Most successful player from Brazil, and one of the most successful from Latin America. Won RG in 97 as 66th-ranked outsider. Ended 2000 at top of rankings for first time by winning first Tennis Masters Cup in Portugal.

LACOSTE, RENÉ
(1904 - 96)
René Lacoste
b. Paris, France
d. Paris, France

7 GS Titles: RG 1925. 27. 29 / Wim 1925. 28 / US 1927. 28.
2 DC Titles: 1927. 28.

One of the four French 'Musketeers' despite poor health which forced him to retire in 29 aged 25. Tremendous tactician who built his victories around an assured baseline game. Won 40 of 51 DC rubbers, most crucially in 27 challenge round when victories over Bill Tilden and Bill Johnston gave France its first DC. Nicknamed 'the crocodile', which he turned to commercial advantage when he adopted a little green crocodile as emblem of his Lacoste clothing range.

LAMBERT CHAMBERS, DOROTHEA
(1878 - 1960)
Dorothea Katharine Douglass
Later Chambers
b. London, England
d. London, England

7 GS Titles: Wim 1903. 04. 06. 10. 11. 13. 14.

One of the great names in Wim and early tennis history. Won first 3 titles as Dorothea Douglass and remaining four after marrying Robert Lambert Chambers. Almost won 8th Wim title in 19 when aged 40 she held 2 match points against 20-year-old Suzanne Lenglen. Also played badminton and field hockey to high standard.

LARNED, BILL
(1872 - 1926)
William Augustus Larned
b. Summit, New Jersey
d. New York

7 GS Titles: US 1901. 02. 07. 08. 09. 10. 11.
1 DC Title: 1902.

Came late to tennis, winning first US championship aged 28 and last at 38, making him still the oldest champion in US Open history. Played all 14 DC rubbers in singles, winning 14. Later enjoyed success in ice hockey, golf, and shooting, but committed suicide after being paralysed by spiral meningitis.

LAVER, ROD
(1938 -)
Rodney George Laver
b. Rockhampton Qld, Australia

11 GS Titles: Aus 1960. 62. 69 / RG 1962. 69 / Wim 1961. 62. 68. 69 / US 1962. 69.
5 DC Titles: 1959. 60. 61. 62. 73.

The only player to complete two Grand Slams, one as amateur, one as professional. Turned pro after 62 US victory after winning every tournament he entered that year. Won first 'open' Wim in 68 and completed second GS in 69. Won 20 of 24 DC rubbers, including all 6 in 73 comeback after 10 years' absence. Split amateur/professional circuits make it impossible to call anyone 'the greatest-ever player', but certainly greatest left-hander ever, and more seem to nominate him as all-time greatest-ever than any other player.

LENDL, IVAN
(1960 -)
Ivan Lendl
b. Ostrava, (then) Czechoslovakia

8 GS Titles: Aus 1989. 90 / RG 1984. 86. 87 / US 1985. 86. 87.
1 DC Title: 1980.

Dominated men's tennis in second half of 1980s, reaching 19 GS singles finals, winning five Masters titles, and spending 270 weeks at top of rankings. Dominant from back of court, his shaky volleys left him uncertain on grass, and never won Wim despite reaching two finals and five semis. Though being witty off-court, his dour on-court presence prevented him from gaining the recognition his results suggested. Became naturalised American citizen. After tennis continues to try to establish himself on the pro golf tour.

LENGLEN, SUZANNE

(1899 - 1938)

Suzanne Rachel Flore Lenglen

b. Compiègne, France
d. Paris, France

12 GS Titles +17 dbls: RG 1920.
21. 22. 23. 25. 26 / Wim 1919. 20.
21. 22. 23. 25.

Some people's choice as greatest-ever woman player, most people's as most elegant. Her magnetic personality, relatively risqué clothing and balletic style of play with flourishing follow-throughs often took attention from her precision groundstrokes. Achieved notoriety on several counts, two in particular: in 21 playing what proved her only match at the US championships withdrew early in second set against Molla Mallory saying she felt ill; and in 26 walked out of amateur tennis after mix-up with Wim officials led to king and queen of England being kept waiting. Died of anaemia aged 39.

LIZANA, ANITA

(1915 -)

Anita Lizana

Later Ellis
b. Santiago, Chile

1 GS Title: US 1937.

First world-class player to come from South America, her shock win at 37 US championships plus quarter-final showing at Wim helped establish tennis in Latin America. Included in The Book of Tennis Hall of Fame because of the impact her success had in promoting the sport.

MALLORY, MOLLA

see Bjurstedt

MANDLIKOVA, HANA

(1962 -)

Hana Mandlíková

b. Prague, (then) Czechoslovakia

4 GS Titles: Aus 1980. 87 / RG 1981 /
US 1985.
3 FC Title: 1983. 84. 85.

Graceful strokemaker who became Czechoslovak No1 after Martina Navratilova's defection in 75. Reached finals of all four GS events, winning 4 of 8, but only won 1 GS dbls title and 3 was highest singles ranking. Married Sydney restaurateur Jan Sedlek during 86 FC tournament but divorced in 88. Later coached Jana Novotna to Wim title.

MARBLE, ALICE

(1913 - 90)

Alice Marble

b. Beckwith, California
d. Palm Springs, California

5 GS Titles +13 dbls: Wim 1939 /
US 1936. 38. 39. 40.

First woman to win GS titles serving and volleying, but noted for remarkable comeback from tuberculosis that left her virtually an invalid after collapsing in 34. Won all GS titles at Wim and US, but career halted by second world war. Turned professional in 41. Glamorous personality, first woman to wear shorts at Wim.

McCORMACK, MARK

(1930 -)

Mark Hume McCormack

b. Chicago, Illinois

Leading figure behind commercialisation of tennis. After graduating from Yale Law School he became business agent of golf legend Arnold Palmer. Expanded into other sports, notably tennis, and founded International Management Group, one of three leading agencies representing tennis players. Pioneered use of corporate hospitality tents at major sporting events. Married tennis professional Betsy Nagelsen in 86.

MCENROE, JOHN

(1959 -)

John Patrick McEnroe

b. Wiesbaden, (then) West Germany

7 GS Titles +10 dbls: Wim 1981.
83. 84 / US 1979. 80. 81. 84.
5 DC Titles: 1978. 79. 81. 82. 92.

One of the most gifted strokemakers ever, whose volatile temperament was so explosive it took his and tennis' reputation beyond boundaries of the sport. Won 77 singles and 77 doubles titles (57 with Peter Fleming, including 7 GS). Virtually invincible in 84, winning 82 of 85 singles matches. One he lost was RG final to Lendl having led by two sets. Loyal servant to DC, still USA's most successful DC player. Married actress Tatum O'Neal, and later singer Patti Smith.

MCKANE, KITTY

(1896 -1992)

Kathleen McKane

Later Godfree
b. London, England
d. London, England

2 GS Titles: Wim 1924. 26.

One of the finest players of the 1920s who would probably have won more but for domination of Lenglen and Wills. Only player to beat Wills at Wim en route to 24 title (in Lenglen's absence). Finalist at US in 25, won 5 GS dbls titles, including becoming only married couple to win Wim in 26 when she won with husband Leslie Godfree after marriage in 26. Also Olympic doubles gold medallist in 20. She was English national champion in badminton four times.

MEMORABLE MATCHES
Ivan Lendl v Michael Chang French Open Fourth Round 1989

There is always a sense of interest and smug satisfaction when great players at the top of their powers lose unexpectedly, but this 4-6 4-6 6-3 6-3 defeat for Lendl was one of the most astonishing and added to the list of matches he should never have lost.

He was 29 and world No1; Chang was 17, ranked 19 and only just squeezed into the seedings. Even when Chang had made good Lendl's two-sets lead, it seemed impossible for Lendl to lose – the American was exhausted, and when he started cramping Lendl only had to pat the ball away. Yet somehow he couldn't, as Chang used every legitimate tactic available. At one stage he served underarm, he got everything back, and he induced Lendl to double-fault on match point by standing virtually on the service line to receive.

Remarkably, Chang still had enough reserves to bounce back from this four-hour 37-minute marathon to win three more rounds, including a five-set final against Stefan Edberg, making him the first American to win the French for 34 years – and at 17 years and three months, he is still the youngest Grand Slam men's champion. It remains his only Grand Slam title to date.

MCLOUGHLIN, MAURICE
(1890 - 1957)
Maurice Evans McLoughlin
b. Carson City, Nevada
d. Hermosa Beach, California

2 GS Titles: US 1912. 13.

Despite limited success partly due to serving in first world war, had a major impact on growth of tennis for two reasons: first player to rely on serve-volley game based on most powerful serve seen at the time, earning him the nickname 'California Comet' and first American champion to come from public parks as opposed to social elite. Sole appearance at Wim in 1913 attracted record crowds.

MCMILLAN, FREW
(1942 -)
Frew Donald McMillan
b. Springs, South Africa

10 GS dbls Titles
1 DC Title: 1974.

Doubles specialist whose superb hand-eye coordination, quick reflexes and calm personality blended with the short-fused Bob Hewitt to create one of tennis's greatest doubles teams. They won 57 titles, including Wim 3 times, and once each at RG and US. Formed powerful mixed partnership with Betty Stove, winning Wim and US twice each. Noted for wearing white cap in all competitive matches.

MOFFITT, BILLIE-JEAN
see King

MOODY, HELEN WILLS
see Wills

MORTIMER, ANGELA
(1932 -)
Florence Angela Margaret Mortimer
Later Barrett
b. Plymouth, England

3 GS Titles: Aus 1958 / RG 1955 / Wim 1961.

Remarkably efficient player whose groundstrokes made up for relative physical frailty. Won Wim in 61 at 11th attempt beating Christine Truman in first all-British Wim final since 1914. Later British FC captain. Married John Barrett in 67.

NASTASE, ILIE
(1946 -)
Ilie Nastase
b. Bucharest, Romania

2 GS Titles: RG 1972 / US 1971.

Brilliantly fluent strokemaker who did much more to take tennis beyond core tennis fans as one of the first publicly recognised characters. His mischievous character made him great to watch but frequently undermined his pursuit of victory, and on one occasion earned him disqualification (v Patrick Proisy, Bournemouth 74). Won 4 Masters titles and spent 40 weeks as world No1 in 73-74. Steered Romania to DC final in 72 with mixture of brilliance and gamesmanship; lost to USA. Won 5 GS dbls titles.

NAVRATILOVA, MARTINA
(1956 -)
Martina Subert
Adopted stepfather's name
Navrátil(ova) at age 10
b. Prague, (then) Czechoslovakia

18 GS Titles +38 dbls: Aus 1981. 83. 85 / RG 1982. 84 / Wim 1978. 79. 82. 83. 84. 85. 86. 87. 90 / US 1983. 84. 86. 87.
4 FC Titles: 1975 (Czechoslovakia) 82. 86. 89 (for USA).

Rivals Lenglen, Court and King for title of greatest-ever female player, and earns title in most people's eyes for supreme fitness, all-court ability and off-court charisma. Holds record 9 singles titles at Wim and reached last final age 38. Won 6 successive GS singles titles 83-84 but never completed calendar year GS. Went unbeaten in dbls with Shriver for 109 matches in two-year span, achieving pure GS 3 times. Took fitness and diet in women's tennis to new level. Defected from Czechoslovakia at 75 US Open, became US citizen 81. Outgoing personality well known for lesbianism and views on social issues.

NEWCOMBE, JOHN
(1944 -)
John David Newcombe
b. Sydney, Australia

7 GS Titles +18 dbls: Aus 1973. 75 / Wim 1967. 70. 71 / US 1967. 73.
5 DC Titles: 1964. 65. 66. 67. 73.

Powerful all-round player who straddled amateur and professional eras, winning Wim and US in last year before 'open' tennis arrived – his decision to turn professional with effect from 68 proved catalyst in decision to go 'open'. Big serve saw him win all GS singles titles on grass, but also powerful from baseline. Forged superb doubles partnership with Tony Roche, winning 12 GS titles and 3 DC final dbls rubbers. Australia DC captain 93-2000, winning in 99.

OSBORNE, MARGARET
(1918 -)
Margaret Evelyn Osborne
Later du Pont
b. Joseph, Oregon

6 GS Titles +30 dbls: RG 1926. 49 / Wim 1947 / US 1948. 49. 50.

One of generation of Americans who dominated women's tennis before and after second world war. Formed spectacularly successful doubles partnership with Louise Brough, winning 20 GS dbls titles. Became oldest Wim champion of either sex in 62 in winning mixed dbls with Neale Fraser aged 44 yrs 125 days. Won all 18 Wightman Cup rubbers. Married William du Pont Jr in 47.

Martina Navratilova at her peak in 1983

Top: Ilie Nastase

Right: John Newcombe

PALFREY, SARAH
(1912 - 96)
Sarah Hammond Palfrey
b. Sharon, Massachussetts
d. New York

2 GS Titles +16 dbls: US 1941. 45.

Superb volleyer with sweeping backhand who might have won more as her peak coincided with second world war. Won 6 of 11 women's dbls GS titles with Alice Marble, 3 with Helen Jacobs. Married 3 times: Marshal Fabyan (34), Elwood Cooke (40), Jerry Danzig (51).

PARKER, FRANK
(1916 - 97)
Frank Andrew Parker
Born Franciszek Andrzej Paikowski
b. Milwaukee, Wisconsin
d. Chicago, Illinois

4 GS Titles: RG 1948. 49 /
US 1944. 45.
2 DC Titles: 1937. 48.

Thoughtful player who compensated for lack of power in groundstrokes (especially forehand) by shrewd tactics and accurate shotmaking. Best on slower surfaces, became first American man and only third in history (with Trabert and Courier) to win RG singles title twice, and won US claycourt title 5 times. Ranked in top 10 in USA for 17 years 33-49. Served in US army in second world war.

PATTERSON, GERALD
(1895 - 1967)
Gerald Leighton Patterson
b. Melbourne, Australia
d. Melbourne, Australia

3 GS Titles: Aus 1927 / Wim 1919. 22.
1 DC Title: 1919.

Dominant player in world tennis after first world war, powerful player with big serve. Was first post-war Wim champion and first to 'play through' full draw in 22 after challenge round abolished. Despite playing 46 DC rubbers, winning 32, only once on winning team. Was Australia DC captain in 46. Later became influential businessman in Australia.

PATTY, BUDGE
(1924 -)
Jesse Edward Patty
b. Fort Smith, Arkansas

2 GS Titles: RG 1950 / Wim 1950.

American who spent most of playing days living in Paris, he was known for one of the best forehand volleys in the game. Won RG and Wim back-to-back in 50. Enjoyed great rivalry with Jaroslav Drobny, including 93-game match at Wim 53.

PERRY, FRED
(1909 - 95)
Frederick John Perry
b. Stockport, England
d. Melbourne, Australia

8 GS Titles: Aus 1934 / RG 1935 /
Wim 1934. 35. 36 / US 1933. 34. 36.
4 DC Titles: 1933. 34. 35. 36.

First player to win all 4 GS titles and one of greatest in history of tennis. Dominant player of mid-30s with powerful game crowned by running forehand. Turned professional after 36 season and toured with Ellsworth Vines and later Don Budge. Father was Labour parliamentarian, Perry rare for not coming from wealthy background – this plus aggressive style of play led to strained relations with Wim for many years, but now honoured there. Later founded sportswear range, and commentated for radio.

PIERCE, MARY
(1975 -)
Mary Pierce
b. Montreal, Canada

2 GS Titles: Aus 1995 / RG 2000.

Statuesque woman who opted to play for France after troublesome childhood that saw her born in Canada and raised in America. Became famous for notorious temperamental father Bobby Glenn (later known as 'Jim' Pierce) who was banned from attending tournaments because of courtside outbursts and alleged off-court intimidation. Broke out of father's shadow with 4 GS finals, starting RG 94. Deadly groundstrokes make up for limited movement and net game.

PIETRANGELI, NICOLA
(1933 -)
Nicola Pietrangeli
b. Tunis, Tunisia

2 GS Titles: RG 1959. 60.

Italian claycourt specialist with French father and Russian mother, his main claim to fame lies in DC. Played 164 rubbers in 66 titles for Italy, winning 78 of 110 singles, 42 of 54 dbls – all records. Reached just 1 DC final, losing to Australia in 60. Captained Italy to sole DC triumph in 76. Later official DC 'ambassador'.

QUIST, ADRIAN
(1913 - 91)
Adrian Karl Quist
b. Medindie SA, Australia
d. Sydney, Australia

3 GS Titles +14 dbls: Aus 1936.
40. 48.
1 DC Title: 1939.

One of all-time great doubles players, notably with John Bromwich with whom he won 10 GS titles. Won Aus dbls 10 times in succession 36-50 (not played 41-45). Despite 3 Aus singles titles never beyond quarter-finals in other Slams.

Mary Pierce won the French Open as a Frenchwoman though never fully won the hearts of the Roland Garros crowd

Left: Fred Perry and his autograph

Adrian Quist won Australian singles titles 12 years apart

MEMORABLE MATCHES
Björn Borg v John McEnroe Wimbledon Final 1980

The tiebreak gained acceptance within a relatively short space of time, but its most dramatic moment came in the 1980 Wimbledon final.

Borg, going for a fifth successive title, looked in danger when McEnroe cruised through the first set and seemed comfortable in the second. But a bad game by the American late in the second turned the tide, and McEnroe was lucky to force a tiebreak in the fourth. What a tiebreak it was! Borg had seven championship points, McEnroe missed six set points, before Borg netted a forehand volley to give McEnroe the tiebreak 18-16.

Most people, including the players, felt McEnroe would go on to win, but even away from the drama of the tiebreak this was a superb contest, and Borg still had reserves. He broke the American in the 14th game of the final set to win 1-6 7-5 6-3 6-7 8-6.

It was to be his last title, McEnroe beating him in four sets in the following year's final.

Above centre: Ken Rosewall

Above right: A Player's cigarettes card of Dorothy Round from the 1930s

---

RAFTER, PATRICK
(1972 -)
Patrick Rafter
b. Mount Isa Qld, Australia

2 GS Titles: US 1997. 98.
1 DC Title: 1999.

Top Australian of 1990s, but happiest on concrete hardcourts despite having one of the best volleys in modern game. Peaked at 98 US Open with near perfect displays to beat Pete Sampras and Mark Philippousssis. Finalist at Wim 2000 and 01, semi-finalist at RG (97) and Aus (2001). Immensely popular player who seems unaffected by success. Known for calling 'sorry mate' after bad service ball toss.

RENSHAW, WILLIAM
(1861 -1904)
William Charles Renshaw
b. Leamington Spa
d. Swanage, England

7 GS Titles: Wim 1881. 82. 83. 84. 85. 86. 89.

One of twins, he and brother Ernest took lawn tennis a major step forward by perfecting overarm serve and smash, and generally being more competitive and spectacular, such that Wim's popularity declined after their retirement. William much more successful of the two, winning 7 Wim titles to Ernest's 1. Renshaw twins won 5 Wim dbls titles in 1880s.

RIGGS, BOBBY
(1918 -95)
Robert Larimore Riggs
b. Los Angeles, California
d. Leucadia, California

2 GS Titles: Wim 1939. US 1939.
1 DC Title: 1938.

Precocious talent who won singles, doubles and mixed titles on first visit to Wim, and reached 3 GS singles finals in 39, before turning professional in 41. Prominent figure on pro circuit, but gained notoriety aged 55 when he challenged Billie-Jean King to 'battle of sexes' match in Houston which King won (see page 19).

ROCHE, TONY
(1945 -)
Anthony Dalton Roche
b. Wagga Wagga, NSW, Australia

1 GS Title +14 dbls: RG 1966.
5 DC Titles: 1964. 65. 66. 67. 77.

Left-hander who played left court in one of all-time great doubles partnerships with John Newcombe. Newcombe-Roche won 12 GS titles, including first three successive titles at Wim (68-70) since Doherty brothers in 03-05. Reached four GS singles finals, but lost 3 in 'open' era. Career thought to be over following elbow problems in early 70s, but returned following remarkable anasthetic-free operation in Philippines.

ROSEWALL, KEN
(1934 -)
Kenneth Robert Rosewall
b. Sydney, NSW, Australia

8 GS Titles +10 dbls: Aus 1953. 55. 71. 72 / RG 1953. 68 / US 1956. 70.
4 DC Titles: 1953. 55. 56. 73.

One of tennis' all-time greats, he would have won more but for peaking during split amateur/professional circuits. Small in height by modern standards (1.73m, 5ft 8in) his economy of effort, tactical awareness and extreme determination made him a remarkable player over 27-year top-level career. Won Aus and RG titles aged 18. US title in 56 prevented dbls partner Lew Hoad from achieving calendar GS. Turned pro after 56 season but was still at top at start of 'open' era, and reached Wim and US finals aged 39. Never won Wim singles despite 4 finals. Holds record as oldest winner of full tour match from Melbourne indoors 80, 13 days short of his 46th birthday.

ROUND, DOROTHY
(1909 - 82)
Dorothy Edith Round
Later Little
b. Dudley, England
d. Kidderminster, England

3 GS Titles: Aus 1935 / Wim 1934. 37.

The outstanding British player of 30s, winning Wim in 34 in same year as Fred Perry won men's and Great Britain won DC. Game based around forehand and shrewd drop shot. Became first non-Australian to win Aus in 35. Won mixed dbls at Wim with Perry 35 & 36. Strong religious faith caused her to refuse Sunday play. Married Dr Douglas Little in 37.

RYAN, BUNNY
(1892 - 1979)
Elizabeth Montague Ryan
b. Anaheim, California
d. Wimbledon, England

26 GS dbls Titles

Arguably best player never to have won a GS singles title. Initially known as Suzanne Lenglen's doubles partner, winning Wim dbls 6 times, later won 4 GS titles with Helen Wills Moody. In singles lost Wim finals of 21 & 30, US of 26. Prolific tournament player characterised by chopped forehand. Settled in England. Died night before Billie-Jean King beat Ryan's record of 19 Wim titles.

SAMPRAS, PETE
(1971 -)
Pete Sampras
b. Washington, DC

13 GS Titles: Aus 1994. 97 /
Wim 1993. 94. 95. 97. 98. 99. 2000 /
US 1990. 93. 95. 96.
2 DC Titles: 1992. 95.

Greatest grasscourt player ever,
winning Wim 7 times, in 2000 beating
Roy Emerson's male record of
12 GS singles titles. All-court game
led by great disguise on powerful
serve, and characterised by
spectacular running forehand and
own 'slam dunk' smash.

Rivals Laver for 'greatest-ever'
tag, though still dogged by failure to
win RG. Showed impressive dbls skills
in limited DC career, but played
mostly singles. Intensely competitive,
but sometimes cricitised for lacking
charisma, but involved in some of the
most emotional matches of his era.

SANCHEZ VICARIO, ARANTXA
(1971 -)
Aranzazu Isabel Sánchez Vicario
b. Barcelona, Spain

4 GS Titles +10 dbls: RG 1989.
94. 98 / US 1994.
5 FC Titles: 1991. 93. 94. 95. 98.

Most successful female player
from Spain. Used energy, fitness,
tactical awareness and enthusiastic
competitive spirit to make up for
less natural talent than many
contemporaries. Broke Steffi Graf's
run of 5 successive GS titles to win
RG 89 aged 17. Though best on
clay, did well on all surfaces.

Topped rankings for 12 weeks.
Also topped dbls rankings after
working hard on net game. Brothers
Emilio and Javier played successfully
on men's tour.

SANTANA, MANOLO
(1938 -)
Manuel Martinez Santana
b. Madrid, Spain

4 GS Titles: RG 1961. 64 /
Wim 1966 / US 1965.

Greatest ever Spanish player,
first Spaniard to win GS title, and
his success from modest background
helped take tennis in Spain out
of affluent circles and make it a
people's sport. Inspired to play after
being ball boy, developed superb
touch game backed up by effective
forehand. Coined 'grass is for cows'
maxim despite winning Wim in 66.
Steered Spain single-handedly to 65
& 67 DC finals, losing to Australia
both times. Later DC captain 96-99
but deposed at start of year Spain
won title.

SEDGMAN, FRANK
(1927 -)
Francis Arthur Sedgman
b. Mount Albert Vic, Australia

5 GS Titles +17 dbls: Aus 1949. 50 /
Wim 1952 / US 1951. 52.
3 DC Titles: 1950. 51. 52.

Superbly agile player with great
volleys, dominated men's tennis in
early 50s but lost to amateur game
at age 24. First Australian Wim
champion for 19 years in 52.
Did Grand Slam in doubles with
Ken McGregor in 51, and only failed
in US final to repeat feat in 52.
Won all 8 GS mixed dbls titles with
Doris Hart. Unbeaten in 9 DC
dbls rubbers, won 16 of 19 in singles.

SEGURA, PANCHO
(1921 -)
Francisco Segura
b. Guayaquil, Ecuador

Always thought of as one of all-time
greats despite never winning GS
title - grew up in poverty so turned
pro as soon as he could in 47 without
having won much as amateur.
Small in height, he had great speed
around court and forged reputation
as great entertainer. Two-handed
forehand one of great shots of his
day. Only player to win three NCAA
(American university) singles titles
43-45. Best GS: RG dbls final in
46 with Enrique Morea. Had short
spell as coach to Andre Agassi in 92.
Included here because of boost he
gave to growth of tennis in Ecuador.

SEIXAS, VIC
(1923 -)
Elias Victor Seixas
b. Philadelphia, Pennsylvania

3 GS Titles +13 dbls: RG 1954 /
Wim 1953 / US 1954.
1 DC Title: 1954.

Dogged though gentlemanly
competitor whose best results came
around age 30 as one of few players
of his era not to turn professional.
Most notable successes came in dbls.
Won Wim mixed 4 years running,
3 with Doris Hart, and formed
dominant men's dbls partnership with
Tony Trabert in 54-55. Beat Rosewall
and won dbls with Trabert in 54 DC
final as USA beat Australia to avenge
losing previous 4 finals.

*Manolo Santana was noted for
not liking grass but won
Wimbledon and US titles on grass
and steered Spain to two Davis
Cup finals*

Top: Arantxa Sanchez Vicario

Left: Pete Sampras

SELES, MONICA
(1973 -)
Monica Seles
b. Novi Sad, (then) Yugoslavia

9 GS Titles: Aus 1991. 92. 93. 96 /
RG 1990. 91. 92 / US 1991. 92.
3 FC Titles: for USA 1996. 99. 2000.

Bubbly precocious talent from
Yugoslavia who became youngest
(at the time) winner of GS title in
winning RG 90 aged 16 yrs 169 days.
Won 7 more GS titles and was
clear world No1 when stabbed by
mentally unstable fan of Steffi Graf
in Hamburg 93. Returned to tour
27 months later (as US citizen), and
initially looked ready to dominate
women's tennis with 2 GS finals and
4th Aus title. But couldn't add to
178 weeks as No1, and has reached
just 1 more GS final since.

Unorthodox playing style with
powerful two-handed forehand and
backhand. Intensity of shotmaking
made grunting an issue.

SHRIVER, PAM
(1962 -)
Pamela Howard Shriver
b. Baltimore, Maryland

22 GS dbls Titles
2 FC Titles: 1986. 89.

One of the greatest women's dbls
players, part of arguably greatest-
ever pair with Martina Navratilova.
They won 79 titles together,
including 20 GS, and calendar GS 3
times (84, 85, 87). Unbeaten in
109 matches over 2 years 83-85.
Shriver was youngest women's
singles finalist at US 78 aged 16 but
never reached another GS singles
final. Successful television
commentator and part-time political
activist for Republican party.

SMITH, MARGARET
see Court

SMITH, STAN
(1946 -)
Stanley Roger Smith
b. Pasadena, California

2* GS Titles: Wim 1972 / US 71.*
7 DC Titles: 1968. 69. 70. 71. 72.
78. 79.

Tall, attacking player whose
serve-volley style compensated for
only average groundstrokes.
Best remembered for two matches v
Ilie Nastase: 72 Wim final won over
5 sets, and first rubber of 72 DC
final when Smith won in 3 despite
hostile crowd and dubious officiating
on clay in Bucharest. Also won
first Masters title in 70. Formed
impressive long-lasting dbls team
with Bob Lutz, winning 5 GS titles,
and winning all 5 rubbers played in
DC finals.

* Smith is listed as the US Open's
amateur champion for 1969 as two
stagings of the competition (amateur
and open) were held in 68 and 69,
but Rod Laver counts as the 69
US Open champion, the tournament
at which he completed his second
pure Grand Slam

STERRY, CHARLOTTE
see Cooper

STOLLE, FRED
(1938 -)
Frederick Sydney Stolle
b. Hornsby NSW, Australia

2 GS Titles +14 dbls: RG 1965 /
US 1966.
3 DC Titles: 1964. 65. 66.

Statistically more a dbls player
then singles, but reached 8 GS finals,
losing 6, including 3 in succession
at Wim. Won 8 GS men's dbls titles,
4 each with Bob Hewitt and
Roy Emerson, and 6 mixed. Played
serve-volley game, but noted for
great backhand return of serve.
Started as bank clerk in amateur
days, turned pro in 67. Later became
television commentator. Son Sandon
plays on pro circuit.

SUTTON, MAY
(1886 - 1975)
May Godfray Sutton
Later Bundy
b. Plymouth, England
d. Santa Monica, California

3 GS Titles: Wim 1905. 07 / US 1904.

English-born but grew up in
California, became first non-Briton
to win Wim. Won US singles & dbls
aged 17 with great speed around
court, top-spin forehand and
'masculine' serve. Played sporadically,
reached quarter-finals at Wim in
29 aged 42. Coached her daughter
Dorothy Bundy, who in 38 became
first American to win Aus title.

TILDEN, BILL
(1893 - 1953)
William Tatem Tilden
b. Germantown, Pennsylvania
d. Los Angeles, California

10 GS Titles +11 dbls:
Wim 1920. 21. 30 / US 1920. 21. 22.
23. 24. 25. 29.
7 DC Titles: 1920. 21. 22. 23. 24.
25. 26.

Rivals Budge, Laver, McEnroe and
Sampras for tag of greatest-ever
player. Tall charismatic figure who
brought sense of theatre to matches
and helped revitalise tennis after
first world war. Won first GS title at
27, last at 37, and missed 5 yrs at
Wim in 20s. Turned pro in 31 and
won pro titles till 45. Aspired to
acting and play writing, he was twice
jailed for homosexual activities.

*Monica Seles dominated
women's tennis up to her stabbing
in 1993*

Above centre: Stan Smith

Right: Bill Tilden

TINLING, TED
(1910 - 90)
b. Eastbourne, England
d. Cambridge, England

Umpire and dress designer.
Appalled by lack of fashion in
functional tennis clothes worn by
1940s champions Louise Brough and
Margaret Osborne, designed lace
panties for Gussy Moran which
she wore at Wim in 48. They caused
a furore, which ended Tinling's career
as an umpire but launched him as
dress designer. Later designed for
Maria Bueno, Billie-Jean King and
other leading players as official
designer to Virginia Slims women's
circuit in 70s.

TRABERT, TONY
(1930 -)
Marion Anthony Trabert
b. Cincinatti, Ohio

5 GS Titles: RG 1954. 55 /
Wim 1955 / US 1953. 55.
I DC Title: 1954.

Attractive player who was world's
leading amateur for 3 years till
turned pro after 55 season. Won Wim
and US titles without dropping a set.
He and Vic Seixas brought DC back
to America after absence of 5 yrs.
Later USA DC captain and television
commentator.

VAN ALEN, JAMES
(1902 -91)
James Henry van Alen
b. Newport, Rhode Island
d. Newport, Rhode Island

Known as the founder of the
modern tiebreak, but also worked
out a simplified scoring system, and
founded the International Tennis
Hall of Fame in Rhode Island.
Three times US national champion
at real tennis, he worked out a set
made up of points rather than games
as a way of shortening long sets;
first used in 1965 on the professional
circuit, 1970 in Slams. Also worked
out Van Alen Simplified Scoring
System (VASSS) which is used in
US inter-collegiate matches whereby
first player to four points wins the
game (so no deuce).

VILAS, GUILLERMO
(1952 -)
Guillermo Vilas
b. Buenos Aires, Argentina

4 GS Titles: Aus 1978. 79 / RG 1977 /
US 1977.

Most successful player to come
from South America, would have
been ranked No1 in 77 under today's
ranking system after winning
15 titles and 50-match unbeaten run.
Beat Newcombe, Borg & Nastase to
win 74 Masters on grass. Peaked at
77 US when he outpsyched Connors
in final. Led Argentina to DC final
in 81. Reclusive player who wrote
poetry, some of which was published.

VINES, ELLSWORTH
(1911 - 94)
Henry Ellsworth Vines
b. Los Angeles, California
d. La Quinta, California

3 GS Titles: Wim 1932 / US 1931. 32.

Regarded in 30s as hardest-ever
hitter of a tennis ball, and still
considered one of fastest servers in
tennis despite no measurements.
Won 13 of 16 singles in DC but lost
to Borotra in 32 final and never
won cup. Turned pro after 33 US,
dominating pro circuit. After 39
switched to golf, turning pro in 42,
winning five 'open' tournaments
and reaching semi-finals of 51 PGA
Championship.

VON CRAMM, GOTTFRIED
(1909 - 76)
Gottfried Alexander
Maximilian Walter Kurt
Baron von Cramm
b. Nettlingen, Germany
d. Alexandria, Egypt

2 GS Titles: RG 1934. 36.

German aristocrat, classic stylish
player noted for exemplary
sportsmanship. Lost 5 of 7 GS singles
finals, including 3 in succession at
Wim (35-37). Played 37 DC ties,
winning 82 of 102 rubbers.
Refused to support Nazi policies and
imprisoned for 6 months on politically
motivated homosexuality charges.
Spent last years in Egypt, died in car
crash.

WADE, VIRGINIA
(1945 -)
Sarah Virginia Wade
b. Bournemouth, England

3 GS Titles: Aus 1972 / Wim 1977 /
US 1968.

Top British player of 70s, greatest
moment came in winning Wim in
centenary year 77 aged 31. Won 3 of
4 GS dbls titles with Margaret Court
in 73 but didn't play Wim together.
Holds record for most FC matches
(100 rubbers, 57 ties) but never
on winning side in 4 finals. Aggressive
player with big serve, but volatile
temperament. Played record 25
Wims, first woman elected to Wim
championships committee (83).

Above: Gottfried von Cramm

Left: Ted Tinling

Tony Trabert pictured in the
early 1950s

WILANDER, MATS
(1964 -)
Mats Arne Olof Wilander
b. Växjö, Sweden

7 GS Titles: Aus 1983. 84. 88 /
RG 1982. 85. 88 / US 1988.
3 DC Titles: 1984. 85. 87.

Often underestimated Swede who
was world's top player in 88 and
topped rankings for 20 weeks,
but energy-intensive style of play
prevented lengthy period of
dominance. 82 RG title made him
first unseeded GS winner in 'open'
era, youngest (then) male GS winner,
and still only man to win 4 GS titles
before age 21. 88 US title ended
Lendl's 157-week run as No1.
Won GS titles on grass, clay and
hard with intelligent and relentless
defensive play. Holds record with
John McEnroe for longest DC rubber
in 82: 6hrs 22 minutes.

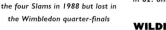

Mats Wilander won three of
the four Slams in 1988 but lost in
the Wimbledon quarter-finals

Right centre: Venus Williams

Far right: 'The Woodies',
Mark Woodforde (left) and Todd
Woodbridge

WILDING, ANTHONY
(1883 - 1915)
Anthony Frederick Wilding
b. Christchurch, New Zealand
d. Neuve Chapelle, France

6 GS Titles: Aus 1906. 09 /
Wim 1910. 11. 12. 13.
4 DC Titles: 1907. 08. 09. 14.

Athletic, dashing barrister and pilot
with impeccable manners, was one
of the most popular figures in tennis
and much mourned after death by
shell fire on western front in first
world war. Came to England to study
at Cambridge University 02.
Dominated Wim before first world
war. Only New Zealand national to
win DC as Australia and NZ played
as Australasia till 25.

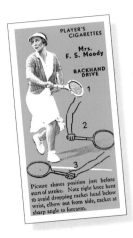

A Player's cigarettes
card of Helen Wills from
the 1930s

WILLIAMS, DICK
(1891 - 1968)
Richard Norris Williams
b. Geneva, Switzerland
d. Bryn Mawr, Pennsylvania

2 GS Titles: US 1914. 16.
5 DC Titles: 1913. 21. 23. 25. 26.

Buccaneering American who played
out-and-out attacking tennis,
sometimes foolishly. Won 3 GS dbls
titles between 12 and 26, and won
Olympic mixed title in 24. Sailed with
father on Titanic – he survived but
father died. Became army captain in
first world war.

WILLIAMS, VENUS
(1980 -)
Venus Ebone Starr Williams
b. Palm Beach Gardens, Florida

4 GS Titles +6 dbls: Wim 2000. 01 /
US 2000. 01.
2 FC Titles: 1999. 2000.

Charismatic player who has
taken power-hitting to new level and
broadened appeal of tennis,
particularly to black community.
Won 35 matches in succession to win
Wim, US and Olympic gold in 2000.
Achieved career dbls GS plus Olympic
gold with younger sister Serena.

WILLS, HELEN
(1905 - 88)
b. Berkeley, California
d. Carmel, California

19 GS Titles +12 dbls: RG 1928. 29.
30. 32 / Wim 1927. 28. 29. 30. 32.
33. 35. 38 / US 1923. 24. 25. 26. 27.
29. 31.

Dominated women's tennis after
Suzanne Lenglen, and would
probably have achieved first pure
GS but she never went to Australia.
Between 27 and 32 never dropped
a set. Also won gold medals in
singles and doubles at 1924 Olympics.
Intense baseliner, her emotionless
demeanour earned her 'Little
Miss Poker Face' nickname.
Played under name Moody after
29 following marriage to Freddie
Moody, divorced 37. Later an artist,
illustrator and writer, publishing
3 books.

WINGFIELD,
MAJOR WALTER
CLOPTON
(1833 - 1912)
b. Ruabon, Wales
d. London, England

Certainly the first marketer of the
modern form of tennis, if not the
inventor of lawn tennis. Sold the
sport in boxes of equipment to be
installed on a lawn; received a patent
for his 'portable' tennis court in
1874.

WOODBRIDGE, TODD
(1971 -)
Todd Andrew Woodbridge
b. Sydney, Australia

17 GS dbls Titles
1 DC Title: 1999.

Right-court player in 'Woodies'
dbls partnership with Woodforde,
winning 61 titles (inc 11 GS), more
than any other pair. Won Wim 5
years running (93-97), but really only
gained recognition in Australia after
winning 96 Olympic dbls gold.

Won Olympic silver in Sydney 2000.
5 mixed dbls GS titles. Best in singles
Wim semi-final 97.

WOODFORDE, MARK
(1965 -)
Mark Raymond Woodforde
b. Adelaide SA, Australia

17 GS dbls Titles
1 DC Title: 1999.

Left-hander in 'Woodies' dbls
partnership with Woodbridge, winning
61 titles (inc 11 GS), more than any
other pair. Won Wim 5 years running,
(93-97), but really only gained
recognition in Australia after winning
96 Olympic dbls gold.

Won Olympic silver in Sydney 2000.
5 mixed dbls GS titles.
Best in singles Aus semi-final 96.

A CENTURY OF CHAMPIONS

Every tournament looks for the chance to have a parade of champions, and there have been some very impressive ones in recent years. The most recent was the Millennium Parade at Wimbledon in 2000, which attracted 64 champions and multiple doubles winners.

It was a very moving occasion, with Björn Borg (middle row, sixth from left) returning to Wimbledon for the first time since his defeat in the 1981 final, and Bunny Austin (bottom row left, with blue blanket) hanging on to be present despite the ill health which caused his death a few weeks later on his 94th birthday.

Austin was never a singles champion, the oldest champion present was Sidney Wood at 88 (sitting next to Austin), and it was to be Jaroslav Drobny's (bottom row right, with stick) last appearance at a tennis event before his death a year later.

With Laver, Emerson, Rosewall, Borg, McEnroe, Becker, Edberg, Court, King, Betz, Goolagong, Navratilova, Graf and others all in attendance, it was probably as close to a who's who of 20th century tennis as is ever likely to happen.

BELOW LEFT TO RIGHT
BACK ROW:
Goran Ivanisevic, Fred Stolle,
Ken Rosewall, Kurt Nielsen,
Peter Fleming, Pam Shriver,
Helena Sukova, Hana Mandlikova,
Darlene Hard, Gigi Fernandez,
Natasha Zvereva, Rosie Casals,
Frew McMillan, Owen Davidson,
Tony Roche, Ken Fletcher,
Bob Hewitt, Ken McGregor

MIDDLE ROW: Michael Stich,
Stefan Edberg, Pat Cash,
Boris Becker, John McEnroe,
Björn Borg, Jan Kodes, Stan Smith,
John Newcombe, Manolo Santana,
Roy Emerson, Rod Laver,
Neale Fraser, Alex Olmedo,
Ashley Cooper, Tony Trabert,
Frank Sedgman, Dick Savitt,
Budge Patty

FRONT ROW: Bunny Austin,
Sidney Wood, Jana Novotna,
Conchita Martinez, Martina
Navratilova, Chris Evert,
Ann Jones, Margaret Court,
Maria Bueno, Pauline Betz,
The Duchess of Gloucester
(who made the presentations),
Shirley Fry, Angela Mortimer,
Billie-Jean King, Evonne Goolagong,
Virginia Wade, Steffi Graf,
Bob Falkenburg, Ted Schroeder,
Vic Seixas, Jaroslav Drobny

THE COMEBACK KIDS

Any sport has stories of players who come back from a major setback to hit the heights again. Here are a few of these from the modern tennis era.

Thomas Muster – The brightest hope ever to come out of Austria had just beaten Yannick Noah to reach the final of 'the Lipton' tournament in Key Biscayne in March 1989 and was due to face Ivan Lendl in the final the following day. He was putting his bags in the back of a car when a drunken driver rammed the car behind Muster, crushing his knee.

His coach Ronnie Leitgeb flew him back to Vienna for specialist knee surgery, and Muster defied initial fears that he would never walk again by returning to the tennis circuit just five months later.

Though he later won the French Open (1995) and for a few weeks was world No1 in early 1996, perhaps his most poignant moment was in winning the Lipton in 1997 to finish the unfinished business.

Monica Seles – On top of the world in early 1993 Seles was the undisputed world No1. But on 30 April on the centre court at the Rothenbaum club in Hamburg, Seles was stabbed in the back by Günther Parche, a mentally unstable 'fan' of Steffi Graf.

Seles was relatively lucky, the wound wasn't deep, but the emotional scars were deeper. She was off the tour for 27 months, and after Parche had been given a two-year suspended sentence for the attack, she felt so betrayed by German justice that even now she still won't play in Germany.

Her comeback was initially impressive, and she won her ninth Grand Slam title at the 1996 Australian Open. But she couldn't keep up the momentum, and has reached just two more Grand Slam finals since.

Andre Agassi – Agassi refused to think of his rise from 141 in the rankings in November 1997 to No1 in July 1999 as a comeback, and his career does testify to a man who until the age of 30 found it hard to sustain his motivation and top form for long. After becoming a French Open semi-finalist at 18, he had been written off for lack of application by the time he won Wimbledon in 1992.

He was then written off again in 1993 before hitting a seam of superb form to win the 1994 US Open and the 1995 Australian, which took him to No1 in the rankings. But he again lost his way in 1996 and by the end of 1997 had been written off again. He went back to the Challenger circuit and worked his way back to No1, completing a career Grand Slam on the way.

Jennifer Capriati – Capriati was the prodigy who was going to conquer the world, but only did so after plumbing the depths of personal failure and humiliation. She was so promising that the women's authorities twisted their age eligibility rules to allow Capriati to play her first tournament (Boca Raton) before her 14th birthday.

When she became the youngest Grand Slam semi-finalist at her first event (Roland Garros 1990) and won an Olympic gold medal, the sky really was the limit. But the pressure caused her to lose interest, and when she was arrested on shoplifting and drugs charges and a glum-faced police photo appeared in the papers, she had become a symbol for teenage burnout, and the WTA Tour rewrote its age eligibility rule to prevent 14-year-olds playing as much as Capriati had done.

It proved a slow road back, but in 2001 she won her first Grand Slam tournament in Australia, followed it up with a second in Paris, and in October took over from Martina Hingis as world No1.

THE RULES OF TENNIS

THE RULES OF TENNIS

MATCHES PLAYED WITHOUT AN UMPIRE

THE RULES OF TENNIS

Includes changes with effect from 1.1.02.

THE SINGLES GAME

1. THE COURT

The Court shall be a rectangle 78 feet (23.77m) long and 27 feet (8.23m) wide. It shall be divided across the middle by a net suspended from a cord or metal cable of a maximum diameter of one-third of an inch (0.8cm), the ends of which shall be attached to, or pass over, the tops of the two posts, which shall be not more than 6 inches (15cm) square or 6 inches (15cm) in diameter. These posts shall not be higher than 1 inch (2.5cm) above the top of the net cord. The centres of the posts shall be 3 feet (.914m) outside the Court on each side and the height of the posts shall be such that the top of the cord or metal cable shall be 3 feet 6 inches (1.07m) above the ground.

When a combined doubles (see Rule 34) and singles Court with a doubles net is used for singles, the net must be supported to a height of 3 feet 6 inches (1.07m) by means of two posts, called "singles sticks", which shall be not more than 3 inches (7.5cm) square or 3 inches (7.5cm) in diameter. The centres of the singles sticks shall be 3 feet (.914m) outside the singles Court on each side.

The net shall be extended fully so that it fills completely the space between the two posts and shall be of sufficiently small mesh to prevent the ball passing through. The height of the net shall be 3 feet (.914m) at the centre, where it shall be held down taut by a strap not more than 2 inches (5cm) wide and completely white in colour. There shall be a band covering the cord or metal cable and the top of the net of not less than 2 inches (5cm) nor more than 2¹/₂ inches (6.35cm) in depth on each side and completely white in colour. There shall be no advertisement on the net, strap band or singles sticks.

The lines bounding the ends and sides of the Court shall respectively be called the base-lines and the side-lines. On each side of the net, at a distance of 21 feet (6.40m) from it and parallel with it, shall be drawn the service-lines. The space on each side of the net between the service-line and the side-lines shall be divided into two equal parts called the service-courts by the centre service-line, which must be 2 inches (5cm) in width, drawn half-way between, and parallel with, the side-line.

Each base-line shall be bisected by an imaginary continuation of the centre service-line to a line 4 inches (10cm) in length and 2 inches (5cm) in width called "the centre mark" drawn inside the Court, at right angles to and in contact with such base-lines. All other lines shall be not less than 1 inch (2.5cm) nor more than 2 inches (5cm) in width, except the base-line which may be not more than 4 inches (10cm) in width, and all measurements shall be made to the outside of the lines.

All lines shall be of uniform colour. If advertising or any other material is placed at the back of the Court, it may not contain white, or yellow. A light colour may only be used if this does not interfere with the vision of the players. If advertisements are placed on the chairs of the linesmen sitting at the back of the court, they may not contain white or yellow. A light colour may only be used if this does not interfere with the vision of the players.

Note 1: In Davis Cup, Fed Cup and the Official Championships of the International Tennis Federation, specific requirements with regard to the space behind the baseline and at the sides are included in the respective Regulations for these events.

Note 2: At club or recreational level, the space behind each baseline should be not less than 18 feet (5.5m) and at the sides not less than 10 feet (3.05m).

2. PERMANENT FIXTURES

The permanent fixtures of the Court shall include not only the net, posts, singles sticks, cord or metal cable, strap and band, but also, where there are any such, the back and side stops, the stands, fixed or movable seats and chairs round the Court, and their occupants, all other fixtures around and above the Court, and the Umpire, Net-cord Judge, Footfault Judge, Linesmen and Ball Boys when in their respective places.

Note: For the purpose of this Rule, the word "Umpire" comprehends the Umpire, the persons entitled to a seat on the Court, and all those persons designated to assist the Umpire in the conduct of a match.

3. THE BALL

Balls that are approved for play under the Rules of Tennis must comply with the following specifications:

3a. The ball shall have a uniform outer surface consisting of a fabric cover and shall be white or yellow in colour. If there are any seams they shall be stitchless.

3b. The ball shall conform to the requirements specified in Appendix I (Regulations for making tests specified in Rule 3) Section iv for size and be more than 1.975 ounces (56.0 grams) and less than 2.095 ounces (59.4 grams) in weight.

3c. More than one type of ball is specified. Each ball shall have a bound of more than 53 inches (134.62cm) and less than 58 inches (147.32cm) when dropped 100 inches (254.00cm) upon a flat, rigid surface e.g. concrete. Ball type 1 (fast speed) shall have a forward deformation of more than .195 inches (.495cm) and less than .235 inches (.597cm) and return deformation of more than .295 inches (.749 cm) and less than .380 inches (.965 cm) at 18lb (8.165kg) load.

Ball types 2 (medium speed) and 3 (slow speed) shall have a forward deformation of more than .220 of an inch (.559cm) and less than .290 of an inch (.737cm) and return deformation of more than .315 of an inch (.800cm) and less than .425 of an inch (1.080cm) at 18 lb. (8.165kg) load.

The two deformation figures shall be the averages of three individual readings along three axes of the ball and no two individual readings shall differ by more than .030 of an inch (.076cm) in each case.

3d. For play above 4,000 feet (1219m) in altitude above sea level, two additional types of ball may be used.

3di. The first type is identical to ball type 2 (medium speed) as defined above except that the ball shall have a bound of more than 48 inches (121.92cm) and less than 53 inches (134.62cm) and shall have an internal pressure that is greater than the external pressure. This type of tennis ball is commonly known as a pressurised ball.

3dii. The second type is identical to ball type 2 (medium speed) as defined above except that the ball shall have a bound of more than 53 inches (134.62cm) and less than 58 inches (147.32cm) and shall have an internal pressure that is approximately equal to the external pressure and have been acclimatised for 60 days or more at the altitude of the specific tournament.

This type of tennis ball is commonly known as a zero-pressure or non-pressurised ball. The third type of ball which is recommended for use for play on any court surface type above 4,000 feet (1219m) in altitude is the ball type 3 (slow speed), as defined above.

3e. All tests for bound, size and deformation shall be made in accordance with the regulations in Appendix I.

3f. The International Tennis Federation shall rule on the question of whether any ball or prototype complies with the above specifications or is otherwise approved, for play. Such ruling may be taken on its own initiative, or upon application by any party with a bona fide interest therein, including any player, equipment manufacturer or National Association or members thereof.

Such rulings and applications shall be made in accordance with the applicable Review and Hearing Procedures of the International Tennis Federation (see Appendix III).

Note 1: Any ball to be used in a tournament which is played under the Rules of Tennis, must be named on the official ITF list of approved balls issued by the International Tennis Federation.

Case 1: Which ball type should be used on which court surface?

Decision: 3 different types of ball are approved for play under the Rules of Tennis. However:

a. Ball type 1 (fast speed) is intended for play on slow pace court surfaces (see Appendix I).

b. Ball type 2 (medium speed) is intended for play on medium/medium-fast paced court surfaces (see Appendix I).

c. Ball type 3 (slow speed) is intended for play on fast pace court surfaces (see Appendix I).

4. THE RACKET

Rackets failing to comply with the following specifications are not approved for play under the Rules of Tennis:

4a. The hitting surface of the racket shall be flat and consist of a pattern of crossed strings connected to a frame and alternately interlaced or bonded where they cross; and the stringing pattern shall be generally uniform, and in particular not less dense in the centre than in any other area. The racket shall be designed and strung such that the playing characteristics are identical on both faces.

The strings shall be free of attached objects and protrusions other than those utilised solely and specifically to limit or prevent wear and tear or vibration, and which are reasonable in size and placement for such purposes.

4b. The frame of the racket shall not exceed 29 inches (73.66cm) in overall length, including the handle. The frame of the racket shall not exceed $12^1/2$ inches (31.75cm) in overall width. The hitting surface shall not exceed $15^1/2$ inches (39.37cm) in overall length, and $11^1/2$ inches (29.21cm) in overall width.

4c. The frame, including the handle, shall be free of attached objects and devices other than those utilised solely and specifically to limit or prevent wear and tear or vibration, or to distribute weight. Any objects and devices must be reasonable in size and placement for such purposes.

4d. The frame, including the handle, and the strings, shall be free of any device which makes it possible to change materially the shape of the racket, or to change the weight distribution in the direction of the longitudinal axis of the racket which would alter the swing moment of inertia, or to deliberately change any physical property which may affect the performance of the racket during the playing of a point. No energy source that in any way changes or affects the playing characteristics of a racket may be built into or attached to a racket.

The International Tennis Federation shall rule on the question of whether any racket or prototype complies with the above specifications or is otherwise approved, or not approved, for play.

Such ruling may be undertaken on its own initiative, or upon application by any party with a bona fide interest therein, including any player, equipment manufacturer or National Association or members thereof.

Such rulings and applications shall be made in accordance with the applicable Review and Hearing Procedures of the International Tennis Federation (see Appendix III).

Case 1: Can there be more than one set of strings on the hitting surface of racket?

Decision: No. The rule clearly mentions a pattern, and not patterns, of crossed strings.

Case 2: Is the stringing pattern of a racket considered to be generally uniform and flat if the strings are on more than one plane?

Decision: No.

Case 3: Can vibration dampening devices be placed on the strings of a racket and if so, where can they be placed?

Decision: Yes; but such devices may be placed only outside the pattern of the crossed strings.

Case 4: In the course of play, a player accidentally breaks the strings of his racket. Can he continue to play with the racket in this condition?

Decision: Yes.

Case 5: Can a battery that affects playing characteristics be incorporated into a racket?

Decision. No. A battery is prohibited because it is an energy source, as are solar cells, and other similar devices.

5. SERVER & RECEIVER

The players shall stand on opposite sides of the net; the player who first delivers the ball shall be called the Server, and the other the Receiver.

Case 1: Does a player, attempting a stroke, lose the point if he crosses an imaginary line in the extension of the net:

a. before striking the ball'.

b. after striking the ball?

Decision: He does not lose the point in either case by crossing the imaginary line and provided he does not enter the lines bounding his opponent's Court (Rule 20(e)). In regard to hindrance, his opponent may ask for the decision of the Umpire under Rules 21 and 25.

Case 2: The Server claims that the Receiver must stand within the lines bounding his Court. Is this necessary?

Decision: No. The Receiver may stand wherever he pleases on his own side of the net.

6. CHOICE OF ENDS & SERVICE

The choice of ends and the right to be Server or Receiver in the first game shall be decided by toss. The player winning the toss may choose or require his opponent to choose:

6a. The right to be Server or Receiver, in which case the other player shall choose the end; or

6b. The end, in which case the other player shall choose the right to be Server or Receiver.

Case 1: Do players have the right to new choices if the match is postponed or suspended before it has started?

Decision: Yes. The toss stands, but new choices may be made with respect to service and end.

7. THE SERVICE

The service shall be delivered in the following manner. Immediately before commencing to serve, the Server shall stand with both feet at rest behind (i.e. further from the net than) the base-line, and within the imaginary continuations of the centre-mark and side-line.

The Server shall then project the ball by hand into the air in any direction and before it hits the ground strike it with his racket, and the delivery shall be deemed to have been completed at the moment of the impact of the racket and the ball. A player with the use of only one arm may utilise his racket for the projection.

Case 1: May the Server in a singles game take his stand behind the portion of the base-line between the side-lines of the Singles Court and the Doubles Court?

Decision: No.

Case 2: If a player, when serving, throws up two or more balls instead of one, does he lose that service?

Decision: No. A let should be called, but if the Umpire regards the action as deliberate he may take action under Rule 21.

8. FOOT FAULT

The Server shall throughout the delivery of the Service:

8a. Not change his position by walking or running. The Server shall not by slight movements of the feet which do not materially affect the location originally taken up by him, be deemed "to change his position by walking or running".

8b. Not touch with either foot, any area other than that behind the base-line within the imaginary extension of the centre-mark and side-lines.

9. DELIVERY OF SERVICE

9a. In delivering the service, the Server shall stand alternately behind the right and left halves of the Court beginning from the right in every game. If service from a wrong half of the Court occurs and is undetected, all play resulting from such wrong service or services shall stand, but the inaccuracy of station shall be corrected immediately it is discovered.

9b. The ball served shall pass over the net and hit the ground within the Service Court which is diagonally opposite, or upon any line bounding such Court, before the Receiver returns it.

10. SERVICE FAULT

The Service is a fault:

10a. If the Server commits any breach of Rules 7, 8 or 9 (b);

10b. If he misses the ball in attempting to strike it;

10c. If the ball served touches a permanent fixture (other than the net, strap or band) before it hits the ground.

Case 1: After throwing a ball up preparatory to serving, the Server decides not to strike at it and catches it instead. Is it a fault?

Decision: No.

Case 2: In serving in a singles game played on a Doubles Court with doubles posts and singles sticks, the ball hits a singles stick and then hits the ground within the lines of the correct Service Court. Is this a fault or a let?

Decision: In serving it is a fault, because the singles stick, the doubles post, and that portion of the net or band between them are permanent fixtures. (Rules 2 and 10, and note to Rule 24.)

11. SECOND SERVICE

After a fault (if it is the first fault) the Server shall serve again from behind the same half of the Court from which he served that fault, unless the service was from the wrong half, when, in accordance with Rule 9, the Server shall be entitled to one service only from behind the other half.

Case 1: A player serves from a wrong Court. He loses the point and then claims it was a fault because of his wrong station.

Decision: The point stands as played and the next service should be from the correct station according to the score.

Case 2: The point score being 15 all, the Server, by mistake, serves from the left-hand Court. He wins the point. He then serves again from the right-hand Court, delivering a fault. This mistake in station is then discovered. Is he entitled to the previous point? From which Court should he next serve?

Decision: The previous point stands. The next service should be from the left-hand Court, the score being 30/15, and the Server having served one fault.

12. WHEN TO SERVE

The Server shall not serve until the Receiver is ready. If the latter attempts to return the service, he shall be deemed ready.

If, however, the Receiver signifies that he is not ready, he may not claim a fault because the ball does not hit the ground within the limits fixed for the service.

13. THE LET

In all cases where a let has to be called under the rules, or to provide for an interruption to play, it shall have the following interpretations:

13a. When called solely in respective of a service that one service only shall be replayed.

13b. When called under any other circumstance, the point shall be replayed.

Case 1: A service is interrupted by some cause outside those defined in Rule 14. Should the service only be replayed?

Decision: No. The whole point must be replayed.

Case 2: If a ball in play becomes broken, should a let be called?

Decision: Yes.

14. THE "LET" IN SERVICE

The Service is a let:

14a. If the ball served touches the net, strap or band, and is otherwise good, or, after touching the net, strap or band, touches the Receiver or anything which he wears or carries before hitting the ground.

14b. If a service or a fault is delivered when the Receiver is not ready (see Rule 12). In case of a let, that particular service shall not count, and the Server shall serve again, but a service let does not annul a previous fault.

15. ORDER OF SERVICE

At the end of the first game the Receiver shall become Server, and the Server Receiver; and so on alternately in all the subsequent games of a match. If a player serves out of turn, the player who ought to have served shall serve as soon as the mistake is discovered, but all points scored before such discovery shall stand.

A fault served before such discovery shall not stand. If a game shall have been completed before such discovery, the order of service shall remain as altered.

16. WHEN PLAYERS CHANGE ENDS

The players shall change ends at the end of the first, third and every subsequent alternate game of each set, and at the end of each set unless the total number of games in such set is even, in which case the change is not made until the end of the first game of the next set.

If a mistake is made and the correct sequence is not followed the players must take up their correct station as soon as the discovery is made and follow their original sequence.

17. THE BALL IN PLAY

A ball is in play from the moment at which it is delivered in service. Unless a fault or a let is called it remains in play until the point is decided.

Case 1: A player fails to make a good return. No call is made and the ball remains in play. May his opponent later claim the point after the rally has ended?

Decision: No. The point may not be claimed if the players continue to play after the error has been made, provided the opponent was not hindered.

18. SERVER WINS POINT

The Server wins the Point:

18a. If the ball served, not being a let under Rule 14, touches the Receiver or anything which he wears or carries, before it hits the ground.

18b. If the Receiver otherwise loses the point as provided by Rule 20.

19. RECEIVER WINS POINT

The Receiver wins the Point:

19a. If the Server serves two consecutive faults;

19b. If the Server otherwise loses the point as provided by Rule 20.

20. PLAYER LOSES POINT

A player loses the point if:

20a. He fails, before the ball in play has hit the ground twice consecutively, to return it directly over the net (except as provided in Rule 24 (a) or (c)); or

20b. He returns the ball in play so that it hits the ground, a permanent fixture, or other object, outside any of the lines which bounds his opponent's Court (except as provided in Rule 24 (a) or (c)); or

20c. He volleys the ball and fails to make a good return even when standing outside the Court: or

20d. In playing the ball he deliberately carries or catches it on his racket or deliberately touches it with his racket more than once; or

20e. He or his racket (in his hand or otherwise) or anything which he wears or carries touches the net, posts, singles sticks, cord or metal cable, strap or band, or the ground within his opponent's Court at any time while the ball is in play; or

20f. He volleys the ball before it has passed the net; or

20g. The ball in play touches him or anything that he wears or carries, except his racket in his hand or hands; or

20h. He throws his racket at and hits the ball; or

20i. He deliberately and materially changes the shape of his racket during the playing of the point.

Case 1: In serving, the racket flies from the Server's hand and touches the net before the ball has touched the ground. Is this a fault, or does the player lose the point?

Decision: The Server loses the point because his racket touches the net whilst the ball is in play (Rule 20 (e)).

Case 2: In serving, the racket flies from the Server's hand and touches the net after the ball has touched the ground outside the proper court. Is this a fault, or does the player lose the point?

Decision: This is a fault because the ball was out of play when the racket touched the net.

Case 3: A and B are playing against C and D, A is serving to D, C touches the net before the ball touches the ground. A fault is then called because the service falls outside the Service Court. Do C and D lose the point?

Decision: The call "fault" is an erroneous one. C and D had already lost the point before "fault" could be called, because C touched the net whilst the ball was in play (Rule 20 (e)).

Case 4: May a player jump over the net into his opponent's Court while the ball is in play and not suffer penalty?

Decision: No. He loses the point (Rule 20 (e)).

Case 5: A cuts the ball just over the net, and it returns to A's side. B, unable to reach the ball, throws his racket and hits the ball. Both racket and ball fall over the net on A's court. A returns the ball outside of B's court. Does B win or lose the point?

Decision: B loses the point (Rule 20 (e) and (h).

Case 6: A player standing outside the service Court is struck by a service ball before it has touched the ground. Does he win or lose the point?

Decision: The player struck loses the point (Rule 20 (g)), except as provided under Rule 14 (a).

Case 7: A player standing outside the Court volleys the ball or catches it in his hand and claims the point because the ball was certainly going out of court.

Decision: In no circumstances can he claim the point:

i. If he catches the ball he loses the point under Rule 20 (g).

ii. If he volleys it and makes a bad return he loses the point under Rule 20 (c).

iii. If he volleys it and makes a good return, the rally continues.

21. PLAYER HINDERS OPPONENT

If a player commits any act which hinders his opponent in making a stroke, then, if this is deliberate, he shall lose the point or if involuntary, the point shall be replayed.

Case 1: Is a player liable to a penalty if in making a stroke he touches his opponent?

Decision: No, unless the Umpire deems it necessary to take action under Rule 21.

Case 2: When a ball bounds back over the net, the player concerned may reach over the net in order to play the ball. What is the ruling if the player is hindered from doing this by his opponent?

Decision: In accordance with Rule 21, the Umpire may either award the point to the player hindered, or order the point to be replayed (see also Rule 25).

Case 3: Does an involuntary double hit constitute an act which hinders an opponent within Rule 21?

Decision: No.

22. BALL FALLS ON LINE

A ball falling on a line is regarded as falling in the Court bounded by that line.

23. BALL TOUCHES PERMANENT FIXTURES

If the ball in play touches a permanent fixture (other than the net, posts, singles sticks, cord or metal cable, strap or band) after it has hit the ground, the player who struck it wins the point; if before it hits the ground, his opponent wins the point.

Case 1: A return hits the Umpire or his chair or stand. The player claims that the ball was going into Court.

Decision: He loses the point.

24. A GOOD RETURN

It is a good return:

24a. if the ball touches the net, posts, singles sticks, cord or metal cable, strap or band, provided that it passes over any of them and hits the ground within the Court; or

24b. If the ball, served or returned, hits the ground within the proper Court and rebounds or is blown back over the net, and the player whose turn it is to strike reaches over the net and plays the ball, provided that he does not contravene Rule 20 (e); or

24c. If the ball is returned outside the posts, or singles sticks, either above or below the level of the top to the net, even though it touches the posts or singles sticks, provided that it hits the ground within the proper Court; or

24d. If a player's racket passes over the net after he has returned the ball, provided the ball passes the net before being played and is properly returned; or

24e. If a player succeeds in returning the ball, served or in play, which strikes a ball lying in the Court.

Note: In a singles match, if, for the sake of convenience, a Doubles Court is equipped with singles sticks for the purpose of a singles game, then the doubles posts and those portions of the net, cord or metal cable and the band outside such singles sticks shall at all times be permanent fixtures, and are not regarded as posts or parts of the net of a singles game.

A return that passes under the net cord between the singles stick and adjacent doubles post without touching either net cord, net or doubles post and falls within the court, is a good return.

Case 1: A ball going out of Court hits a net post or singles stick and falls within the lines of the opponent's Court. Is the stroke good?

Decision: If a service: no, under Rule 10(c). If other than a service: yes, under Rule 24 (a).

Case 2: Is it a good return if a player returns the ball holding his racket in both hands?

Decision: Yes.

Case 3: The service, or ball in play, strikes a ball lying in the Court. Is the point won or lost thereby?

Decision: No. Play must continue. If it is not clear to the Umpire that the right ball is returned a let should be called.

Case 4: May a player use more than one racket at any time during play?

Decision: No. The whole implication of the Rules is singular.

Case 5: May a player request that a ball or balls lying in his opponent's Court be removed?

Decision: Yes, but not while a ball is in play.

25. HINDRANCE OF A PLAYER

In case a player is hindered in making a stroke by anything not within his control, except a permanent fixture of the Court, or except as provided for in Rule 21, a let shall be called.

Case 1: A spectator gets into the way of a player, who fails to return the ball. May the player then claim a let?

Decision: Yes. If in the Umpire's opinion he was obstructed by circumstances beyond his control, but not if due to permanent fixtures of the Court or the arrangements of the ground.

Case 2: A player is interfered with as in Case 1, and the Umpire calls a let. The Server had previously served a fault. Has he the right to two services?

Decision: Yes. As the ball is in play, the point, not merely the stroke, must be replayed as the Rule provides.

Case 3: May a player claim a let under Rule 25 because he thought his opponent was being hindered, and consequently did not expect the ball to be returned?

Decision: No.

Case 4: Is a stroke good when a ball in play hits another ball in the air?

Decision: A let should be called unless the other ball is in the air by the act of one of the players, in which case the Umpire will decide under Rule 21.

Case 5: If an Umpire or other judge erroneously calls "fault" or "out", and then corrects himself, which of the calls shall prevail?

Decision: A let must be called unless, in the opinion of the Umpire, neither player is hindered in his game, in which case the corrected call shall prevail.

Case 6: If the first ball served - a fault - rebounds, interfering with the Receiver at the time of the second service, may the Receiver claim a let?

Decision: Yes. But if he had an opportunity to remove the ball from the Court and negligently failed to do so, he may not claim a let.

Case 7: Is it a good stroke if the ball touches a stationary or moving object on the Court

Decision: It is a good stroke unless the stationary object came into Court after the ball was put in to play in which case a let must be called. If the ball in play strikes an object moving along or above the surface of the Court a let must be called.

Case 8: What is the ruling if the first service is a fault, the second service correct, and it becomes necessary to call a let either under the provision of Rule 25 or if the Umpire is unable to decide the point?

Decision: The fault shall be annulled and the whole point replayed.

26. SCORE IN A GAME

26a. If a player wins his first point, the score is called 15 for that player; on winning his second point, the score is called 30 for that player; on winning his third point, the score is called 40 for that player, and the fourth point won by a player is scored game for that player except as below:-

If both players have won three points, the score is called deuce; and the next point won by a player is scored advantage for that player.

If the same player wins the next point, he wins the game; if the other player wins the next point the score is again called deuce; and so on, until a player wins the two points immediately following the score at deuce, when the game is scored for that player. 26b. Optional Alternative Scoring system

The No - Ad System of Scoring may be adopted as an alternative to the traditional scoring system in paragraph (a) of this Rule, provided the decision is announced in advance of the event.

In this case, the following Rules shall be effective:

If a player wins his first point, the score is called 15 for that player; on winning his second point, the score is called 30 for that player; on winning his third point, the score is called 40 for that player, and the fourth point won by a player is scored game for that player except as below:

If both players have won three points, the score is called deuce; one deciding point shall then be played. The receiver shall choose whether he wishes to receive the service from the right-half of the court or the left-half of the court. The player who wins the deciding point is scored the game.

Doubles

In doubles a similar procedure to that for singles shall apply. At deuce the Receiving Team shall choose whether it wishes to receive the Service from the right-half of the court or the left-half of the court. The team who wins the deciding point is scored the game.

Mixed doubles

In mixed doubles, a slightly different procedure will apply as follows: At deuce, with the male player serving, he shall serve to the male player of the opposing team irrespective of which half of the court he is standing, and when the female player is serving, she shall serve to the female player of the opposing team.

27. SCORE IN A SET

27a. A player (or players) who first wins six games wins a set; except that he must win by a margin of two games over his opponent and where necessary a set shall be extended until this margin is achieved.

27b. The tie-break system of scoring may be adopted as an alternative to the advantage set system in paragraph (a) of this Rule provided the decision is announced in advance of the match.

In this case, the following Rules shall be effective:

The tie-break shall operate when the score reaches six games all in any set except in the third or fifth set of a three set or five set match respectively when an ordinary advantage set shall be played, unless otherwise decided and announced in advance of the match.

The following system shall be used in a tie-break game.

Singles

i. A player who first wins seven points shall win the game and the set provided he leads by a margin of two points. If the score reaches six points all the game shall be extended until this margin has been achieved. Numerical scoring shall be used throughout the tie-break game.

ii. The player whose turn it is to serve shall be the Server for the first point. His opponent shall be the Server for the second and third points and thereafter each player shall serve alternately for two consecutive points until the winner of the game and set has been decided.

iii. From the first point, each service shall be delivered alternately from the right and left Courts, beginning from the right court. If service from a wrong half of the Court occurs and is undetected, all play resulting from such wrong service or services shall stand, but the inaccuracy of station shall be corrected immediately it is discovered.

iv. Players shall change ends after every six points and at the conclusion of the tie-break game.

v. The tie-break game shall count as one game for the ball change, except that, if the balls are due to be changed at the beginning of the tie-break, the change shall be delayed until the second game of the following set.

Doubles

In doubles the procedure for singles shall apply. The player whose turn it is to serve shall be the Server for the first point.

Thereafter each player shall serve in rotation for two points, In the same order previously in that set, until the winners of the game and set have been decided.

Rotation of Service

The player (or pair in the case of doubles) whose turn it was to serve first in the tie-break game shall receive service in the first game of the following set.

Case 1: At six all the tie-break is played, although it has been decided and announced in advance of the match that an advantage set will be played. Are the points already played counted?

Decision: If the error is discovered before the ball is put in play for the second point, the first point shall count but the error shall be corrected immediately. If the error is discovered after the ball is put in play for the second point the game shall continue as a tie-break game.

Case 2: At six all, an advantage game is played, although it has been decided and announced in advance of the match that a tie-break will be played. Are the points already played counted?

Decision: If the error is discovered before the ball is put in play for the second point, the first point shall be counted but the error shall be corrected immediately. If the error is discovered after the ball is put in play for the second point an advantage set shall be continued. If the score thereafter reaches eight games all or a higher even number, a tie-break shall be played.

Case 3: If during a tie-break in a singles or doubles game, a player serves out of turn, shall the order of service remain as altered until the end of the game?

Decision: If a player has completed his turn of service the order of service shall remain as altered. If the error is discovered before a player has completed his turn of service the order of service shall be corrected immediately and any points already played shall count.

Alternative scoring methods approved until 31st December 2001 can be found in Appendix II.

28. MAXIMUM NUMBER OF SETS

A match can be played to the best of 3 sets (the player/team needs to win 2 sets to win the match) or to the best of 5 sets (the player/team needs to win 3 sets to win the match).

29. ROLE OF COURT OFFICIALS

In matches where an Umpire is appointed, his decision shall be final; but where a Referee is appointed, an appeal shall lie to him from the decision of an Umpire on a question of law, and in all such cases the decision of the Referee shall be final.

In matches where assistants to the Umpire are appointed (Linespersons, Net-cord Judges, Foot-fault Judges) their decisions shall be final on questions of fact except that if in the opinion of an Umpire a clear mistake has been made he shall have the right to change the decision of an assistant or order a let to be played.

When such an assistant is unable to give a decision he shall indicate this immediately to the Umpire who shall give a decision. When an Umpire is unable to give a decision on a question of fact he shall order a let to be played.

In Davis Cup matches or other team competitions where a Referee is on Court, any decision can be changed by the Referee, who may also instruct an Umpire to order a let to be played.

The Referee, in his discretion, may at any time postpone a match on account of darkness or the condition of the ground or the weather.

In any case of postponement the previous score and previous occupancy of courts shall hold good, unless the Referee and the players unanimously agree otherwise.

Case 1: The Umpire orders a let, but a player claims the point should not be replayed. May the Referee be requested to give a decision?

Decision: Yes. A question of tennis law, that is an issue relating to the application of specific facts, shall first be determined by the Umpire. However, if the Umpire is uncertain or if a player appeals from his determination, then the Referee shall be requested to give a decision, and his decision is final.

Case 2: A ball is called out, but a player claims that the ball was good. May the Referee give a ruling?

Decision: No. This is a question of fact, that is an issue relating to what actually occurred during a specific incident, and the decision of the on-court officials is therefore final.

Case 3: May an Umpire overrule a Linesman at the end of a rally if, in his opinion, a clear mistake has been made during the course of a rally?

Decision: No. An Umpire may overrule a Linesman only if he does so immediately after the mistake has been made.

Case 4: A Linesman calls a ball out. The Umpire was unable to see clearly, although he thought the ball was in. May he overrule the Linesman?

Decision: No. An Umpire may overrule if he considers that a call was incorrect beyond all reasonable doubt. He may overrule a ball determined good by a Linesman only if he has been able to see a space between the ball and the line; and he may overrule a ball determined out, or a fault, by a Linesman only if he has seen the ball hit the line, or fall inside the line.

Case 5: May a Linesman change his call after the Umpire has given the score?

Decision: Yes. If a Linesman realises he has made an error, he may make a correction provided he does so immediately.

Case 6: A player claims his return shot was good after a Linesman called "out". May the Umpire overrule the Linesman?

Decision: No. An Umpire may never overrule as a result of a protest or an appeal by a player.

30. CONTINUOUS PLAY & REST PERIODS

Play shall be continuous from the first service until the match is concluded, in accordance with the following provisions:

30a. If the first service is a fault, the second service must be struck by the Server without delay.

The Receiver must play to the reasonable pace of the Server and must be ready to receive when the Server is ready to serve.

When changing ends a maximum of ninety (90) seconds shall elapse from the moment the ball goes out of play at the end of the game to the time the ball is struck for the first point of the next game.

However, after the first game of each set and during a tie-break, play shall be continuous and the players shall change ends without a rest period. At the conclusion of each set, there shall be a set break of a maximum of one hundred and twenty (120) seconds from the moment the ball goes out of play at the end of the game to the time the ball is struck for the first point of the next game.

The Umpire shall use his discretion when there is interference which makes it impracticable for play to be continuous.

The organisers of international circuits and team events recognised by the ITF may determine the time allowed between points, which shall be a maximum twenty (20) seconds from the moment the ball goes out of play at the end of one point to the time the ball is struck for the next point.

30b. Play shall never be suspended, delayed or interfered with for the purpose of enabling a player to recover his strength, breath, or physical condition. However, in the case of a treatable medical condition, the Umpire may allow a one-time three minute time-out for that medical condition.

30c. If, through circumstances outside the control of the player, his clothing, footwear or equipment (excluding racket) becomes out of adjustment in such a way that it is impossible or undesirable for him to play on, the Umpire may suspend play while the maladjustment is rectified.

30d. The Umpire may suspend or delay play at any time as may be necessary and appropriate.

30e. After the third set, or when women take part the second set, either player shall be entitled to a rest, which shall not exceed 10 minutes, or in countries situated between latitude 15 degrees north and latitude 15 degrees south, 45 minutes and furthermore, when necessitated by circumstances not within the control of the players, the Umpire may suspend play for such a period as he may consider necessary.

If play is suspended and is not resumed until a later day the rest may be taken only after the third set (or when women take part the second set) of play on such a later day, completion of an unfinished set being counted as one set.

If play is suspended and is not resumed until 10 minutes have elapsed in the same day the rest may be taken only after three consecutive sets have been played without interruption (or when women take part two sets), completion of an unfinished set being counted as one set.

Any nation and/or committee organising a tournament, match or competition, is at liberty to modify this provision or omit it from its regulations provided this is announced before the event commences. With respect to the Davis Cup and Fed Cup, only the International Tennis Federation may modify this provision or omit it from its Regulations.

30f. A tournament committee has the discretion to decide the time allowed for a warm-up period prior to a match but this may not exceed five minutes and must be announced before the event commences.

30g. When approved point penalty and non-accumulative point penalty systems are in operation, the Umpire shall make his decisions within the terms of those systems.

30h. Upon violation of the principle that play shall be continuous the Umpire may, after giving due warning, disqualify the offender.

31. COACHING

During the playing of a match in a team competition, a player may receive coaching from a captain who is sitting on the court only when he changes ends at the end of a game, but not when he changes ends during a tie-break game.

A player may not receive coaching during the playing of any other match. The provisions of this rule must be strictly construed. After due warning an offending player may be disqualified.

When an approved point penalty system is in operation, the Umpire shall impose penalties according to that system.

Case 1: Should a warning be given, or the player be disqualified, if the coaching is given by signals in an unobtrusive manner?

Decision: The Umpire must take action as soon as he becomes aware that coaching is being given verbally or by signals. If the Umpire is unaware that coaching is being given, a player may draw his attention to the fact that advice is being given.

Case 2: Can a player receive coaching during an authorised rest period under Rule 30 (e), or when play is interrupted and he leaves the court?

Decision: Yes. In these circumstances, when the player is not on the court, there is no restriction on coaching.

Note: The word "coaching" includes any advice or instruction.

32. BALL CHANGE

In cases where balls are to be changed after a specified number of games, if the balls were not changed in the correct sequence, the mistake shall be corrected when the player, or pair in the case of doubles, who should have served with new balls is next due to serve. Thereafter the balls shall be changed so that the number of games between changes shall be that originally agreed.

THE DOUBLES GAME

33. THE DOUBLES GAME

The above Rules shall apply to the Doubles Game except as below.

34. THE DOUBLES COURT

For the Doubles Game, the court shall be 36 feet (10.97m) in width, i.e. $4\frac{1}{2}$ feet (1.37m) wider on each side than the Court for the Singles Game, and those portions of the singles side-lines which lie between the two service-lines shall be called the service side-lines.

In other respects, the Court shall be similar to that described in Rule 1, but the portions of the singles side-lines between the base-line and service-line on each side of the net may be omitted if desired.

35. ORDER OF SERVICE IN DOUBLES

The order of serving shall be decided at the beginning of each set as follows: The pair who have to serve in the first game of each set shall decide which partner shall do so and the opposing pair shall decide similarly for the second game.

The partner of the player who served in the first game shall serve in the third; the partner of the player who served in the second game shall serve in the fourth, and so on in the same order in all the subsequent games of a set.

Case 1: In doubles, one player does not appear in time to play, and his partner claims to be allowed to play single-handed against the opposing players. May he do so?

Decision: No.

36. ORDER OF RECEIVING IN DOUBLES

The order of receiving the service shall be decided at the beginning of each set as follows:- The pair who have to receive the service in the first game shall decide which partner shall receive the first service, and that partner shall continue to receive the first service in every odd game throughout that set.

The opposing pair shall likewise decide which partner shall receive the first service in the second game and that partner shall continue to receive the first service in every even game throughout that set. Partners shall receive the service alternately throughout each game.

Case 1: Is it allowable in doubles for the Server's partner or the Receiver's partner to stand in a position that obstructs the view of the Receiver?

Decision: Yes. The Server's partner or the Receiver's partner may take any position on his side of the net in or out of the Court that he wishes.

37. SERVICE OUT OF TURN IN DOUBLES

If a partner serves out of his turn, the partner who ought to have served shall serve as soon as the mistake is discovered, but all points scored, and any faults served before such discovery, shall be reckoned. If a game shall have been completed before such discovery, the order of service remains as altered.

38. ERROR IN ORDER OF RECEIVING IN DOUBLES

If during a game the order of receiving the service is changed by the Receivers it shall remain as altered until the end of the game in which the mistake is discovered, but the partners shall resume their original order of receiving in the next game of that set in which they are Receivers of the service.

39. SERVICE FAULT IN DOUBLES

The service is a fault as provided for by Rule 10, or if the ball touches the Server's partner or anything which he wears or carries; but if the ball served touches the partner of the Receiver, or anything which he wears or carries, not being a let under Rule 14 (a) before it hits the ground, the Server wins the point.

40. PLAYING THE BALL IN DOUBLES

The ball shall be struck alternately by one or other player of the opposing pairs, and if a player touches the ball in play with his racket in contravention of this Rule, his opponents win the point.

Note 1: Except where otherwise stated, every reference in these Rules to the masculine includes the feminine gender.

Note 2: See Rule 26(b) with regard to the Optional Alternative Scoring System in Doubles and Mixed.

WHEELCHAIR TENNIS

The game of wheelchair tennis follows the ITF Rules of Tennis with the following exceptions.

I. THE TWO BOUNCE RULE

The wheelchair tennis player is allowed two bounces of the ball. The player must return the ball before it hits the ground a third time. The second bounce can be either in or out of the court boundaries.

2. THE WHEELCHAIR

The wheelchair is considered part of the body and all applicable rules which apply to a player's body shall apply to the wheelchair.

3. THE SERVICE

3i. The service shall be delivered in the following manner. Immediately before commencing the serve, the server shall be in a stationary position. The server shall then be allowed one push before striking the ball.

3ii. The server shall throughout the delivery of the service not touch with any wheel, any area other than that behind the baseline within the imaginary extension of the centre mark and sideline.

3iii. If conventional methods for the service are physically impossible for a quadriplegic player, then the player or an individual may drop the ball for such a player. However, the same method of serving must be used each time.

4. PLAYER LOSES POINT

A player loses a point if:

4i. He fails to return the ball before it has touched the ground three times.

4ii. Subject to rule 4) below. He uses any part of his feet or lower extremities as brakes or as stabilisers while delivering service, stroking a ball, turning or stopping against the ground or against any wheel while the ball is in play.

4iii. He fails to keep one buttock in contact with his wheelchair seat when contacting the ball.

5. PROPELLING THE CHAIR WITH THE FOOT

5i. If due to lack of capacity a player is unable to propel the wheelchair via the wheel then he may propel the wheelchair using one foot.

5ii. Even if in accordance with rule 5i. above a player is permitted to propel the chair using one foot, no part of the player's foot may be in contact with the ground:

a). during the forward motion of the swing, including when the racket strikes the ball.

b). from the initiation of the service motion until the racket strikes the ball.

c). A player in breach of this rule shall lose a point.

6. WHEELCHAIR/ABLE-BODIED TENNIS

Where a wheelchair tennis player is playing with or against an able-bodied person in singles and doubles, the Rules of Wheelchair Tennis shall apply for the wheelchair player while the Rules of Tennis for able-bodied tennis shall apply for the able-bodied player. In this instance, the wheelchair player is allowed two bounces while the able-bodied player is allowed only one bounce.

Note: The definition of lower extremities is: the lower limb, including the buttocks, hip, thigh, leg, ankle and foot.

THE RULES OF TENNIS AMENDMENTS

The official and decisive text to the Rules of Tennis shall be for ever in the English language and no alteration or interpretation of such Rules shall be made except at an Annual General Meeting of the Council, nor unless notice of the resolution embodying such alteration shall have been received by the Federation in accordance with Article 16 of the Constitution of ITF Limited (Notice of Resolutions) and such resolution or one having the like effect shall be carried by a majority of two-thirds of the votes recorded in respect of the same.

Any alteration so made shall take effect as from the first day of January following unless the Meeting shall by the like majority decide otherwise.

The Board of Directors shall have power, however, to settle all urgent questions of interpretation subject to confirmation at the General Meeting next following.

This Rule shall not be altered at any time without the unanimous consent of a General Meeting of the Council.

APPENDIX I
REGULATIONS FOR MAKING TESTS SPECIFIED IN RULE 3

i. Unless otherwise specified all tests shall be made at a temperature of approximately 68 0 Fahrenheit (20 0 Centigrade) and a relative humidity of approximately 60 per cent. All balls shall be removed from their container and kept at the recognised temperature and humidity for 24 hours prior to testing, and shall be at that temperature and humidity when the test is commenced.

ii. Unless otherwise specified the limits are for a test conducted in an atmospheric pressure resulting in a barometric reading of approximately 30 inches (76cm).

iii. Other standards may be fixed for localities where the average temperature, humidity or average barometric pressure at which the game is being played differ materially from 68 0 Fahrenheit (20 0 Centigrade), 60 per cent and 30 inches (76cm) respectively. Applications for such adjusted standards may be made by any National Association to the International Tennis Federation and if approved shall be adopted for such localities.

iv. In all tests for diameter a ring gauge shall be used consisting of a metal plate, preferably non-corrosive, of a uniform thickness of one-eighth of an inch (.318cm). In the case of BALL Type 1 (fast SPEED) and BALL Type 2 (medium SPEED) balls there shall be two circular openings in the plate measuring 2.575 inches (6.541cm) and 2.700 inches (6.858cm) in diameter respectively.

In the case of BALL Type 3 (slow SPEED) balls there shall be two circular openings in the plate measuring 2.750 inches (6.985cm) and 2.875 inches (7.302 cm) in diameter respectively.

The inner surface of the gauge shall have a convex profile with a radius of one-sixteenth of an inch (.159cm). The ball shall not drop through the smaller opening by its own weight and shall drop through the larger opening by its own weight.

v. In all tests for deformation conducted under Rule 3, the machine designed by Percy Herbert Stevens and patented in Great Britain under Patent No.230250, together with the subsequent additions and improvements thereto, including the modifications required to take return deformations, shall be employed.

Other machines may be specified which give equivalent readings to the Stevens machine and these may be used for testing ball deformation where such machines have been given approval by the International Tennis Federation.

6. PROCEDURE FOR CARRYING OUT TESTS:

6a. Pre-compression. Before any ball is tested it shall be steadily compressed by approximately one inch (2.54cm) on each of three diameters at right angles to one another in succession; this process to be carried out three times (nine compressions in all). All tests to be completed within two hours of pre-compression.

6b. Bound test (as in Rule 3). Measurements are to be taken from the concrete base to the bottom of the ball.

6c. Size test (as in paragraph (iv) above).

6d. Weight test (as in Rule 3).

6e. Deformation test. The ball is placed in position on the modified Stevens machine so that neither platen of the machine is in contact with the cover seam. The contact weight is applied, the pointer and the mark brought level, and the dials set to zero.

The test weight equivalent to 18lb. (8.165kg) is placed on the beam and pressure applied by turning the wheel at a uniform speed so that five seconds elapse from the instant the beam leaves its seat until the pointer is brought level with the mark.

When turning ceases the reading is recorded (forward deformation). The wheel is turned again until figure ten is reached on the scale (one inch (2.54cm) deformation). The wheel is then rotated in the opposite direction at a uniform speed (thus releasing pressure) until the beam pointer again coincides with the mark.

After waiting ten seconds the pointer is adjusted to the mark if necessary. The reading is then recorded (return deformation). This procedure is repeated on each ball across the two diameters at right angles to the initial position and to each other.

7. CLASSIFICATION OF COURT SURFACE PACE

The ITF test method used for determining the pace of a court surface is test method ITF CS 01/01 (ITF Surface Pace Rating) as described in the ITF publication entitled "An initial ITF study on performance standards for tennis court surfaces".

Court surfaces which are found to have an ITF Surface Pace Rating of between 0 and 35 shall be classified as being Category 1 (slow pace). Examples of court surface types which conform to this classification will include most clay courts and other types of unbound mineral surface.

Court surfaces which are found to have an ITF Surface Pace Rating of between 30 and 45 shall be classified as being Category 2 (medium/medium-fast pace). Examples of court surface types which conform to this classification will include most hardcourts with various acrylic type coatings plus some textile surfaces.

Court surfaces which are found to have an ITF Surface Pace Rating of over 40 shall be classified as being Category 3 (fast pace). Examples of court surface types which conform to this classification will include most natural grass, artificial turf and some textile surfaces.

N.B. The proposed overlap in ITF Surface Pace Rating values for the above categories is to allow some latitude in ball selection.

APPENDIX II
ALTERNATIVE SCORING METHODS (RULE 27)

1. "SHORT" SETS

The first player/team who wins four games wins that Set, provided there is a margin of two games over the opponent(s). If the score reaches four games all, a tie-break game shall be played.

2. DECIDING TIE-BREAK GAME

When the score in a match is one set all, or two sets all in best of five sets matches, one tie-break game shall be played to decide the match. This tie-break game replaces the deciding final set.

3. DECIDING SUPER TIE-BREAK GAME

When the score in a match is one set all, or two sets all in best of five sets matches, one super tie-break game shall be played to decide the match. This super tie-break game replaces the deciding final set. The player who first wins ten points shall win this super tie-break and the match provided he leads by a margin of two points.

APPENDIX III
PROCEDURES FOR REVIEW AND HEARINGS ON THE RULES OF TENNIS

I. INTRODUCTION

1.1. These procedures were approved by the Board of Directors of the International Tennis Federation ("Board of Directors") on 17 May 1998.

1.2. The Board of Directors may from time to time supplement, amend, or vary these procedures.

2. OBJECTIVES

2.1. The International Tennis Federation is the custodian of the Rules of Tennis and is committed to:

2.1a. Preserving the traditional character and integrity of the game of tennis.

2.1b. Actively preserving the skills traditionally required to play the game.

2.1c. Encouraging improvements, which maintain the challenge of the game.

2.1d. Ensuring fair competition.

2.2 To ensure fair, consistent and expeditious review and hearings in relation to the Rules of Tennis the procedures set out below shall apply.

3. SCOPE

3.1 These Procedures shall apply to Rulings under:

3.1a. Rule 1 – The Court.

3.1b. Rule 3 – The Ball.

3.1c. Rule 4 – The Racket.

3.1d. Appendix 1 of the Rules of Tennis.

3.1e. Any other Rules of Tennis which the International Tennis Federation may decide.

4. STRUCTURE

4.1. Under these procedures Rulings shall be issued by a Ruling Board.

4.2. Such Rulings shall be final save, for an entitlement to appeal to an Appeal Tribunal pursuant to these procedures.

5. APPLICATION

5.1. Rulings shall be taken either:

5.1a. Following a motion of the Board of Directors; or

5.1b. Upon the receipt of an application in accordance with the procedures set out below.

6. APPOINTMENT AND COMPOSITION OF RULING BOARDS

6.1. Ruling Boards shall be appointed by the President of the International Tennis Federation ("President") or his designee and shall comprise of such a number, as the President or his designee shall determine.

6.2. If more than one person is appointed to the Ruling Board the Ruling Board shall nominate one person from amongst themselves to act as Chairperson.

6.3. The Chairperson shall be entitled to regulate the procedures prior to and at any review and/or hearing of a Ruling Board.

7. PROPOSED RULINGS BY THE RULING BOARD

7.1. The details of any proposed Ruling issued upon the motion of the Board of Directors may be provided to any bona fide person or any players, equipment manufacturer or national association or members thereof with an interest in the proposed Ruling.

7.2. Any person so notified shall be given a reasonable period within which to forward comments, objections, or requests for information to the President or his designee in connection with the proposed Ruling.

8. APPLICATION FOR RULINGS

8.1. An application for a Ruling may be made by any party with a bona fide interest in the Ruling including any player, equipment manufacturer or national association or member thereof.

8.2. Any application for a Ruling must be submitted in writing to the President.

8.3. To be valid an application for a Ruling must include the following minimum information:

8.3a. The full name and address of the Applicant.

8.3b. The date of the application.

8.3c. A statement clearly identifying the interest of the Applicant in the question upon which a Ruling is requested.

8.3d. All relevant documentary evidence upon which the Applicant intends to rely at any hearing.

8.3e. If, in the opinion of the Applicant, expert evidence is necessary he shall include a request for such expert evidence to be heard. Such request must identify the name of any expert proposed and their relevant expertise.

8.3f. When an application for a Ruling on a racket or other piece of equipment is made, a prototype or, exact, copy of the equipment in question must be submitted with the application for a Ruling.

8.3g. If, in the opinion of the Applicant, there are extraordinary or unusual circumstances, which require a Ruling to be made within a specified time or before a specified date he shall include a statement describing the extraordinary or unusual circumstances.

8.4. If an application for a Ruling does not contain the information and/or equipment referred to at Clause 8.3 (a)-(g) above the President or his designee shall notify the Applicant giving the Applicant a specified reasonable time within which to remedy the defect.

If the Applicant fails to remedy the defect within the specified time the application shall be dismissed.

9. CONVENING THE RULING BOARD

9.1. On receipt of a valid application or on the motion of the Board of Directors the President or his designee may convene a Ruling Board to deal with the application or motion.

9.2. The Ruling Board need not hold a hearing to deal with an application or motion where the application or motion, in the opinion of the Chairperson can be resolved in a fair manner without a hearing.

10. PROCEDURE OF THE RULING BOARD

10.1. The Chairperson of a Ruling Board shall determine the appropriate form, procedure and date of any review and/or hearing.

10.2. The Chairperson shall provide written notice of those matters set out at 10.1 above to any Applicant or any person or association who has expressed an interest in the proposed Ruling.

10.3. The Chairperson shall determine all matters relating to evidence and shall not be bound by judicial rules governing procedure and admissibility of evidence provided that the review and/or hearing is conducted in a fair manner with a reasonable oppor-tunity for the relevant parties to present their case.

10.4. Under these procedures any review and/or hearings:

10.4a. Shall take place in private.

10.4b. May be adjourned and/or postponed by the Ruling Board.

10.5. The Chairperson shall have the discretion to co-opt from time to time additional members onto the Ruling Board with special skill or experience to deal with specific issues, which require such special skill or experience.

10.6. The Ruling Board shall take its decision by a simple majority. No member of the Ruling Board may abstain.

10.7. The Chairperson shall have the complete discretion to make such order against the Applicant (and/or other individuals or organisations commenting objecting or re-questing information at any review and/or hearing) in relation to the costs of the application and/or the reasonable expenses incurred by the Ruling Board in holding tests or obtaining reports relating to equipment subject to a Ruling as he shall deem appropriate.

11. NOTIFICATION

11.1. Once a Ruling Board has reached a decision it shall provide written notice to the Applicant, or, any person or association who has expressed an interest in the pro-posed Ruling as soon as reasonably practicable.

11.2. Such written notice shall include a summary of the reasoning behind the decision of the Ruling Board.

11.3. Upon notification to the Applicant or upon such other date specified by the Ruling Board the Ruling of the Ruling Board shall be immediately binding under the Rules of Tennis.

12. APPLICATION OF CURRENT RULES OF TENNIS

12.1. Subject to the power of the Ruling Board to issue interim Rulings the current Rules of Tennis shall continue to apply until any review and/or hearing of the Ruling Board is concluded and a Ruling issued by the Ruling Board.

12.2. Prior to and during any review and/or hearing the Chairperson of the Ruling Board may issue such directions as are deemed reasonably necessary in the implementation of the Rules of Tennis and of these procedures including the issue of interim Rulings.

12.3. Such interim Rulings may include restraining orders on the use of any equipment under the Rules of Tennis pending a Ruling by the Ruling Board as to whether or not the equipment meets the specification of the Rules of Tennis.

13. APPOINTMENT AND COMPOSITION OF APPEAL TRIBUNALS

13.1. Appeal Tribunals shall be appointed by the President or his designee from (members of the Board of Directors/Technical Commission).

13.2. No member of the Ruling Board who made the original Ruling shall be a member of the Appeal Tribunal.

13.3. The Appeal Tribunal shall comprise of such number as the President or his designee shall determine but shall be no less than three.

13.4. The Appeal Tribunal shall nominate one person from amongst themselves to act as Chairperson.

13.5. The Chairperson shall be entitled to regulate the procedures prior to and at any appeal hearing.

14. APPLICATION TO APPEAL

14.1. An Applicant (or a person or association who has expressed an interest and forwarded any comments, objections, or requests to a proposed Ruling) may appeal any Ruling of the Ruling Board.

14.2. To be valid an application for an appeal must be:

14.2a. Made in writing to the Chairperson of the Ruling Board who made the Ruling appealed not later than (45) days following notification of the Ruling;

14.2b. Must set out details of the Ruling appealed against; and

14.2c. Must contain the full grounds of the appeal.

14.3. Upon receipt of a valid application to appeal the Chairperson of the Ruling Board making the original Ruling may require a reasonable appeal fee to be paid by the Appellant as a condition of appeal. Such appeal fee shall be repaid to the Appellant if the appeal is successful.

15. CONVENING THE APPEAL TRIBUNAL

15.1. The President or his designee shall convene the Appeal Tribunal following payment by the Appellant of any appeal fee.

16. PROCEDURES OF APPEAL TRIBUNAL

16.1. The Appeal Tribunal and their Chairperson shall conduct procedures and hearings in accordance with those matters set out in sections 10, 11 and 12 above.

16.2. Upon notification to the Appellant or upon such other date specified by the Appeal Tribunal the Ruling of the Appeal Tribunal shall be immediately binding and final under the Rules of Tennis.

17. GENERAL

17.1. If a Ruling Board consists of only one member that single member shall be responsible for regulating the hearing as Chairperson and shall determine the procedures to be followed prior to and during any review and/or hearing.

17.2. All review and/or hearings shall be conducted in English. In any hearing where an Applicant, and/or other individuals or organisations commenting, objecting or re-questing information do not speak English an interpreter must be present. Wherever practicable the interpreter shall be independent.

17.3. The Ruling Board or Appeal Tribunal may publish extracts from its own Rulings.

17.4. All notifications to be made pursuant to these procedures shall be in writing.

17.5. Any notifications made pursuant to these procedures shall be deemed notified upon the date that they were communicated, sent or transmitted to the Applicant or other relevant party.

17.6 A Ruling Board shall have the discretion to dismiss an application if in its reasonable opinion the application is substantially similar to an application or motion upon which a Ruling Board has made a decision and/or Ruling within the 36 months prior to the date of the application.

APPENDIX IV
THE WHEELCHAIR TENNIS PLAYER

CHALLENGES AND PROCEDURES FOR A PLAYER'S ELIGIBILITY

1. CHALLENGES

1a. The following parties have the right to question a player's eligibility:

• ITF Member Nations (through their General Secretary).

• The wheelchair tennis Players' Representatives Committee (through their Chairperson).

• The ITF Wheelchair Tennis Committee.

Note 1: IWTA Member Nations who are not represented by their National Tennis Federation, may submit a challenge through the ITF Wheelchair Tennis Committee who must decide if the challenge should proceed to the Eligibility Sub-Committee.

1b. On receipt of a formal written challenge from any of the parties named in 1a. above, the ITF must inform the player and ask them to submit sufficient objective medical evidence of permanent physical disability in writing to the Eligibility Sub-Committee of the ITF Wheelchair Tennis Committee within 28 days.

The Eligibility Sub-Committee (which shall be made up of at least one medical doctor from the ITF Medical Commission and at least two ITF appointed experts in the Rules of Wheelchair Tennis) must then review the case.

Note 1: The player may continue to play during the Eligibility Sub-Committee's investigation. Should the outcome of the Eligibility Sub-Committee be that the player does not meet the minimum criteria as laid out in Rule 1 of the Rules of Wheelchair Tennis, the player must then cease to play with immediate effect. The only exception to this is in the case of an appeal against the decision by the player as outlined in the Appeals Procedure below.

Note 2: Failure to submit medical evidence as described above within 28 days of the request being made by the ITF, shall result in automatic suspension of that player until such time as evidence is provided.

Note 3: The costs incurred by the player in obtaining the medical evidence shall be borne by the player. All costs incurred in the evaluation of medical evidence provided by the player will be the responsibility of the ITF. The player will be instructed by the ITF, regarding how, when and where to provide the necessary medical evidence.

1c. If the Eligibility Sub-Committee judges that a player is eligible to compete, their eligibility may not be challenged again for a minimum of 12 months. After this time, all challenges shall be subject to the same procedures as laid out above. If, after a second challenge, the player is still deemed eligible to compete, their eligibility may not be challenged again for a further 3 years.

Note 1: If a player is challenged after already having been deemed eligible to compete, they may continue to play while any new challenges are being considered.

2. APPEALS PROCEDURE

2a. If the Eligibility Sub-Committee judges that supporting medical evidence is insufficient, then the player may appeal within 14 days of the decision and request an evaluation by an independent medical doctor appointed by the ITF Member Nation for that player.

Further to receiving the submission from the medical doctor appointed by the ITF Member Nation, the ITF Medical Commission will give a ruling on the eligibility of the player which shall not be subject to further appeal for a minimum of 12 months (see 2b. below).

Note 1: In the case of an appeal being made, the player may continue to play until after the appeal has been heard.

Note 2: The costs of the evaluation for the appeal will be at the player's expense. All costs incurred in the evaluation of medical evidence provided by the medical doctor will be the responsibility of the ITF.

2b. If a person's circumstances change in relation to their physical disability in the future, the person is entitled to submit a request to the ITF to be reconsidered. This request may only be made a minimum of 12 months after the first appeal decision.

Such a request shall be supported by the new medical evidence and shall be subject to the same process as outlined in Rule 1 of the Rules of Wheelchair Tennis and this Appendix IV. If, after the second appeal, the player is still deemed ineligible to compete, their case may not be reconsidered for a further 3 years.

Note 1: If the Eligibility Sub-Committee has already judged that a player is currently ineligible, they may not compete while any new medical evidence is being considered.

PLAN OF THE COURT

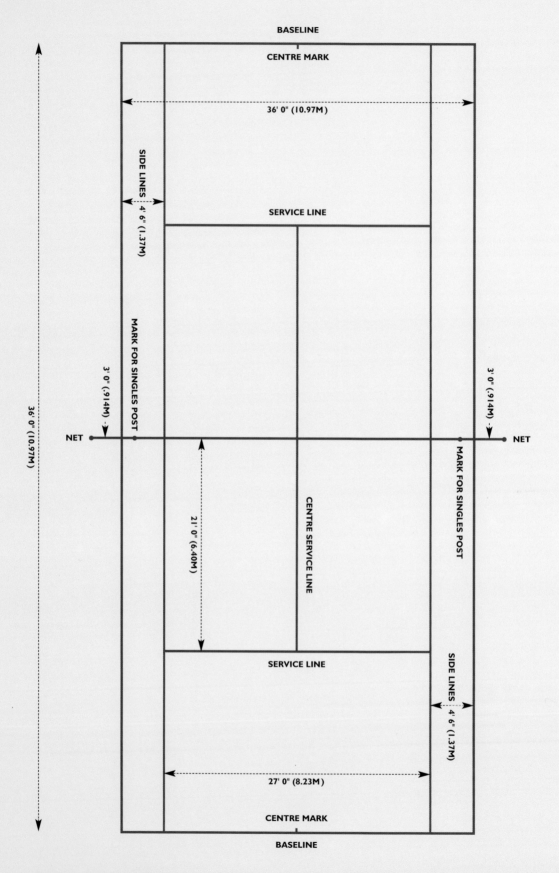

BASELINE

CENTRE MARK

36' 0" (10.97M)

SIDE LINES 4' 6" (1.37M)

SERVICE LINE

MARK FOR SINGLES POST

3' 0" (.914M)

NET

36' 0" (10.97M)

21' 0" (6.40M)

CENTRE SERVICE LINE

MARK FOR SINGLES POST

3' 0" (.914M)

NET

SIDE LINES 4' 6" (1.37M)

SERVICE LINE

27' 0" (8.23M)

CENTRE MARK

BASELINE

HOW TO MARK OUT A COURT

The following procedure is for the usual combined Doubles and Singles Court. (See note at foot for a Court for one purpose only.)

First select the position of the net; a straight line 42 feet (12.8m) long. Mark the centre (X on the diagram above) and, measuring from there in each direction, mark:

- At 13' 6" (4.11m) the points a, b, where the net crosses the inner sidelines.

- At 16' 6" (5.03m) the positions of the singles posts (or sticks) (n, n).

- At 18' 0" (5.49m) the points A, B, where the net crosses the outer sidelines.

- At 21' 0" (6.40m) the positions of the net posts (N, N), being the ends of the original 42' 0" (12.8m) line.

Insert pegs at A and B and attach to them the respective ends of two measuring tapes. On one, which will measure the diagonal of the half-court, take a length 53' 1" (16.18m) and on the other (to measure the sideline) a length of 39' 0" (11.89m). Pull both taut so that at these distances they meet at a point C, which is one corner of the Court. Reverse the measurements to find the other corner D.

As a check on this operation it is advisable at this stage to verify the length of the line CD which, being the baseline, should be found to be 36' 0" (10.97m); and at the same time its centre J can be marked, and also the ends of the inner sidelines (c, d), 4' 6" (1.37m) from C and D.

The centre-line and service-line are now marked by means of the points F, H, G, which are measured 21' 0" (6.40m) from the net down the lines bc, XJ, ad, respectively. Identical procedure the other side of the net completes the Court.

Notes:

i. If a Singles Court only is required, no lines are necessary outside the points a, b, c, d, but the Court can be measured out as above. Alternatively, the corners of the base-line (c, d) can be found if preferred by pegging the two tapes at a and b instead of at A and B, and by then using lengths of 47' 5" (14.46m) and 39' 0" (11.89m). The net posts will be at n, n, and a 33' 0" (10m) singles net should be used.

ii. When a combined doubles and singles Court with a doubles net is used for singles, the net must be supported at the points n, n, to a height of 3 feet 6inches (1.07m) by means of two posts, called "singles sticks", which shall be not more than 3 inches (7.5cm) square or 3 inches (7.5cm) in diameter. The centres of the singles sticks shall be 3 feet (.914m) outside the singles Court on each side.

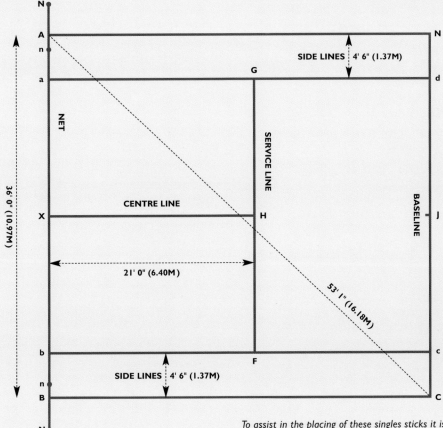

To assist in the placing of these singles sticks it is desirable that the points n, n, should each be shown with a white dot when the Court is marked.

MATCHES PLAYED WITHOUT AN UMPIRE

The Rules of Tennis govern how the game should be played, but who enforces them when there is no on-court arbiter (umpire) as happens in many matches?

Because the rules don't cover every eventuality for matches without an umpire, the ITF has drawn up a list of guidelines for players and referees in tournaments where matches take place without an umpire.

Ultimately the referee is responsible for what happens at a tournament, but any player following these guidelines should find him/herself on the right side of any dispute.

If you have any questions about this, contact either *The Book of Tennis* website, or the ITF's officiating department (details page 162).

ITF RECOMMENDATIONS FOR PLAYERS AND REFEREES

1. For Players

At some tournaments, some matches will be played without a Chair Umpire. All players should be aware of the following basic principles when playing a match in these circumstances:

- *Each player is responsible for all calls on his/her side of the net.*

- *All "out" or "fault" calls should be made promptly after the ball has bounced and loudly enough for the opponent to hear.*

- *If in doubt, the player must give the benefit of the doubt to his/her opponent.*

- *If a player incorrectly calls a ball "out" and then realises that the ball was good, the point should be replayed, unless it was a point winning shot.*

- *The server should call the score before each 1st serve, loudly enough for his/her opponent to hear.*

- *If a player is unhappy with his/her opponent's actions or decisions, he/she should call the Referee (or assistant).*

For matches played on clay courts, there are some additional procedures that all players should follow:

- *A ball mark can be checked on a point ending shot, or when play is stopped (a reflex return is allowed).*

- *If a player is unsure of his/her opponent's call, he/she can ask his/her opponent to show the mark. The player can then cross the net to look at the mark.*

- *If a player erases the mark, he/she is conceding the point If there is a disagreement over a ball mark, the Referee (or assistant) can be called to make a final decision.*

- *If a player incorrectly calls a ball "out" and then realises that the ball was good, the player who called "out" loses the point.*

Players who do not fairly follow these procedures could be subject to the Hindrance Rule and the Unsportsmanlike Conduct provision of the ITF Code of Conduct.

Any questions on these procedures should be referred to the Supervisor/Referee.

2. For Referees

The ITF recognises that at some tournaments it is not possible to have a Chair Umpire for every match. In order to have a consistent approach, these guidelines have been created so that matches can be handled in a similar manner worldwide.

Please find attached a Player Notice, which gives some procedures for players taking part in matches without a Chair Umpire. If you are the Supervisor/Referee at an event where matches will be played in these circumstances, please make sure that this notice is displayed for the players at the tournament site.

Obviously, a number of problems can occur in these matches so it is very important that the Referee (and assistants) walk around the courts as much as possible. The players appreciate having easy access to an official in case of any problems.

Referees (or assistants) should use the following guidelines when handling different situations.

a. Line call disputes

For matches not played on clay courts

If the Referee (or assistant) is called to the court over a disputed line call and he/she was not watching the match, he/she should ask the player who made the call (on his/her own side of the net) if he/she is sure of the call. If the player confirms the call, the point stands with this call.

If it appears that it would be beneficial to have the match officiated, try and find a Chair Umpire who will assume all the duties and call all the lines from the chair. If this is not possible (e.g. no experienced Chair Umpire available, no Umpire's Chair), another option is for the Referee (or assistant) to stay on-court to watch the rest of the match. He/she should then tell the players that he/she will correct any clearly incorrect line calls made by the players.

If the Referee (or assistant) is off-court and happens to be watching a match when a player makes a blatantly incorrect call, he/she can go on-court and tell the player that the incorrect call was an unintentional hindrance to his/her opponent and the point will be replayed.

The Referee (or assistant) must also tell the player that any further clearly incorrect calls may be considered as a deliberate hindrance and the player will lose the point.

In addition a Code Violation for Unsportsmanlike Conduct can be given if the Referee (or assistant) is sure that the player is blatantly calling incorrectly.

Referees (and assistants) must take care not to become too involved in matches when it is not required or necessary, or to use the Hindrance Rule for close calls that are incorrectly called. As a matter of practice, before using the Hindrance Rule, the Referee (or assistant) must be very sure that a very bad call has been made.

b. Ball mark disputes
Clay courts only

If the Referee (or assistant) is called to the court to resolve a dispute, he/she should find out if the players agree on which ball mark it is.

If the players agree on which mark it is, but disagree on their reading of the mark, the Referee (or assistant) should decide if the mark shows the ball was in or out.

If the players disagree on which mark it is, the Referee (or assistant) should find out from the players what kind of shot was played and the direction in which the ball was hit.

This may assist in deciding which mark is the correct one. If this information does not help, the call by the player at the end where the mark is stands.

c. Score disputes

If the Referee (or assistant) is called to court to resolve a score dispute, he/she should discuss the relevant points or games with the players to find out the points or games that the players agree on. All points or games which the players agree on stand and only those in dispute should be replayed.

For example, a player claims the score is 40-30 and his opponent claims the score is 30-40. You discuss the points with the players and discover that they disagree only on who won the first point in the game. The correct decision is to continue the game from 30-30, since both players agree that each of them has won two points in that game.

When a game is in dispute, the same principle applies. For example, a player claims that he is leading 6-5, but his opponent disagrees, claiming that he is leading 6-5.

After discussing the games you discover that both players claim they won the first game. The correct decision is to continue the match with the game score 5-5, since both players agree that each of them has won five games. The player who received in the last game that was played will serve in the next game.

After resolving any score dispute, it is important for the Referee (or assistant) to emphasise the procedure that the server should call the score before each 1st serve, loudly enough for his/her opponent to hear.

d. Other issues

There are a number of other issues that are difficult to handle when there is no Chair Umpire. When there is a dispute regarding lets, not-ups and foul shots, the Referee (or assistant) should try to find out from the players what happened and either confirm the call that was made or replay the point, as he/she deems appropriate.

Foot Faults can only be called by a Referee (or assistant) and not by the receiver. However, to call foot faults the official must be standing on-court for the match. Officials standing off-court are not allowed to make foot fault calls.

Coaching, as well as other Code and Time Violations can only be handled by the Referee (or assistant), so it is extremely important that there are officials observing the conduct of the players and coaches. When issuing a Code or Time Violation, the Referee (or assistant) should go on to court as soon as possible after the violation and briefly inform the players that a Code or Time Violation has been issued.

Players who do not fairly follow these procedures can be subject to the Unsportsmanlike Conduct provision of the Code of Conduct, but this should only be used in clear situations.

If you have any questions on these procedures, please contact the ITF Officiating Department in London (see page 162).

THE USTA CODE

In the 1980s a leading American referee Nick Powel drew up his own guide on how to behave in unofficiated matches which he called 'The Code – The player's guide to unofficiated matches'. It has undergone some revisions since, including a restructuring in 1998 by the USTA. This is the latest version, supplied by the USTA. It goes much further than the ITF's guidelines, though never actually contradicts them (the USTA worked with the ITF in drawing up the ITF's guidelines on the basis of its experience with its own Code).

Only in America could a player quote from the USTA's Code and be confident that it would carry some weight.

The Book of Tennis is happy to reprint it as food for thought, though as much of the Code deals with etiquette we would point out that many experienced players may differ with some aspects of it, and not everything is followed on the professional circuit. For example, contrary to article 4 of the Code, many players at professional and amateur level do practise their returns using their opponent's practice serves – because of time constraints they are trading a few practice serves for a few practice returns, but in most clubs and tournaments this is considered legitimate.

PREFACE

When your serve hits your partner stationed at the net, is it a let, fault, or loss of point? Likewise, what is the ruling when your serve, before touching the ground, hits an opponent who is standing back of the baseline? The answers to these questions are obvious to anyone who knows the fundamentals of tennis, but it is surprising the number of players who don't know these fundamentals. All players have a responsibility to be familiar with the basic rules and customs of tennis.

Further, it can be distressing to your opponent when he makes a decision in accordance with a rule and you protest with the remark: "Well, I never heard of that rule before!" Ignorance of the rules constitutes a delinquency on the part of a player and often spoils an otherwise good match.

What is written here constitutes the essentials of *The Code*, a summary of procedures and unwritten rules which custom and tradition dictate all players should follow. No system of rules will cover every specific problem or situation that may arise. If players of good will follow the principles of *The Code*, they should always be able to reach an agreement, while at the same time making tennis more fun and a better game for all. The principles set forth in *The Code* shall apply in cases not specifically covered by The Rules of Tennis and USTA Regulations.

Before reading this you might well ask yourself: Since we have a book that contains all the rules of tennis, why do we need a code? Isn't it sufficient to know and understand all the rules?

There are a number of things not specifically set forth in the rules that are covered by custom and tradition only. For example, if you have a doubt on a line call, your opponent gets the benefit of the doubt. Can you find that in the rules? Further, custom dictates the standard procedures that players will use in reaching decisions. These are the reasons why we need a code.

Colonel Nick Powel

Note: This edition of The Code *is an adaptation of the original, which was written by Colonel Nicholas E Powel.*

PRINCIPLES

1. *Courtesy.* Tennis is a game that requires cooperation and courtesy from all participants. Make tennis a fun game by praising your opponent's good shots and by not:

- *Conducting loud postmortems after points.*

- *Complaining about shots like lobs and drop shots.*

- *Embarrassing a weak opponent by being overly gracious of condescending.*

- *Losing your temper, using vile language, throwing your racket, or slamming a ball in anger or*

- *Sulking when you are losing.*

2. *Counting points played in good faith.* All points played in good faith stand. For example, if after losing a point, a player discovers that the net was four inches too high, the point stands. If a point is played from the wrong court, there is no replay. If during a point, a player realizes that a mistake was made at the beginning (for example service from the wrong court), he shall continue playing the point. Corrective action may be taken only after a point has been completed.

THE WARM-UP

3. *Warm-up is not practice.* A player should provide his opponent a five-minute warm-up (ten minutes if there are no ball persons). If a player refuses to warm-up his opponent, he forfeits his right to a warm-up. Some players confuse warm-up and practice. A player should make a special effort to hit his shots directly to his opponent. (If partners want to warm each other up while their opponents are warming up, they may do so.)

4. *Warm-up serves.* Take all your warm-up serves before the first serve of the match. Courtesy dictates that you not practice your service return when your opponent practices his serve. If a player has completed his warm-up serves, he shall return warm-up serves directly to his opponent.

MAKING CALLS

5. *Player makes calls on his side of the net.* A player calls all shots landing on, or aimed at, his side of the net.

6. *Opponent gets benefit of doubt.* When a match is played without officials, the players are responsible for making decisions, particularly for line calls. There is a subtle difference between player decisions and those of an on-court official.

An official impartially resolves a problem involving a call, whereas a player is guided by the unwritten law that any doubt must be resolved in favor of his opponent. A player in attempting to be scrupulously honest on line calls frequently will find himself keeping a ball in play that might have been out or that he discovers too late was out. Even so, the game is much better played this way.

7. *Ball touching any part of line is good.* If any part of the ball touches the line, the ball is good. A ball 99% out is still 100% good.

8. *Ball that cannot be called out is good.* Any ball that cannot be called out is considered to have been good. A player may not claim a let on the basis that he did not see a ball. One of tennis' most infuriating moments occurs after a long hard rally when a player makes a clean placement and his opponent says: "I'm not sure if it it was good or out. Let's play a let."

Remember, it is each player's responsibility to call all balls landing on, or aimed at, his side of the net. If a ball can't be called out with certainty, it is good. When you say your opponent's shot was really out but you offer to replay the point to give him a break, you are deluding yourself because you must have had some doubt.

9. *Calls when looking across a line or when far away.* The call of a player looking down a line is much more likely to be accurate than that of a player looking across a line. When you are looking across a line, don't call a ball out unless you can clearly see part of the court between where the ball hit and the line. It is difficult for a player who stands on one baseline to question a call on a ball that landed near the other baseline.

10. *Treat all points the same regardless of their importance.* All points in a match should be treated the same. There is no justification for considering a match point differently than the first point.

11. *Requesting opponent's help.* When an opponent's opinion is requested and he gives a positive opinion, it must be accepted. If neither player has an opinion, the ball is considered good. Aid from an opponent is available only on a call that ends a point.

12. *Out calls corrected.* If a player mistakenly calls a ball "out" and then realizes it was good, the point shall be replayed if he returned the ball within the proper court. Nonetheless, if the player's return of the ball results in a "weak sitter", the player should give his opponent the point. If the player failed to make the return, his opponent wins the point. If the mistake was made on the second serve, the server is entitled to two serves.

13. *Player calls his own shots out.* With the exception of the first serve, a player should call against himself any ball he clearly sees out regardless of whether he is requested to do so by his opponent. The prime objective in making calls is accuracy. All players should cooperate to attain this objective.

14. *Partners' disagreement on calls.* If a player and his partner disagree about whether their opponents' ball was out, they shall call it good. It is more important to give your opponents the benefit of the doubt than to avoid possibly hurting your partner's feelings by not overruling. The tactful way to achieve the desired result is to tell your partner quietly that he has made a mistake and then let him overrule himself. If a call is changed from out to good, the point is replayed only if the out ball was put back in play.

15. *Audible or visible calls.* No matter how obviously it is to a player that his opponent's ball is out, the opponent is entitled to a prompt audible or visible out call.

16. *Opponent's calls questioned.* When a player genuinely doubts his opponent's call, the player may ask: "Are you sure of your call?" If the opponent reaffirms that the ball was out, his call shall be accepted. If the opponent acknowledges that he is uncertain, he loses the point. There shall be no further delay or discussion.

17. *Spectators never to make calls.* A player shall not enlist the aid of a spectator in making a call. No spectator has a part in the match.

18. *Prompt calls eliminate two chance option.* A player shall make all calls promptly after the ball has hit the court. A call shall be made either before the player's return shot has gone out of play or before the opponent has had the opportunity to play the return shot. Prompt calls will quickly eliminate the "two chances to win the point" option that some players practice.

To illustrate, a player is advancing to the net for an easy put away when he sees a ball from an adjoining court rolling toward him. He continues his advance and hits the shot, only to have his supposed easy put away fly over the baseline. The player then claims a let. The claim is not valid because he forfeited his right to call a let by choosing instead to play the ball. He took his chance to win or lose, and he is not entitled to a second chance.

19. *Lets called when balls roll on the court.* When a ball from an adjacent court enters the playing area, any player shall call a let as soon as he becomes aware of the ball. The player loses the right to call a let if he unreasonably delays in making the call.

20. *Touches, hitting the ball before it crosses net, invasion of opponent's court, double hits, and double bounces.* A player shall promptly acknowledge if:

• *A ball touches him.*

• *He touches the net.*

• *He touches his opponent's court.*

• *He hits a ball before it crosses the net.*

• *He deliberately carries or double hits the ball or*

• *The ball bounces more than once in his court.*

21. *Balls hit through the net or into the ground.*

A player shall make the ruling on a ball that his opponent hits:

• *Through the net or*

• *Into the ground before it goes over the net.*

22. *Calling balls on clay courts.* If any part of the ball mark touches the line on a clay court, the ball shall be called good. If you can see only part of the mark on the court, this means that the missing part is on the line or tape. A player should take a careful second look at any point-ending placement that is close to a line on a clay court. Occasionally a ball will strike the tape, jump, and then leave a full mark behind the line.

The player should listen for the sound of the ball striking the tape and look for a clean spot on the tape near the mark. If these conditions exist, the player should give the point to his opponent.

SERVING

23. *Server's request for third ball.* When a server requests three balls, the receiver shall comply when the third ball is readily available. Distant balls shall be retrieved at the end of a game.

24. *Foot faults.* A player may warn his opponent that the opponent has committed a flagrant foot fault. If the foot faulting continues, the player may attempt to locate an official. If no official is available, the player may call flagrant foot faults. Compliance with the foot fault rule is very much a function of a player's personal honor system. The plea that he should not be penalized because he only just touched the line and did not rush the net is not acceptable.

Habitual foot faulting, whether intentional or careless, is just as surely cheating as is making a deliberate bad line call.

25. *Service calls in doubles.* In doubles the receiver's partner should call the service line, and the receiver should call the sideline and the center service line. Nonetheless, either partner may call a ball that he clearly sees.

26. *Service calls by serving team.* Neither the server not his partner shall make a fault call on the first service even if they think it is out because the receiver maybe giving the server the benefit of the doubt. But the server and his partner shall call out any second serve that either of them clearly sees out.

27. *Service let calls.* Any player may call a service let. The call shall be made before the return of serve goes out of play or is hit by the server or his partner. If the serve is an apparent or near ace, any let shall be called promptly.

28. *Obvious faults.* A player shall not put into play or hit over the net an obvious fault. To do so constitutes rudeness and may even be a form of gamesmanship. On the other hand, if a player believes that he cannot call a serve a fault and gives his opponent the benefit of a close call, the server is not entitled to replay the point.

29. *Receiver readiness.* The receiver shall play to the reasonable pace of the server. The receiver should make no effort to return a serve when he is not ready. If a player attempts to return a serve (even if it is a "quick" serve), then he (or his team) is presumed to be ready.

30. *Delays during service.* When the server's second service motion is interrupted by a ball coming onto the court, he is entitled to two serves. When there is a delay between the first and second serves:

• *The server gets one serve if he was the cause of the delay.*

• *The server gets two serves if the delay was caused by the receiver or there was outside interference.*

The time it takes to clear a ball that comes onto the court between the first and second serves is not considered sufficient time to warrant the server receiving two services unless this time is so prolonged as to constitute an interruption.

The receiver is the judge of whether the delay is sufficiently prolonged to justify giving the server two serves.

SCORING

31. *Server announces score.* The server shall announce the game score before the first point of the game and the point score before each subsequent point of the game.

32. *Disputes.* Disputes over the score shall be resolved by using one of the following methods, which are listed in the order of preference:

• *Count all points and games agreed upon by the players and replay only the disputed points or games.*

• *Play from a score mutually agreeable to all players.*

• *Spin a racket or toss a coin.*

HINDRANCE ISSUES

33. *Talking during a point.* A player shall not talk while the ball is moving toward his opponent's side of the court. If the player's talking interferes with his opponent's ability to play the ball, the player loses the point. Consider the situation where a player hits a weak lob and loudly yells at his partner to get back.
If the shout is loud enough to distract his opponent, then the opponent may claim the point based on a deliberate hindrance. If the opponent chooses to hit the lob and misses it, the opponent loses the point because he did not make a timely claim of hindrance.

34. *Feinting with the body.* A player may feint with his body while the ball is in play. He may change position at any time, including while the server is tossing the ball. Any movement or sound that is made solely to distract an opponent, including but not limited to waving the arms or racket or stamping the feet, is not allowed.

35. *Lets due to hindrance.* A let is not automatically granted because of hindrance. A let is authorized only if the player could have made the shot had he not been hindered. At let is also not authorized for a hindrance caused by something within a player's control. For example a request for a let because the player tripped over his own hat should be denied.

36. *Grunting.* A player should avoid grunting and making other loud noises. Grunting and other loud noises may bother not only opponents but also players on adjacent courts. In an extreme case, an opponent or a player on an adjacent court may seek the assistance of the referee or a roving official. The referee or official may treat grunting and the making of loud noises as a hindrance. Depending upon the circumstance, this could result in a let or loss of point.

37. *Injury caused by a player.* When a player accidentally injures his opponent, the opponent suffers the consequences. Consider the situation where the server's racket accidentally strikes the receiver and incapacitates him. The receiver is unable to resume play within the time limit.

Even though the server caused the injury, the server wins the match by retirement. On the other hand, when a player deliberately injures his opponent and affects the opponent's ability to play, then the opponent wins the match by default. Hitting a ball or throwing a racket in anger is considered a deliberate act.

WHEN TO CONTACT AN OFFICIAL

38. *Withdrawing from a match or tournament.* A player shall not enter a tournament and then withdraw when he discovers that tough opponent have also entered. A player may withdraw from a match or tournament only because of injury, illness, personal emergency, or another bona fide reason. If a player cannot play a match, he shall notify the referee at once so that his opponent may be saved a trip.

A player who withdraws from a tournament is not entitled to the return of his entry fee unless he withdrew before the draw was made.

Stalling. The following actions constitute stalling:

• *Warming up for more than the allotted time.*

• *Playing at about one-third a player's normal pace.*

• *Taking more than the allotted 90 seconds on the odd-game changeover.*

• *Taking a rest at the end of a set that contains an even number of games.*

• *Taking more than the authorized ten minutes during an authorized rest period between sets.*

- *Starting a discussion or argument in order for a player to catch his breath.*

- *Clearing a missed first serve that doesn't need to be cleared and*

- *Bouncing the ball ten times before each serve.*

Contact an official if you encounter a problem with stalling. It is subject to penalty under the Point Penalty System.

40. *Requesting an official.* While normally a player may not leave the playing area, he may visit the referee or seek a roving official to request assistance. Some reasons for visiting the referee include:

- *Stalling.*

- *Chronic flagrant foot faults.*

- *A medical time-out.*

- *A scoring dispute and*

- *A pattern of bad calls.*

A player may refuse to play until an official responds.

BALL ISSUES

41. *Retrieving stray balls.* Each player is responsible for removing stray balls and other objects from his end of the court. A player shall not go behind players on an adjacent court until their point is over. When a player returns a ball that comes from an adjacent court, he shall wait until their point is over and then return it directly to one of the players, preferably the server.

42. *Catching a ball.* Unless you have made a local ground rule, if you catch a ball before it bounces, you lose the point regardless of where you are standing.

43. *New balls for a third set.* When a tournament specifies new balls for a third set, new balls shall be used unless all the players agree otherwise.

MISCELLANEOUS

44. *Clothing and equipment malfunction.* If clothing or equipment other than a racket becomes unusable through circumstances outside the control of the player, play may be suspended for a reasonable period. The player may leave the court after the point is over to correct the problem. If a racket or string is broken, the player may leave the court to get a replacement, but he is subject to code violations under the Point Penalty System.

45. *Placement of towels.* Place towels on the ground outside the net post or at the back fence. Clothing and towels should never be placed on the net.

If you have any questions or observations, visit either *The Book of Tennis* website: www.thebookoftennis.com, or contact the USTA's officiating department (details page 169).

The Book of Tennis

TENNIS ASSOCIATIONS

GLOBAL

ATP
201 ATP Tour Boulevard
Ponte Vedra Beach
Florida 32082
USA
Telephone: +1 904 285 8000
Fax: +1 904 285 5966
Website: www.atptour.com
Chief Executive Officer:
    Mark Miles
Chief Operating Officer:
    Larry Scott

TENNIS
PROPERTIES LIMITED
TPL*
Bank Lane
London
SW15 5XZ
England
Telephone: +44 20 8392 4722
Fax: +44 20 8392 4725
Director: Mark Webster
* TPL is the company set up by
the tournament directors of the
Tennis Masters Series, the nine elite
tournaments on the ATP tour

SANEX WTA TOUR
1266 East Main Street
Stamford
Connecticut 06902-3546
USA
Telephone: +1 203 978 1740
Fax: +1 203 978 1702
Website: www.sanexwta.com
Chief Executive Officer:
    Bart McGuire

INTERNATIONAL
TENNIS FEDERATION
ITF
Bank Lane
London
SW15 5XZ
England
Telephone: +44 20 8878 6464
Fax: +44 20 8878 7799
E-mail: reception@itftennis.com
Website: www.itftennis.com
President: Francesco Ricci Bitti
Executive Vice-President:
    Juan Margets

REGIONAL

ASIAN
TENNIS FEDERATION
ATF
131 Tanglin Road
Tudor Court
Unit F
Singapore 247924
Telephone: +65 738 3258
Fax: +65 738 9278
E-mail: atf@asiantennis.com
Website: www.asiantennis.com
President: Eiichi Kawatei
Secretary: Herman Hu

CONFEDERACION DE
TENIS DE
CONTROAMERICA
CARIBE
COTECC
c/o Federacion Salvadorena
Apartado Postal (01) 110
San Salvador
El Salvador
Telephone: +503 278 8087
Fax: +503 221 0564
E-mail: chilancalmo@aol.com
President: Enrique Molins
Secretary: Frank Liautaud

CONFEDERACION
SUDAMERICANA DE
TENIS
COSAT
Casa de Federaciones
Calle Mexico No 1638
La Paz 14752
Bolivia
Telephone: +591 2 313334
Fax: +591 2 313323
E-mail:
    seccosat@ceibo.entelnet.bo
President:
    Vicento Calderon Zeballos
Secretary: Ms Janett la Fuente

CONFEDERATION
OF AFRICAN TENNIS
CAT
BP 1712
Dakar
Senegal
Telephone: +221 822 5855
Fax: +221 823 1222
E-mail: catennis@telecomplus.sn
Website: www.cat.sn
President: Diagna N'Diaye
Secretary: Nicolas Ayeboua

TENNIS EUROPE
ETA
Formerly the
European Tennis Association
Seltisbergerstrasse 6
4059 Basel
Switzerland
Telephone: +41 61 331 7675
Fax: +41 61 331 7253
Website: www.etatennis.com
President: Augustin Pujol Niubo
Secretary: Ms Charlotte Ferrari

OCEANIA
TENNIS FEDERATION
OTF
Private Bag 6060
Richmond South
Victoria 3121
Australia
Telephone: +61 3 9286 1177
Fax: +61 3 9650 2743
President: Geoff Pollard
Secretary: Patrick Rourke

NATIONAL
Full ITF members
(Class B)
with voting rights

ALGERIA
ALG
Fédération Algérienne de Tennis
Centre des Fédérations Sportives
Cité Olympique BP 88 El Biar
Algers 16030
Algeria
Telephone: +213 21 922970
Fax: +213 21 924613
E-mail: fat.tennis@caramail.com
Website:
    www.multimania.com/tennisdz
President: Mohammed Bouabdallah
Secretary: Sellami Mebarek

ANDORRA
AND
Federacion Andorrana de Tenis
Sant Antoni
C/ Verge del Pilar 5 3er
    desp no 10
Andorra la Vella
Andorra
Telephone: +376 861381
Fax: +376 868381
President: Antoni Ricart
Secretary: Joan Grau

ANGOLA
ANG
Federacao Angolana de Tenis
Cidadeia Desportive
PO Box 3677
Luanda
Angola
Telephone: +244 2 399650
Fax: +244 2 399650
E-mail: luisrosa.lopes@snet.co.ao
President: Luis Rosa Lopes
Secretary: Francisco Barros

ANTIGUA & BARBUDA
ANT
Antigua & Barbuda Tennis
    Association
PO Box 2758
St Johns
Antigua & Barbuda
Telephone: +1 268 460 5573
Fax: +1 268 462 4658
E-mail: a_btennis@hotmail.com
President: Cordell Williams
Secretary: Derald Williams

ARGENTINA
ARG
Asociacion Argentina de Tenis
Avenida San Juan 1307
1148 Buenos Aires
Argentina
Telephone: +54 114 304 2470
Fax: +54 114 305 0296
E-mail: info@aat.com.ar
Website: www.tenisargentina.com
President: Enrique Morea
Secretary: Roberto Fernandaz

ARMENIA
ARM
Armenian Tennis Association
Arshakunyats 9
Yerevan 375023
Armenia
Telephone: +3741 548 171
Fax: +3741 548 191
E-mail:
   armeniantennis@hotmail.com
President: Harutyun Pambukian
Secretary: George Karamanoukian

AUSTRALIA
AUS
Tennis Australia
Bag 6060
Richmond South
Victoria 3121
Australia
Telephone: +61 3 9286 1177
Fax: +61 3 9650 2743
Website:
   www.tennisaustralia.com.au
President: Geoff Pollard
Secretary: Fenton Coull

AUSTRIA
AUT
Österreichischer Tennisverband
Haecklstrasse 33
1235 Vienna
Austria
Telephone: +43 1 865 4506
Fax: +43 1 865 450685
E-mail: info@oetv.at
Website: www.asn.or.at/oetv
President: Ernst Wolner
Secretary: Martin Reiter

AZERBAIJAN
AZE
Azerbaijan Tennis Federation
Flat 46
44-46B Madjedov Str
Baku 370002
Azerbaijan
Telephone: +994 12 395172
Fax: +994 12 394023
President: Nazim Ibragimov
Secretary: Djavanshir Ibragimov

BAHAMAS
BAH
Bahamas Lawn Tennis Association
PO Box N-10169
Nassau
Bahamas
Telephone: +1 242 328 7238
Fax: +1 242 323 3934
E-mail: chappy@bahamas.net.bs
President: Ms Edith Powell
Secretary: Ms Vicky Knowles

BAHRAIN
BRN
Bahrain Tennis Federation
PO Box 26985
Bahrain
Telephone: +973 687236
Fax: +973 781533
E-mail: btennisf@batelco.com.bh
President: Ahmed Alkalifa
Secretary:
   Mohammad Saleh Abdul Latif

BANGLADESH
BAN
Bangladesh Tennis Federation
Tennis Complex
Ramna Green
Dhaka 1000
Bangladesh
Telephone: +880 2 862 6287
Fax: +880 2 966 2711
E-mail: btf@bttb.net.bd
President: Sayed Chowdhury
Secretary: Sanaul Haque

BARBADOS
BAR
Barbados Lawn Tennis Association
PO Box 615C
Bridgetown
Barbados
Telephone: +1 246 426 6453
Fax: +1 246 429 3342
E-mail: blta@sunbeach.net
President: Raymond Forde
Secretary: Ms Jean Date

BELARUS
BLR
Belarus Tennis Association
63 Masherov Avenue
Minsk 220035
Belarus
Telephone: +375 17 2269374
Fax: +375 17 226 9823
E-mail: beltennis@yahoo.com
President: Simon Kagan
Secretary: Georgy Matsuk

BELGIUM
BEL
Royal Belgian Tennis
   Federation
Galérie de la Porte Louise 203
(8ème étage)
1050 Brussels
Belgium
Telephone: +32 2 513 2927
Fax: +32 2 513 7950
E-mail: aft@pophost.eunet.be
President: Yves Freson
Secretary: Franz Lemaire

BENIN
BEN
Fédération Beninoise de
   Lawn Tennis
BP 2709
Cotonoui
Benin
Telephone: +229 315153
Fax: +229 311252
President: Edgar-Yves Monnou
Secretary: Ladami Gafari

BERMUDA
BER
Bermuda Lawn Tennis
   Association
PO Box HM342
Hamilton HM BX
Bermuda
Telephone: +1 441 296 0834
Fax: +1 441 295 3056
E-mail: aes@ibl.bm
President: David Lambert
Secretary: Ms Airlie Arton

BOLIVIA
BOL
Federacion Boliviana de Tenis
Calle Rene Moreno 552
Casilla Postale No 1041
Santa Cruz
Bolivia
Telephone: +591 336 8625
Fax: +591 911 2976
E-mail:
   fbtenis@bibosi.scz.entelnet.bo
Website: www.fbtenis.org.bo
President: Edmundo Rodriguez
Secretary:
   Ms Maria Eugenia Oporto

BOSNIA
HERZEGOVINA
BIH
Tennis Association of Bosnia
   & Herzegovina
Obalni Bulevar 30A
72000 Zenica
Bosnia Herzegovina
Telephone: +387 32 286610
Fax: +387 32 411077
E-mail: tsbih@hotmail.com
President: Neven Tomic
Secretary: Haris Barucija

BOTSWANA
BOT
Botswana Tennis Association
PO Box 1174
Gaorone
Botswana
Telephone: +267 373193
Fax: +267 373193
E-mail: lightbooks@it.bw
President: Botsang Tshenyego
Secretary: Charles Bewlay

BRAZIL
BRA
Confederacão Brasileira
de Tenis
Av Paulista Nr 326-2
CJ 26/27
01310-902 São Paulo
Brazil
Telephone: +55 11 283 1788
Fax: +55 11 283 0768
E-mail: cbt@zaz.com.br
Website: www.cbtennis.com.br
President: Nelson Nastas
Secretary:
   Carlos Alberto Martelotte

BRUNEI
BRU
Brunei Darussalam Tennis
Association
National Tennis Centre
Hassanal Bolkiah Sports Complex
PO Box 859 Gadong Post Office
Bandar Seri Begawan
Negara Be 7938
Brunei
Telephone: +673 2 381205
Fax: +673 2 381 205
E-mail: bdta@brunet.bn
President: Pg Kamaruddin Radin
Secretary: Hj Zuraimi Abd San

BULGARIA
BUL
Bulgarian Tennis Federation
Bul. Vasil Levsky 75
Sofia 1040
Bulgaria
Telephone: +359 2 963 1310
Fax: +359 2 981 5728
E-mail: bft@mail.techno-link.com
President: Krassimir Angarski
Secretary: Chavdar Ganev

BURKINA FASO
BUR
Fédération Burkinabe de Tennis
01 BP 45
Ouadougou 1
Burkina Faso
Telephone: +226 312733
Fax: +226 304031
President: Zambo Martin Zongo
Secretary: André Batiana

CAMEROON
CMR
Fédération Camerounaise
de Tennis
BP 1121
Yaounde
Cameroon
Telephone: +237 370790
Fax: +237 230319
President: Paul Kemadjou
Secretary: Victor Momha

CANADA
CAN
Tennis Canada
3111 Steeles Avenue West
Downsview
Ontario M3J 3H2
Canada
Telephone: +1 416 665 9777
Fax: +1 416 665 9017
E-mail:
compcoord@tenniscanada.com
Website: www.tenniscanada.com
President: Robert H Moffatt
Secretary: Ms Kim Ali

CHILE
CHI
Federacion de Tenis de Chile
Jose Joaquin
Prieto No 4040, Paradero 7
Gran Avenida
Santtiago
Chile
Telephone: +56 25 540068
Fax: +56 25 541078
E-mail: ftch@entelchile.net
Website: www.fedtenis.cl
President: Ms Jimena Espinoza
Secretary: Andres Fazio Molina

CHINA HONG KONG
HKG
Hong Kong Tennis
Association Limited
Sports House (Room 1021)
1 Stadium Path
So Kon Po
Causeway Bay
Telephone: +852 2 504 8277
Fax: +852 2 894 8704
E-mail: stellapn@tennishk.org
President: Philip Kwok
Secretary: Ms Stella Poon

CHINA
PEOPLE'S REPUBLIC
CHN
Chinese Tennis Association
5' Tiyuguan Road
Beijing 100763
China
Telephone: +86 10 6718 0176
Fax: +86 10 6711 4096
E-mail: cta@tennis.org.cn
President: Lu Zhenchao
Secretary: Zhang Xiaoning

CHINESE TAIPEI
TPE
Chinese Taipei Tennis Association
Room 705, 7th floor
20 Chu-Lun Street
Taipei
Taiwan
Telephone: +886 2 2772 0298
Fax: +886 2 2771 1696
E-mail: ctta@gcn.net.tw
President: F T Hsieh
Secretary: Samuel Mu

COLOMBIA
COL
Federacion Colombiana de Tenis
Centro de Alto Rendimiento
Calle 63 No 47-06
Santa Fe de Bogota DC
Colombia
Telephone: +571 314 3885
Fax: +571 660 4234
E-mail: fedtenis@multi.net.co
Website: www.fedetenis.com
President: Ricardo Mejia Pelaez
Secretary: David Murillo

CONGO
CGO
Fédération Congolaise de
Lawn Tennis
BP 550
Brazzaville
Democratic Republic of Congo
Telephone: +242 411222
Fax: +242 810330
E-mail: fecoten@hotmail.com
President:
Germain Ickonga Akindou
Secretary: Antoine Ouabonzi

COSTA RICA
CRC
Federacion Costarricense
de Tenis
Apartado 1815-1250
Escazu
San Jose
Costa Rica
Telephone: +506 221 7882
Fax: +506 221 5597
E-mail: fedtenis@racsa.co.cr
Website: www.mercury.2kweb.net/
11414/tennis/ftenniscosta
President: Xavier Roca
Secretary: Jürgen G Nanne-Koberg

CROATIA
CRO
Croatian Tennis Association
Gundulieeva 3
10 000 Zagreb
Croatia
Telephone: +385 1 4830 756
Fax: +385 1 4830 720
E-mail: cro-tennis@zg.tel.hr
Website: www.tenis.ccb.hr
President: Slaven Ledica
Secretary: Ms Suzana Knezevic

CUBA
CUB
Federacion Cubana de Tenis
de Campo
Calle 13NR 601 esq AC
Vedado Habana 4
Cuba
Telephone: +53 7 951694
Fax: +53 7 972121
E-mail: fctennis@inder.co.cu
President: Rolando Martinez Perez
Secretary: Juan Baez

CYPRUS
CYP
Cyprus Tennis Federation
Ionos Str 30
PO Box 3931
Nicosia 1687
Cyprus
Telephone: +357 2 666822
Fax: +357 2 668016
E-mail: cytennis@spidernet.com.cy
President: Philios Christodoulou
Secretary: Stavros Ioannou

CZECH REPUBLIC
CZE
Czech Tenisova Asociace
Ostrov Stvanice 38
17000 Praha 7
Czech Republic
Telephone: +42 0224 810272
Fax: +42 0224 810301
E-mail: cts@cta.cz
Website: www.cztenis.cz
President: Ivo Kaderka
Secretary: Marek Moravec

DENMARK
DEN
Dansk Tennis Forbund
Idraettens Hus
Broendby Stadion 20
2605 Broendby
Denmark
Telephone: +45 43 262660
Fax: +45 43 262670
E-mail: dtf@dtftennis.dk
Website: www.dtftennis.dk
President: Peter Schak Larsen
Secretary: Niels Persson

DJIBOUTI
DJI
Fédéderation Djiboutienne
de Tennis
BP 728
Djibouti
Telephone: +253 352536
Fax: +253 352536
E-mail: oned@intneet.dj
President: Houmed Houssein
Secretary: Bourham Daoud

DOMINICAN REPUBLIC
DOM
Federacion Dominicana de Tenis
Club Deportivo Naco
Calle Central
Ens Naco
Santo Domingo
Dominican Republic
Telephone: +1 809 549 5031
Fax: +1 809 549 5131
E-mail: fedotenis@hotmail.com
President: Mario Emilio Guerrero
Secretary: J Ravelo

ECUADOR
ECU
Federacion Ecuatoriana de Tenis
Lomas de Urdesa
Tres Cerritos
Guayaquil
Ecuador
Telephone: +593 4 610467
Fax: +593 4 610466
E-mail: fetenis@gye.satnet.net
President:
Jaime Guzman Maspons
Secretary:
Ms Nuria Guzman de Ferretti

EGYPT
EGY
Egyptian Tennis Federation
13 Kasr el Nile Street
Cairo
Egypt
Telephone: +20 2 574 7697
Fax: +20 2 575 3235
E-mail: etf@urgentmail.com
President: Mohamed Halawa
Secretary: Motaz Sonbol

EL SALVADOR
ESA
Federacion Salvadorena de Tenis
Apartado Postal (01) 110
San Salvador
El Salvador
Telephone: +503 278 3278
Fax: +503 221 0564
President: Enrique Molins Rubio
Secretary: Miguel Irigoyen

ESTONIA
EST
Estonian Tennis Association
1-5P Regati Ave
11911 Tallinn
Estonia
Telephone: +372 6 398637
Fax: +372 6 398635
E-mail: Estonian.tennis@tennis.ee
President: Endel Siff
Secretary: Ms Ene Vahter

ETHIOPIA
ETH
Ethiopian Tennis Federation
PO Box 3241
Addis Ababa
Ethiopia
Telephone: +251 1 152028
Fax: +251 1513345
President: Negussie Mamo
Secretary: Seifu W/yohannes

FIJI
FIJ
Fiji Tennis Association
c/o Mr Paras Daidu
PO Box 3664
Lautoka
Fiji
Telephone: +679 315988
Fax: +679 667082
E-mail: parasfta@is.com.fj
President: Cliff Benson
Secretary: Paras Naidu

FINLAND
FIN
Suomen Tennisliitto
Varikkotie 4
00900 Helsinki
Finland
Telephone: +358 9 3417 1533
Fax: +358 9 323 1105
E-mail:
*   mika.bono@tennisliitto.inet.fi*
Website: www.infopiste.fi/tennis
President: Mauri Elovainio
Secretary: Mika Bono

FRANCE
FRA
Fédération Française de Tennis
Stade Roland Garros
2 avenue Gordon Bennett
75016 Paris
France
Telephone: +33 1 4743 4800
Fax: +33 1 4743 0494
E-mail: fft@fft.fr
Website: www.fft.fr
President: Christian Bîmes
Secretary: J Dupré

GABON
GAB
Fédération Gabonaise de Tennis
PO Box 4241
Libreville
Gabon
Telephone: +241 247344
Fax: +241 703190
E-mail: fedgabten@hotmail.com
Website:
*   www.rdd.rddgabon.gouv.ga.*
*   fegaten*
President: Samuel Minko Mindong
Secretary: Marcel Desire Mebale

GEORGIA
GEO
Georgian Tennis Federation
K Marjanishvili St 29
Tbilisi
Georgia
Telephone: +995 32 952781
Fax: +995 32 953829
E-mail: gtf@global-erty.net
President: Ms Leila Meskhi
Secretary: Zurab Katsarava

GERMANY
GER
Deutscher Tennis Bund e.V.
Hallerstr 89
20149 Hamburg
Germany
Telephone: +49 40 4117 8260
Fax: +49 40 4117 8233
E-mail: dtb@dtb-tennis.de
Website: www.dtb-tennis.de
President: Georg von Waldenfels
Secretary: Reimund Schneider

GHANA
GHA
Ghana Tennis Association
PO Box T-95
Sports Stadium Post Office
Accra
Ghana
Telephone: +233 21 667267
Fax: +233 21 662281
E-mail:
*   gtennis@africaonline.com.gh*
President: Eddie Annan
Secretary: Charles James Aryeh

GREAT BRITAIN
GBR
The Lawn Tennis Association
The Queen's Club
Palliser Road
London W14 9EG
Great Britain
Telephone: +44 20 7381 7000
Fax: +44 20 7381 5965
E-mail: info@lta.org.uk
Website: www.lta.org.uk
President: Malcolm Gracie
Secretary: John James

GREECE
GRE
Hellenic Tennis Federation
267 Imitou Street
11631 Pagrati
Athens
Greece
Telephone: +30 1 756 3170
Fax: +30 1 756 3173
E-mail: efoa@otenet.gr
President: Spyros Zannias
Secretary: Ntinos Nikolaidis

GUATEMALA
GUA
Federacion Nacionale de
    Tenis de Guatemala
Section 1551
PO Box 02-5339
Miami Fl 33102-5339
USA
Telephone: +502 361 8206
Fax: +502 331 0261
E-mail: fedtenis@terra.com.gt
President: Ms Anarrosa de Padilla
Secretary: Francis Bruderer

HAITI
HAI
Fédération Haitienne de Tennis
PO Box 1442
Port au Prince
Haiti
Telephone: +509 2501 317
Fax: +509 2491 233
E-mail: patrick@abhardware.com
President: Frantz Liautaud
Secretary: Hulzer Adolphe

HONDURAS
HON
Federacion Hondurena de Tenis
PO Box 30152
Toncontin
Comayaguela MDC
Honduras
Telephone: +504 2 396890
Fax: +504 2 396887
President: Humerto Rodriguez
Secretary: Rodulio Perdomo

HUNGARY
HUN
Magyar Tenisz Szovetseg
Dozsa Gyorgy Ut 1-3
1143 Budapest
Hungary
Telephone: +36 1 252 6687
Fax: +36 1 251 0107
E-mail: tennis@mail.matav.hu
Website: www.tennis.hu
President: Janos Berenyi
Secretary: Steve Szedlar

ICELAND
ISL
Icelandic Tennis Association
Ithrotamidstoedinni
I Laugardal
104 Reykjavik
Iceland
Telephone: +354 5 813377
Fax: +354 5 888848
E-mail: jongg@islandia.is
President:
*   Skjoldur Vatnar Bjornsson*
Secretary: Jón Gunnar Grjetarsson

INDIA
IND
All India Tennis Association
R K Khanna Tennis Stadium
Africa Avenue
110029 New Delhi
India
Telephone: +91 11 617 9062
Fax: +91 11 617 3159
E-mail: aita@vsnl.com
President: Yashwant Sinha
Secretary: Anil Khanna

INDONESIA
INA
Indonesian Tennis Association
Gelora Senayan Tennis Stadium
Jakarta 10270
Indonesia
Telephone: +62 21 571 0298
Fax: +62 21 570 0157
E-mail: pelti@vision.net.id
President:Tanri Abeng
Secretary: Soegeng Sarjadi

IRAN
IRI
Tennis Federation of Islamic
Republic of Iran
PO Box 15815-1881
Tehran
Iran
Telephone: +98 21 884 4731
Fax: +98 21 884 4731
President: Abbas Khazei
Secretary: Hamid R Shayesteh Zad

IRAQ
IRQ
Iraqi Tennis Federation
PO Box 440
Baghdad
Iraq
Telephone: +964 1 774 8261
Fax: +964 1 772 8424
E-mail: inoc@mail.uruklink.net
President: Harith Ahmed al-Ayash
Secretary: Laith al-Ani

IRELAND
IRL
Tennis Ireland
Dublin City University
Glasnevin
Dublin 9
Ireland
Telephone: +353 16 681841
Fax: +353 16 683411
E-mail: tennis@iol.ie
Website: www.tennisireland.ie
President: Walter Hall
Secretary: Ciaran O'Donovan

ISRAEL
ISR
Israel Tennis Association
2 Shitrit Street
Hader Yosef
69482 Tel Aviv
Israel
Telephone: +972 36 499440
Fax: +972 36 499144
E-mail: igutenis@netvision.net.il
President: David Harnik
Secretary: Yoram Baron

ITALY
ITA
Federazione Italiana Tennis
Viale Tiziano 74
00196 Rome
Italy
Telephone: +39 06 3685 8406
Fax: +39 06 3685 8166
E-mail: fit_segr@gisa.net
Website: www.federtennis.it
President: Angelo Binaghi
Secretary: Mario Orienti

IVORY COAST
CIV
Fédération Ivoirienne de Tennis
01 BPV 273
Abidjan 01
Côte d'Ivoire
Telephone: +225 22 441354
Fax: +225 22 441354
President: Jean-Claude Delafosse
Secretary: Ouattara Souleymane

JAMAICA
JAM
Tennis Jamaica
68 Lady Musgrave Road
Kingston 10
Jamaica
Telephone: +1 876 927 9466
Fax: +1 876 927 9436
E-mail: tennisjam@cwjamaica.com
President: Ken Morgan
Secretary: Ms Joycelin Morgan

JORDAN
JOR
Jordan Tennis Federation
PO Box 961046
Amman
Jordan
Telephone: +962 65 682796
Fax: +962 65 682796
E-mail: tennisfed@tennisfed.org.jo
President: Saad Hijjawi
Secretary: Ms Tamara Qunash

KAZAKHSTAN
KAZ
Kazakhstan Tennis Federation
Central Sports Club of the Army
480051 Almaty
Kazakhstan
Telephone: +7 3272 641621
Fax: +7 3272 640469
President: Pavel Novikov
Secretary: Valery Kovalev

KENYA
KEN
Kenya Lawn Tennis Association
PO Box 43184
Nairobi Club
Upperhill
Nairobi
Kenya
Telephone: +254 2 725672
Fax: +254 2 725672
E-mail: kenyatennis@habarinet.net
President: John Warambo
Secretary: Baldev Aggarwal

KOREA
KOR
Korea Tennis Association
Room 108 Olympic Gym No 2
88-2 Oryun-Dong
Songpa-Gu
Seoul 138-151
South Korea
Telephone: +82 2 420 4285
Fax: +82 2 420 4284
E-mail: tennis@aports.or.kr
President: Yong-Duck Park
Secretary: Yeong-Moo Huh

KUWAIT
KUW
Kuwait Tennis Federation
PO Box 1462
Hawalli 32015
Kuwait
Telephone: +965 539 7261
Fax: +965 539 0671
E-mail: ruizbry@hotmail.com
President: Sheik Ahmed al-Sabah
Secretary: Abdul-Ridha Ghareeb

LATVIA
LAT
Latvian Tennis Union
Oskara Kalpaka Pr 16
LV 2010 Jurmala
Latvia
Telephone: +371 775 2121
Fax: +371 775 5021
E-mail: teniss@parks.lv
President: Juris Savickis
Secretary: Janis Pliens

LEBANON
LIB
Fédération Libanaise de Tennis
Beirut-Lebanon & Kuwait Building
(1st Floor)
Dora Main Street
Beirut
Lebanon
Telephone: +961 1 879288
Fax: +961 1 879277
E-mail: nvs@leb-online.com
President: Riad Haddad
Secretary: Nohad V Schoucair

LESOTHO
LES
Lesotho Lawn Tennis Association
PO Box 156
Maseru 100
Lesotho
Telephone: +266 321543
Fax: +266 321543
E-mail: tennis@ilesotho.com
President: Makase Nyaphisii
Secretary: Mokhali Lithebe

LIBYA
LBA
Libyan Arab Tennis & Squash
   Federation
PO Box 879-2729
Tripoli
Libya
Telephone: +218 21 333 9150
Fax: +218 21 333 9150
E-mail:
   libyan_tennis_fed@hotmail.com
President: Abdul-Hamid M Shamash
Secretary: Abdulssalam A Bellel

LIECHTENSTEIN
LIE
Liechtensteiner Tennisverband
Heiligkreuz 28
9490 Vaduz
Liechtenstein
Telephone: +423 232 1166
Fax: +423 392 4418
President: Daniel Kieber
Secretary: Ms Vanessa Schurte

LITHUANIA
LTU
Lithuanian Tennis Union
Zemaites G 6
2675 Vilnius
Lithuania
Telephone: +3702 333898
Fax: +3702 333898
E-mail: lts@takas.lt
Website: www.tennis.lt
Secretary: Mindaugas Dagys

LUXEMBOURG
LUX
Fédération Luxembourgeoise
   de Tennis
Boite Postale 134
4002 Esch sur Alzette
Luxembourg
Telephone: +352 574470
Fax: +352 574473
E-mail: fltennis@pt.lu
Website: www.flt.lu
President: Paul Helminger
Secretary: Erny Betzen

MACEDONIA
MKD
Macedonian Tennis Association
Gradski Park bb
92000 Skopje
Macedonia
Telephone: +389 91 118530
Fax: +389 91 131361
E-mail: mta@unet.com.mk
President: Geroge Gurkovic
Secretary: Ms Marija Gavrilovska

MADAGASCAR
MAD
Fédération Malgache de Tennis
BP 8410
101 Antananarivo
Madagascar
Telephone: +261 202 263198
Fax: +261 202 263199
E-mail: jserger@simicro.mg
President: Serge Ramiandrasoa
Secretary:
   Emma Lisiarisoa Rabodomalala

MALAYSIE
MAS
Lawn Tennis Association
   of Malaysia
National Tennis Centre
Jalan Duta
50480 Kuala Lumpur
Malaysia
Telephone: +603 620 16173
Fax: +603 620 16167
E-mail: ltam@first.net.my
President:
   Tan Sri Sallehuddin Mohamed
Secretary: Musaladin Dahalan

MALI
MLI
Fédération Malienne de Tennis
IFA-BACO
425 Avenue de l'Yser
Bamako
Mali
Telephone: +223 232326
Fax: +223 232324
E-mail: ifabaco@cefib.com
President: Mohamed Traore

MALTA
MLT
Malta Tennis Federation
PO Box 50
Sleima Post Office
Malta
Telephone: +356 330757
Fax: +356 331259
E-mail: pjz@maltatennis.org.mt
President: Peter Zammit
Secretary: Ms Tanya Gravina

MAURITIUS
MRI
Mauritius Tennis Federation
La Croix Street
Curepipe
Mauritius
Telephone: +230 670 2603
Fax: +230 670 2539
E-mail: mltate@intnet.mu
President: Jean-Michel Giraud
Secretary: Akhtar Toorawa

MEXICO
MEX
Federacion Mexicana de Tenis
Miguel Angel de Quevedo 953
Mexico City 04330 DF
Mexico
Telephone: +52 5689 9733
Fax: +52 5689 6307
E-mail: federacion@fmttenis.com
Website: www.fmt.com.mx
President: Francisco Maciel
Secretary: Antonio Vargas

MOLDOVA
MDA
Moldova Republic Tennis
  Federation
59 Coca Street
Chisinau 2039
Moldova
Telephone: +3732 727772
Fax: +3732 727781
Website:
  www.angelfire.com/vt/mtennis
President: Sergei Sava
Secretary: Ms Larisa Mitrofanova

MONACO
MON
Fédération Monegasque de
  Lawn Tennis
BP No 253
98005 Monaco Cedex
Telephone: +377 9325 5574
Fax: +377 9330 5482
E-mail: info@monaco-tennis.com
President: Ms Elisabeth de Massy
Secretary: Alain Manigley

MOROCCO
MAR
Fédération Royale Marocaine
  de Tennis
BP 15794
Casablanca Principale
Morocco
Telephone: +212 22 981266
Fax: +212 22 981265
E-mail: frmt@casanet.net.ma
President: Mohamed M'Jid
Secretary: Hachem Kacimi My

NAMIBIA
NAM
Namibia Tennis Association
PO Box 479
Windhoek 9000
Namibia
Telephone: +264 61 244495
Fax: +264 61 251718
E-mail: cariena@iafrica.com.na
President: Pietie Loubser
Secretary: Ms Carien du Plessis

NETHERLANDS
NED
Koninklijke Nederlandse Lawn
  Tennis Bond
PO Box 1617
3800 BP Amersfoort
Netherlands
Telephone: +31 33 454 2600
Fax: +31 33 454 2645
E-mail: knltb@knltb.nl
Website: www.knltb.nl
President: Klaas Rijpma
Secretary: Evert-Jan Hulshof

NETHERLANDS
ANTILLES
AHO
Netherlands Antilles Tennis
  Association
PO Box 3571
Curaçao
Netherlands Antilles
Telephone: +599 9 737 2613
Fax: +599 9 737 2613
E-mail: info@natf.an
President: Randall Rojer
Secretary: Norman Macares

NEW ZEALAND
NZL
New Zealand Tennis Inc
PO Box 11-541
Level 7 Compudigm House
49 Boulcott Street
Wellington
New Zealand
Telephone: +64 4 473 1115
Fax: +64 4 473 5267
E-mail: info@tennis.org.nz
Website: www.tennis.org.nz
President: David Howman
Secretary: Ms Christine Burr

NIGERIA
NGR
Nigeria Tennis Federation
National Stadium
Surulere
PO Box 145
Lagos
Nigeria
Telephone: +234 1 264 6444
Fax: +234 1 545 4471
E-mail: nigtennis@hyperia.com
President: Chuka Momah
Secretary: Ms Funmi Koya-Adako

NORWAY
NOR
Norges Tennisforbund
Haslevangen 33
PO Box 287 – Okern
0511 Oslo
Norway
Telephone: +47 2 265 7550
Fax: +47 2 264 6409
E-mail: tennis@nif.idrett.no
Website: www.nif.idrett.no/tennis
President: Jarl Whist
Secretary: Sissel Sivertsen

OMAN
OMA
Oman Tennis Association
PO Box 2226
Ruwi 112
Oman
Telephone: +968 751402
Fax: +968 751394
E-mail: tennis@gto.net.om
President:
  Rashad Mohammed al Zubair
Secretary:
  Mohamad Salim Khawwar

PAKISTAN
PAK
Pakistan Tennis Federation
39-A Jinnah Stadium
Pakistan Sports Complex
Kashmir Highway
Islamabad
Pakistan
Telephone: +92 519 212846
Fax: +92 519 212846
E-mail:
  pktenfed@isb.comsats.net.pk
President: Anwar Saifullah Khan
Secretary: Mohammad Ali Akbar

PANAMA
PAN
Federacion Panamena de Tenis
Apartado 6-4965
El Dorado
Panama
Telephone: +507 232 5196
Fax: +507 232 6841
E-mail: fedepate@sinfo.net
President: Ms Norma Maduro
Secretary: Juan B Quintero

PARAGUAY
PAR
Asociacion Paraguaya de Tenis
Centro Nacional de Tenis
Consejo Nacional de Deportes
Avda Eusebio Ayala KM 5 1/2
Y R.I.6 Boqueron
Asuncion
Paraguay
Telephone: +595 21 520574
Fax: +595 21 520674
E-mail: apt@pla.net.py
Website: www.apt.com.py
President: Miguel Carrizosa
Secretary: Ms Esther Tami

PERU
PER
Federacion de Tenis de Peru
Cercado Campo de Marte S/N
Casilla NRO 11-0488
Lima 11
Peru
Telephone: +511 424 9979
Fax: +511 431 0533
E-mail: tenisperu@terra.com.pe
President: Alfredo Acuna
Secretary: Julio Chang

PHILIPPINES
PHI
Philippine Tennis Association
Rizal Memorial Sports Complex
Pablo Ocampo Sr. Street
Manila
Philippines
Telephone: +63 2 525 6434
Fax: +63 2 525 2016
E-mail: philta@info.com.ph
President: Salvador H Andrada
Secretary: Romeo Magat

POLAND
POL
Polski Zwiazek Tenisowy
Ul. Marszalkowska 2 (3rd floor)
00-581 Warsaw
Poland
Telephone: +48 22 629 2621
Fax: +48 22 621 8001
E-mail: pzt@pzt.top.pl
President: Lew Rywin
Secretary: Stefan Makarczyk

PORTUGAL
POR
Federaçao Portuguese de Tenis
Rua Actor Chaby
Pinheiro 7-A
2795-060 Linda-a-Velha
Portugal
Telephone: +351 21 415 1356
Fax: +351 21 414 1520
E-mail: fptenis@mail.telepac.pt
Website: www.fptenis.pt
President: Pedro Coelho
Secretary: Jose Costa

PUERTO RICO
PUR
Asociacion de Tenis de
    Puerto Rico
1611 Fernandez Juncos Avenue
Santurce
00909
Puerto Rico
Telephone: +1 787 982 7782
Fax: +1 787 982 7783
E-mail: rodriguez@cta.usta.com
President: Pedro Beauchamp
Secretary: Carlos Rivera

QATAR
QAT
Qatar Tennis & Squash Federation
PO Box 4959
Doha
Qatar
Telephone: +974 4 409666
Fax: +974 4 832990
President: Ali Hussein al Fardan
Secretary: Mohammed Ismail

ROMANIA
ROM
Federatia Romana de Tenis
Str Vasile Conta 16
Sector 2
70139 Bucharest
Romania
Telephone: +40 1 324 5330
Fax: +40 1 324 5329
E-mail: frtenis@mts-gw.pub.ro
President: Ilie Nastase
Secretary: Lucian Vasiliu

RUSSIA
RUS
All Russia Tennis Association
Lutzhnetskaya Nab 8
119871 Moscow
Russia
Telephone: +7 095 956 3360
Fax: +7 095 956 3361
President: Shamil Tarpischev
Secretary: Alexander Kalivod

RWANDA
RWA
Fédération Rwandaise de Tennis
Stade National Amahoro
BP 3321
Kigali
Rwanda
Telephone: +250 74521
Fax: +250 74074
E-mail: ntwalit@hotmail.com
President: Charles Ruadkubana
Secretary:
    Freddy Somayire Rubona

SAINT LUCIA
LCA
St Lucia Lawn Tennis Association
PO Box 189
20 Micoud Street
Castries
Saint Lucia
Telephone: +1 758 452 2662
Fax: +1 758 452 3885
E-mail: mcnmara.co@candw.lc
President: Stephen McNamara
Secretary:
    Ms Pauline Erlinger-Ford

SAN MARINO
SMR
San Marino Tennis Federation
Parco di Montecchio 1
47890 San Marino
Telephone: +378 0549 990578
Fax: +378 0549 990584
E-mail: fst@omniway.sm
Website: www.fst.sm
President: Christian Forcellini
Secretary: Marino Guardigli

SAUDI ARABIA
KSA
Saudia Arabian Tennis Federation
PO Box 29454
Riyadh 11457
Saudi Arabia
Telephone: +966 1 482 0188
Fax: +966 1 482 2829
E-mail: sf@nournet.com.sa
President: Abdulaziz S Kridis
Secretary: Rasheed Abu Rasheed

SENEGAL
SEN
Fédération Sénégalaise de Tennis
BP 510
Dakar
Senegal
Telephone: +221 820 3269
Fax: +221 869 0019
E-mail: fst@arc.sn
President: Amadou Ndiaye
Secretary: Layti Ndiaye

SINGAPORE
SIN
Singapore Lawn Tennis
    Association
Unit 10
National Stadium
Stadium Road
397718 Singapore
Telephone: +65 348 0124
Fax: +65 348 2414
E-mail: slta@pacific.net.sg
President: Edwin Lee
Secretary: Ling Khoon Chow

SLOVAK REPUBLIC
SVK
Slovak Tennis Association
Junacka 6
832 80 Bratislava
Slovakia
Telephone: +421 2 4924 9134
Fax: +421 2 4924 9533
E-mail: stz@stz.sk
Website: www.stz.sk
President: Tibor Macko
Secretary: Igor Moska

SLOVENIA
SLO
Slovene Tennis Association
Vurnikova 2/VI
1000 Ljubljana
Slovenia
Telephone: +386 1 430 6370
Fax: +386 1 430 6695
E-mail: teniska.zveza@sting.si
Website: www.slotenis.negahit.si
President: Drasko Veselinovic
Secretary: Tone Preseren

SOUTH AFRICA
RSA
South African Tennis Association
PO Box 15978
Doornfontein
Johannesburg 2028
South Africa
Telephone: +27 11 402 3608
Fax: +27 11 402 0242
E-mail: satennis@mweb.co.za
Website: www.supertennis.co.za
President: Gordon Forbes
Secretary: Mohamed Sheik

SPAIN
ESP
Real Federacion Espanola de Tenis
Avenida Diagonal 618 3 D
08021 Barcelona
Spain
Telephone: +34 93 200 5355
Fax: +34 93 202 1279
E-mail: rfet@fedetenis.es
Website: www.fedetenis.es
President: Agustin Pujob Niubo
Secretary:
    Thomas Garcia Balmaseda

SRI LANKA
SRI
Sri Lanka Tennis Association
45 Sir Marcus Fernando Mawatha
Colombo 7
Sri Lanka
Telephone: +94 1 686174
Fax: +94 1 686174
E-mail: slta@eureka.lk
President: Lalith Withana
Secretary: Maxwell de Silva

SUDAN
SUD
Sudan Lawn Tennis Association
PO Box 3792
Africa House
Khartoum
Sudan
Telephone: +249 11 770246
Fax: +249 11 770246
President: Khalid Talaat Farid
Secretary:
    Ahmed Abuelgasim Hasim

SWEDEN
SWE
Swedish Tennis Association
Box 1064
269 21 Båstad
Sweden
Telephone: +46 43 178390
Fax: +46 43 175684
E-mail: info@tennis.se
Website: www.tennis.se
President: Jan Carlzon
Secretary: Anders Wetterberg

SWITZERLAND
SUI
Swiss Tennis
Solothurnstrasse 112
2501 Biel
Switzerland
Telephone: +41 32 344 0707
Fax: +41 32 344 0700
daniel.monnin@swisstennis.com
Website: www.swisstennis.com
President: Ms Christine Ungricht
Secretary: Pierre-Alain Morard

SYRIA
SYR
Syrian Arab Tennis Federation
PO Box 967 421
Baramke
Damascus
Syria
Telephone: +963 11 212 5026
Fax: +963 11 212 3346
President: Samer Mourad
Secretary: Safa Sarakbi

TAJIKISTAN
TJK
National Tennis Federation
    of the Republic of Tajikistan
Tennis Palace
A/B 308
Dushanbe 734001
Tajikistan
Telephone: +992 377 2361 206
Fax: +992 377 2361 206
E-mail: aj.atoev@tajik.net
President: Amircul Azimov
Secretary: Vazirbek Nazirov

THAILAND
THA
Lawn Tennis Association
    of Thailand
Muang Thong Thani Tennis
Complex
Pak-Kred
Chaengwatana Road
Nonthaburi 11120
Thailand
Telephone: +662 504 0383
Fax: +662 504 0381
E-mail: ltat@ksc.th.com
President: Akaradej Sasiprapha
Secretary: Wichar Siritham

TOGO
TOG
Fédération Togolaise de Tennis
BP 12720
Lome
Togo
Telephone: +228 215181
Fax: +228 222397
E-mail: fttennis@togo-imet.com
President: Kouassi Luc Dofontien
Secretary: Koffi Galokpo

TRINIDAD & TOBAGO
TBI
Tennis Association of Trinidad
    & Tobago
21 Taylor Street
Woodbrook
Port of Spain
Trinidad
Telephone: +1 868 628 0783
Fax: +1 868 628 0783
E-mail: tatt@tstt.net.tt
President: Oswald Downes
Secretary: Ms Christine Alexis

TUNISIA
TUN
Fédération Tunisienne de Tennis
BP 350
El Menzah
1004 Tunis
Tunisia
Telephone: +216 1 844144
Fax: +216 1 798844
President: Tarak Cherif
Secretary: Zohra Bouhafa

TURKEY
TUR
Turkiye Tenis Federasyonu
Ulus is Hani
Ankara
Turkey
Telephone: +90 312 310 7345
Fax: +90 312 310 7345
E-mail: tenis@ttf.org.tr
Website: www.ttf.org.tr
President: Sadi Toker
Secretary: Yener Dogru

UGANDA
UGA
Uganda Tennis Association
PO Box 9825
Kampala
Uganda
Telephone: +256 41 236688
Fax: +256 41 236333
E-mail: ncl@infocom.co.ug
President: Peter Ntaki
Secretary: Gideon M Karyoko

UKRAINE
UKR
Ukrainian Tennis Federation
A/C B-2
PO 252001
Kiev
Ukraine
Telephone: +38 044 224 8782
Fax: +38 044 290 4062
President: German Benyaminov
Secretary: Igor Hohlov

UNITED
ARAB EMIRATES
UAE
United Arab Emirates Tennis
    Association
PO Box 22466
Dubai
UAE
Telephone: +971 4 269 0393
Fax: +971 4 266 9290
President:
    Sheika Hasher al-Maktoum
Secretary: Mohammed al-Merry

UNITED STATES
OF AMERICA
USA
United States Tennis Association
70 West Red Oak Lane
White Plains
New York 10604-3602
USA
Telephone: +1 914 696 7000
Fax: +1 914 696 7167
Website: www.usta.com
President: Mervin A Heller
Secretary: Rick Ferman

UNITED STATES
VIRGIN ISLANDS
ISV
Virgin Islands Tennis Association
4236 La Grande Princesse
St Croix 00820-4449
US Virgin Islands
Telephone: +1 340 773 1448
Fax: +1 340 773 3651
E-mail: manor@viaccess.net
President: Prospero Lewis
Secretary: Ms Judith Gadd

URUGUAY
URU
Asociacion Uruguaya de Tenis
Galicia 1392
CP 11.200
Montevideo
Uruguay
Telephone: +598 2 901 5020
Fax: +598 2 902 1809
E-mail: aut@montevideo.com.uy
President: Gilberto Saenz
Secretary: Elbio Arias

UZBEKISTAN
UZB
Uzbekistan Tennis Federation
1 Ulyanovskiy Pereulok
House 14
Tashkent 700035
Uzbekistan
Telephone: +99 871 137 2554
Fax: +99 871 230 2272
E-mail: shepelev@uzbektennis.uz
Website: www.uzbektennis.uz
President: R Inoyatov
Secretary: I Shepelev

VENEZUELA
VEN
Federacion Venezolana de Tenis
Complejo Nacional de Tenis
Calle A Apartado 70539
Urb Santa Rosa de Lima
Caracas 1070-A
Venezuela
Telephone: +582 979 2421
Fax: +582 979 2694
E-mail: cmenores@cantv.net
President: Rene Herrera
Secretary: Deva de Gonzalez

YUGOSLAVIA
YUG
Tenis Savez Yugoslavije
Aleksandra Stamboliskog 26
11000 Beograd
Yugoslavia
Telephone: +381 11 667540
Fax: +381 11 661635
E-mail: yugtenis@verat.net
President: Predrag Mitrovic
Secretary: Petar Marinkovic

ZAMBIA
ZAM
Zambia Lawn Tennis Association
PO Box 40408
Mufulira
Zambia
Telephone: +260 2 441832
Fax: +260 2 447005
E-mail: zimbam@mcm.com.zm
President: John Mupeta
Secretary: Masauso Zimba

ZIMBABWE
ZIM
Tennis Zimbabwe
PO Box A575
Avondale
Harare
Zimbabwe
Telephone: +263 4 740509
Fax: +263 4 740351
E-mail:
    teniszim@africaonline.co.zw
President: Paul Chingoka
Secretary: Ms Patricia Mavunduke

NATIONAL
Associate
ITF members
(Class C)
without voting rights

AFGHANISTAN
AFG
Afghanistan Tennis Federation
c/o Afghanistan NOC
PO Box 1824 or 1775
Kabul
Afghanistan
Telephone: +932 290009
Fax: +932 290009
President:
Sher Mohammad Abass Stanikzai
Secretary: Abdul Azim Niazi

ALBANIA
ALB
Federata Shqiptare e Tenisit
Rruga Siri Kodra
Shtypshkronja Psh 2015
Blloku I Magazinave
Tirana
Albania
Telephone: +355 423 0895
Fax: +355 424 5564
E-mail: atf@abissnet.com.al
President: Perlat Voshtina
Secretary: Arben Alushi

AMERICAN SAMOA
ASA
American Samoa Tennis
Association
PO Box 3501
Pago Pago
AS 96799
American Samoa
Telephone: +684 699 2100
Fax: +684 699 2105
E-mail: perelini@ntamar.com
President: Ms Jennifer Joneson
Secretary: Jerome Amoa

ARUBA
ARU
Aruba Lawn Tennis Bond
Fergusonstraat 40-A
PO Box 1151
Oranjestad
Aruba
Telephone: +297 821271
Fax: +297 821271
E-mail: valastar@setarnet.aw
President: Frank Velazquez
Secretary: Peter Mohamed

BELIZE
BIZ
Belize Tennis Association
PO Box 365
Belize City
Belize
Telephone: +501 277070
Fax: +501 275593
President: Edward Nabil Musa
Secretary: Clement Usher

BHUTAN
BHU
Bhutan Tennis Federation
PO Box 939
Thimphu
Bhutan
Telephone: +975 232 2138
Fax: +975 232 3937
E-mail: bhusport@druknet.net.bt
President: Dasho Passang Dorji
Secretary: Tshering Namgay

BRITISH
VIRGIN ISLANDS
IVB
British Virgin Islands Lawn
Tennis Association
PO Box 158
Road Town
Tortola
British Virgin Islands
Telephone: +1 284 494 3340
E-mail: cbecarvin@aol.com
President: Carvin Malone
Secretary: Clive Gumbs

BURMA see Myanmar

BURUNDI
BDI
Fédération de Tennis du Burundi
BP 2221
Bujumbura
Burundi
Telephone: +257 242443
Fax: +257 222247
E-mail: ftb@cbinf.com
President: Edouard Hicintuka
Secretary: Salvator Matata

CAPE VERDE ISLANDS
CPV
Federaçao Cabo-Verdiana de Tenis
Ministerio da Informaçao
Cultura e Desportos
Rua 5 de Julho
Praia
Cape Verde Islands
Telephone: +238 613309
Fax: +238 621312
E-mail: fedcabtenis@cvtelecom.cv
President: Hugo Albeida
Secretary: Antonia Ferreira

CAYMAN ISLANDS
CAY
Tennis Federation of the
Cayman Islands
PO Box 219 GT
Grand Cayman
Cayman Islands
Telephone: +1 345 946 3425
Fax: +1 345 945 4237
President: Chris Johnson
Secretary: John Smith

CENTRAL
AFRICAN REPUBLIC
CAF
Fédération Centrafricaine
de Tennis
BP 804
Bangui
Central African Republic
Telephone: +236 611805
Fax: +236 615660
President: I Kamach
Secretary: Jean Ombi

CONGO
COD
Fédération Congolaise
Democratique de Lawn Tennis
BP 11 497 Kin 1
Kinshasa
Democratic Republic of Congo
Telephone: +243 884 3469
E-mail: gam7@raga.net
President: Ndombe Jacob
Secretary: Geroges Koshi

COOK ISLANDS
COK
Tennis Cook Islands
PO Box 303
Avarua
Rarotonga
Cook Islands
Telephone: +682 24249
Fax: +682 24248
E-mail: t&m@gatepoly.co.ck
President: Chris McKinley
Secretary: Brendan Stone

DOMINICA
DMA
Dominica Lawn Tennis Association
PO Box 138
Roseau
Dominica
Telephone: +1 767 448 2681
Fax: +1 767 448 7010
E-mail: tomd@cwdom.dm
President: Kenny Alleyne
Secretary: Thomas Dorsett

EQUATORIAL GUINEA
GEQ
Equatorial Guinea Tennis
Federation
PO Box 980 BN
Malabo
Equatorial Guinea
Telephone: +240 9 2866
Fax: +240 9 3313
President: Enrique Mercader Costa
Secretary: Francisco Sibita

ERITREA
ERI
Eritrean Tennis Federation
c/o Eritrean Olympic Committee
PO Box 3665
Asmara
Eritrea
Telephone: +291 1 120762
Fax: +291 1 120967
E-mail: tesat@tse.com.er
President: Tewoldeberhan Mehari
Secretary: Fesseha Haile

GAMBIA
GAM
Gambia Lawn Tennis Association
PMB 664
Serekunda
Gambia
Telephone: +220 495834
Fax: +220 496270
E-mail: gnosc@commit.gm
President: Charles Thomas
Secretary: Geoffrey Renner

GRENADA
GRN
Grenada Tennis Association
PO Box 514
St George's
Grenada
Telephone: +1 473 440 1977
Fax: +1 473 440 1977
E-mail: interact@caribsurf.net.com
President: Ken Aberdeen
Secretary: Ms Salesh Patrick

GUAM
GUM
Guam National Tennis Federation
PO Box 4379
Agana 96932
Guam
Telephone: +1 671 472 6270
Fax: +1 671 472 0997
E-mail: yasnit@hotmail.com
Website: www.tennis.guam.org
President: Rick Ninete
Secretary: Ms Analiza Tubal

GUINÉE CONAKRY
GUI
Fédération Guinéenne de Tennis
BP 4897
Guinée Conakry
Telephone: +224 444019
Fax: +224 411926
President:
    Ms Magass-Malado Diallo
Secretary: Baba Bayo

GUAYANA
GUY
Guyana Lawn Tennis Association
PO Box 10205
Georgetown
Guayana
Telephone: +592 225403
Fax: +592 267559
President: William Skeete
Secretary: Ms Georgia Inniss

KIRIBATI
KIR
Kiribati Tennis Association
PO Box 66
Bairiki
Tarawa
Kiribati
Telephone: +686 26541
Fax: +686 26606
President: Tangitang Kaureta
Secretary: Eritibete Tomizuka

KYRGYZSTAN
KGZ
Kyrgyzstan Tennis Federation
Moskovskey Str 121/58
Bishkek 720000
Kyrgyzstan
Telephone: +996 312 214756
Fax: +996 312 214756
E-mail: tfkr@elcat.kg
President: Nikolai Tanaev
Secretary: Valentin Akinshin

LAOS
LAO
Lao Tennis Federation
PO Box 6280
Vientiane
Democratic People's Republic
    of Laos
Telephone: +856 212956
Fax: +856 212 5274
President: Kikham Vongsay
Secretary: Khounno Phonesomdeth

LIBERIA
LBR
Liberia Tennis Association
PO Box 10-1742
Buchannan Street
Monrovia
Liberia
Telephone: +231 225626
Fax: +231 226219
President: Siake Toure
Secretary: Edmund Dassin

MALAWI
MAW
Lawn Tennis Association of Malawi
PO Box 1417
Blantyre
Malawi
Telephone: +265 673460
Fax: +265 672417
E-mail: fjumbe@admarc.malawi.net
President: Friday Jumbe
Secretary: Ms Barbara Halse

MALDIVES
MDV
Tennis Association of the Maldives
PO Box 20175
Male
Maldives
Telephone: +960 317018
Fax: +960 310325
E-mail: info@tennismaldives.com.mv
Secretary: Abdul Aleem

MARSHALL ISLANDS
MSH
Marshall Island Tennis Federation
PO Box 197
Marjuro MH96960
Marshall Islands
Telephone: +692 625 5275
Fax: +692 625 5277
E-mail: troyb@ntamar.com
President: Oscar Debrum
Secretary: Ms Netty Nathan

MAURITANIA
MTN
Fédération Mauritanienne
    de Tennis
BP 40 161
Nouakchott
Mauritania
Telephone: +222 525 8587
Fax: +222 525 2455
President: Isaac Ould Rajel
Secretary: Cheickh Ould Horomtala

MICRONESIA
FSM
FSM Lawn Tennis Association
PO Box PS319
Paliker
Pohnpei
FM 96941
Federated States of Micronesia
Telephone: +691 320619
Fax: +691 320 8915
E-mail: fsmnoc@mail.fm
President: Richard Alex
Secretary: James Tobin

MONGOLIA
MGL
Mongolian Tennis Association
PO Box 522
Ulaanbaatar 44
Mongolia
Telephone: +976 11 350071
Fax: +976 11 343611
E-mail: mta@magicnet.mn
President: Ch. Ganzorig
Secretary: Janchiv Batjargal

MOZAMBIQUE
MOZ
Federaçao Moçambicana de Tenis
Caixa Postal 4531
Maputo
Mozambique
Telephone: +258 1 427027
Fax: +258 1 303665
E-mail: fmtenis@hotmail.com
President: Arao Nhancale
Secretary: Armindo Nhavene

MYANMAR
MYA
Myanmar Tennis Federation
Theinbyu Tennis Plaza
Mingalar Taung Nyunt Township
Yangon
Myanmar
Telephone: +951 72731
Fax: +951 571061
President: U Chit Swe
Secretary: Myint Soe

NAURU
NRU
Nauru Tennis Association
PO Box 274
Aiwo District
Nauru
Telephone: +674 444 3118
Fax: +674 444 3231
E-mail: naurutennis_@yahoo.com
President: Chief Paul Aingimea
Secretary: Preston Itaia

NEPAL
NEP
All Nepal Tennis Association
PO Box 3943
Kathmandu
Nepal
Telephone: +977 1 426002
Fax: +977 1 416427
E-mail: anlta@mos.com.np
President: Siddheshwar K Singh
Secretary: Ramji Thapa

NICARAGUA
NCA
Federacion Nicaraguense de Tenis
PO Box 2878
Sucursal Jorge Navarro
Managua
Nicaragua
Telephone: +505 265 1572
Fax: +505 278 7039
E-mail: deloitte@cablenet.com.ni
President: Jose Antonia Arguello

NIGER
NIG
Fédération Nigérienne de Tennis
Stade du 29 Juillet 1991
Avenue du Zarmaganda
BP 10 788 Niamey
Niger
Telephone: +227 735893
Fax: +227 732876
E-mail: nigertennis@hotmail.com
President: Ahmed Ousman Diallo
Secretary: Boubacar Djibo

NORFOLK ISLANDS
NFK
Norfolk Islands Tennis Association
Queen Elizabeth Avenue
South Pacific
Norfolk Islands
Telephone: +67 23 22966
Fax: +67 23 23226
E-mail: emaisey@ni.net.nf
President: Thomas Greening
Secretary: Ms Emma Maisey

NORTHERN
MARIANA ISLANDS
NMI
Northern Mariana Islands
Tennis Association
PO Box 10,000
Saipan
MP 96950-9504
Northern Mariana Islands
Telephone: +1 670 234 8438
Fax: +1 670 234 5545
E-mail: race@saipan.com
President: Jeff Race
Secretary: Ed Johnson

PALAU
PAL
Palau Amateur Tennis Association
PO Box 44
Koror 96940
Democratic Republic of Palau
Telephone: +680 488 2690
Fax: +680 488 1310
E-mail: ekrengiil@palaunet.com
President: Ms Christina Michelsen
Secretary: Ms Annabel Lyman

PALESTINE
PLE
Palestine Tennis Association
Beit Sahour
POB 131
Palestine
Telephone: +972 2 277 2833
Fax: +972 2 277 4677
E-mail: pta@p-ol.com
Website: www.paltennis.org
President: Issa Rishmawi
Secretary: Ms Samar Mousa Araj

PAPUA NEW GUINEA
PNG
Papua New Guinea Lawn
   Tennis Association
PO Box 160
Port Moresby
Papua New Guinea
Telephone: +675 321 1533
Fax: +675 321 3086
E-mail: raisi@online.net.pg
President: Robert Aisi

SAINT KITTS & NEVIS
SKN
St Kitts Lawn Tennis Association
Cayon Street
Basseterre
St Kitts & Nevis
Telephone: +1 869 465 6809
Fax: +1 869 465 1190
President: Raphael Jenkins
Secretary: Ms Connie Marsham

SAINT VINCENT &
THE GRENADINES
VIN
St Vincent & The Grenadines
Lawn Tennis Association
PO Box 1487
Kingstown
St Vincent & The Grenadines
Telephone: +1 784 457 1018
Fax: +1 784 457 2901
E-mail: svgtennis@vincysurf.com
President: Michael Nanton
Secretary: Peter Nanton

SAMOA
SAM
Tennis Samoa Inc
PO Box 6402
Apia
Samoa
Telephone: +685 22115
Fax: +685 21145
President:
   Waikaremoana Soonalole
Secretary: Ms Fiaapia Devoe

SEYCHELLES
SEY
Seychelles Tennis Association
PO Box 580
Mahe
Victoria
Seychelles
Telephone: +248 323908
Fax: +248 324066
E-mail: tennisey@seychelles.net
President: John Adam
Secretary: André Derjacques

SIERRA LEONE
SLE
Sierra Leone Lawn Tennis
Association
National Sports Council
PO Box 1181
Freetown
Sierra Leone
Telephone: +232 22 226874
Fax: +232 22 229083
President: John Benjamin
Secretary: E T Ngandi

SOLOMON ISLANDS
SOL
Solomon Islands Tennis
Association
PO Box 111
Honiara
Solomon Islands
Telephone: +677 21616
Fax: +677 25498
President: Ranjit Hewagama
Secretary: Selwyn Miduku

SOMALIA
SOM
Somali Tennis Association
c/o Gabalaya Street
11567 El Borg
Cairo
Eqypt
Telephone: +252 1 280042
Fax: +252 1 216516
President:
   Osman Mohiadin Moallim
Secretary:
   Abdurahman Warsame Abdulle

SURINAM
SUR
Surinaamse Tennisbond
c/o Ann Meyer
Verlengde
Gemenelandsweg 167
Paramibo
Surinam
Telephone: +597 491741
Fax: +597 471047
E-mail: surtennis@cq-link.sr
President: Manodj Hindori
Secretary: Ms Ann Meyer

SWAZILAND
SWZ
Swaziland National Tennis Union
PO Box 2397
Manzini
Swaziland
Telephone: +268 54564
Fax: +268 31472
E-mail: djele@hotmail.com
President: L Nxumalo
Secretary: J Mazibuko

TANZANIA
TAN
Tanzania Lawn Tennis Association
PO Box 965
Dar es Salaam
Tanzania
Telephone: +255 742 782561
Fax: +255 222 116656
E-mail: rugimbana@ud.co.tz
President: Richard Rugimbaba
Secretary: Godfrey Zimba

TONGA
TGA
Tonga Tennis Association
PO Box 816
Nuku'Alofa
Tonga
Telephone: +676 23933
Fax: +676 24127
President: Fuka Kitekeiaho
Secretary: Ms Kiu Tatafu

TURKMENISTAN
TKM
Turkmenistan Tennis Association
30 MKRN PR 2
Bulvarny
744020 Ashgabat
Turkmenistan
Telephone: +993 12 390856
Fax: +993 12 393187
President: Berdimurad Redjepov
Secretary: Bjashimov Serdar

VANUATU
VAN
Fédération de Tennis de Vanuatu
BP 563
Port Vila
Vanuatu
Telephone: +678 24817
Fax: +678 26133
E-mail: jacobe@vanuatu.com.vu
President: Ms Evelyne Jacobe
Secretary: Michel Mainguy

VIETNAM
VIE
Vietnam Tennis Federation
175 Nguyen Thai Hoe Street
Ba Dinh District
Hanoi
Vietnam
Telephone: +844 733 0036
Fax: +844 733 0036
E-mail: vtf@fpt.vn
President: Dang Huu Hai
Secretary: Nguyen Van Manh

YEMEN
YEM
Yemen Tennis Federation
PO Box 19816
Sanaa
Yemen
Telephone: +967 1 268456
Fax: +967 1 268456
President: Abdul Wali Nasher
Secretary:
   Osama Ahmed al Haithami

SELECTED TENNIS BODIES

CLIFF RICHARD TENNIS FOUNDATION
PO Box 46C
Claygate
Surrey KT10 0RB
England
Telephone: +44 1372 470648
Fax: +44 1372 470645
Website: www.cliffrichardtennis.org

INTERCOLLEGIATE TENNIS ASSOCIATION
PO Box 71
Princeton University
Princeton
New Jersey 08544
USA
Telephone: +1 609 258 1686
Fax: +1 609 258 2935
E-mail: ita@tennisonline.com

INTERNATIONAL HEALTH, RACQUET & SPORTSCLUB ASSOCIATION
263 Summer St
Boston
Massachussetts 02210
USA
Telephone: +1 617 951 0055
Fax: +1 617 951 0056
E-mail: info@ihrsa.org

INTERNATIONAL OLYMPIC ASSOCIATION
Chateau de Videy
1007 Lausanne
Switzerland
Website: www.olympic.org

MAUREEN CONNOLLY BRINKER FOUNDATION
PO Box 7065
Dallas
Texas 75209
USA
Telephone: +1 214 352 7978
Fax: +1 214 352 9708

NATIONAL ASSOCIATION OF INTERCOLLEGIATE ATHLETICS NAIA
Suite 1450
6120 South Yale Ave
Tulsa
Oklahoma 74136
USA
Telephone: +1 918 494 8828

NATIONAL FOUNDATION OF WHEELCHAIR TENNIS
Suite B
940 Calle Amanecer
San Clementa
California 92672
USA
Telephone: +1 714 361 3663
Fax: +1 714 361 6822
E-mail: nfwt@aol.com

NATIONAL COLLEGIATE ATHLETIC ASSOCIATION NCAA
6201 College Blvd
Overland Park
Kansas 66221
USA
Telephone: +1 913 339 1906
Fax: +1 913 339 1950

SPECIAL OLYMPICS INTERNATIONAL
1325 G Street NW
Suite 500
Washington
DC 20005-4709
USA
Telephone: +1 202 628 3630
Fax: +1 202 824 0200

TENNIS AGAINST BREAST CANCER
Suite 8
328 East 59th St
New York
NY 10022
USA
Telephone: +1 212 752 1789
Fax: +1 212 752 1780

US PROFESSIONAL TENNIS ASSOCIATIOM
1 USPTAA Centre
3535 Briarpark Drive
Houston
Texas 77042
USA
Telephone: +1 713 978 7782
Fax: +1 713 978 7780
E-mail: uspta@uspta.org

US RACQUET STRINGERS ASSOCIATION
PO Box 40
Del Mar
California 92014-9959
USA
Telephone: +1 619 481 3543
Fax: +1 619 481 0624
E-mail: usrsa@aol.com

WOMEN'S SPORTS FOUNDATION
Eisenhower Park
East Meadow
NY 11554
USA
Telephone: +1 516 542 4700
E-mail: wosport@aol.com

WORLDWIDE SENIOR TENNIS CIRCUIT
(formerly The Nuveen Tour)
Suite 100
1320 18th St NW
Washington
DC 20036
USA
Telephone: +1 202 785 4464
Fax: +1 202 785 4468

THE TENNIS SUPERMARKET

There are thousands of companies involved in the business of tennis, so there's no way we can include them all here.
Yet here are the major ones in the major fields.

Many of these companies have national offices, so go to their website to find out if a company you want to contact has an office in your country.

RACKETS
BALLS
CLOTHING
SHOES

The following is a list of the top names in tennis which market rackets, balls, clothes and shoes.

Note the word 'market' – some of these companies don't manufacture their own products but merely buy them from a maker and put their own name and logo on them.

Market Key:

R = Markets Rackets

B = Markets Balls

C = Markets Tennis Clothing

S = Markets Tennis Shoes

St = Markets Strings & Grips

ADIDAS
Adidas AG
Adi-Dassler Str 2
Postfach 11-20
91072 Herzogenaurach
Germany
Telephone: +49 9132 842378
Fax: +49 9132 842241
Website: www.adidas.com
Key: C / S

ASICS
Asics Corporation Japan
1-1 N
Minatojima Nakamachi 7 chome
650 Kobe
Japan
Telephone: +817 830 32298
Fax: +817 830 32244
E-mail: info@asics.co.jp
Key: C / S

BABOLAT
Babolat VS SA
93 rue André Bollier
69007 Lyon
France
Telephone: +33 4 7869 7869
Fax: +33 4 7869 7879
Website: www.babolat.com
Key: R / St

DIADORA
Diadora Spa
Via Mazzini 20
31031 Caerano di San Marco
Treviso
Italy
Telephone: +39 04 236581
Fax: +39 04 23 858512
Website: www.diadora.it
Key: C / S

DONNAY
Donnay International
Route Charlemagne 20
5660 Couvin
Belgium
Telephone: +32 60 347593
Fax: +32 60 347599
Key: R / St / C

DUNLOP/SLAZENGER
Dunlop Slazenger Group
Maxfli Court
Riverside Way
Camberley GU15 3YL
England
Telephone: +44 1276 803 399
Fax: +44 1276 679 680
Website: www.dunlopsports.com
Website: www.slazenger.com
Key: R / B / C / S

ELLESSE
Ellesse International Spa
Via Filippo Tuyrati 32
06074 Corciano
Perugia
Italy
Telephone: +39 075 50391
E-mail: ellesse@ellesse.it
Key: C

FILA
Fila Sport Spa
Via Cesare Batisti 26
Biella
Italy
Telephone: +39 01 53 5061
Fax: +39 01 53 506399
Website: www.fila.it
Key: C / S

FISCHER
Fischer GmbH
Fischerstrasse 8
4910 Ried im Innkreis
Austria
Telephone: +43 7752 909
Fax: +43 7752 909376
Website: www.fischer-ski.com
Key: R / St

FRED PERRY
Fred Perry Limited
19 Margaret Street
London WIN 7LD
England
Telephone: +44 20 7307 3500
Website: www.fredperry.com
Key: C

GAMMA
Gamma Racquet Sports
200 Waterfront Drive
Pittsburgh
Pennsylvania 15222
USA
Telephone: +1 412 323 0335
E-mail: gsi@gammasports.com
Key: R / B / C / St

GOSEN
Gosen America Limited Inc
Suite B
15791 Rockfield Boulevard
Irvine
California 92618
USA
Telephone: +1 949 380 0677
gosen@gte.net
Website: www.gosen.com
Key: R / St

HEAD
Head Sport AG
Wuhrkopfweg 1
6921 Kennelbach
Austria
Telephone: +43 5574 6080
Fax: +43 5574 608 130
Website: www.head.com
Key: R / C

HI-TEC
Hi-Tec Sports Distributors Limited
10 Kya Sand Road
Kya Sand
PO Box 3066
Honeydew 2040
South Africa
Telephone: +27 11 462 7100
E-mail: sales@hi-tec.co.za
Website: www.hi-tec.com
Key: S

K-SWISS
K-Swiss BV
4th floor
The Spring Building
Overschiestraat 186f
1062 XK Amsterdam
Netherlands
Telephone: +31 20 669 3859
Fax: +31 20 617 4176
E-mail: kscs@k-swiss.com
Website: www.k-swiss.com
Key: C / S

KAPPA
EC Basic SRL
Via Padova 55
10152 Torino
Italy
Telephone: +39 01 12 617207
Fax: +39 01 12 617370
Website: www.kappa.com
Key: C / S

KARAKAL
Karakal UK
PO Box 11
Bristol BS11 0AS
England
Telephone: +44 117 982 9057
Fax: +44 117 982 9004
Website: www.karakal.com
Key: C / R / B

LACOSTE
La Chemise Lacoste
8 rue de Castiglione
75001 Paris
France
Telephone: +33 1 4458 1212
Fax: +33 1 4261 1849
Website: www.lacoste.com
Key: C

LE COQ SPORTIF

Le Coq Sportif
France
57bis rue des Romains
68390 Sausheim
France
Telephone: +33 1 3087 4111
E-mail: info@lecoqsportif.fr
Key: C / S

LOTTO

Lotto Sport Italia Spa
Via San Gaetano 200
31044 Montebelluna (TV)
Italy
Telephone: +39 04 23 6181
Fax: +39 04 23 600402
E-mail: email@lotto.it www.lotto.it
Key: C / S

MAJOR

Major Sports
Route Départementale 307
Boite Postale 5
78810 Feucherolles
France
Telephone: +33 1 3054 9710
Fax: +33 1 3054 9739
Key: R / B

MIZUNO

Mizuno Corporation
12-35
1 chome
Nanko-kita
Suminoe-ku
Osaka 541-8538
Japan
Telephone: +81 666 148315
Fax: +81 666 483589
Website: www.mizuno.com
Key: C / S

NEW BALANCE

New Balance
   Athletic Shoe Company
International Inc
20 Guest Street
Brighton
Massachussetts 02135-2088
USA
Telephone: +1 617 746 2201
Website: www.newbalance.com
Key: S

NIKE

Nike International
World Campus
1 Bowerman Drive
Beaverton
Oregon 97005
USA
Telephone: +1 503 671 6453
Fax: +1 503 671 6300
Website: www.nike.com
Key: C / S

PENN

Penn Racquet Sports
306 South 45th Avenue
Phoenix
Arizona 85043
USA
Telephone: +1 602 447 2300
Fax: +1 602 447 2365
Website: www.pennracquet.com
Key: R / B

PRINCE/BENETTON

Prince Sports Group
One Sportsystem Plaza
Bordertown
New Jersey 08585
USA
Telephone: +1 609 291 5800
Fax: +1 609 291 5795
Website: www.bssusa.com
Key: R / B / St / C / S

PRO-KENNEX

World Pro-Kennex International
5F 752-4 SEC.4 Wen-Shin Road
403 Taichung
Taiwan
Telephone: +88 64 22347371
Fax: +119
Website: www.prokennex.com
Key: R / B / St

PUMA

Puma AG
PO Box 1420
91072 Herzogenaurach
Germany
Telephone: +49 913 2810
Fax: +49 913
Website: www.puma.com
Key: C / S

REEBOK

Reebok USA
1895 JW Foster Boulevard
Canton
Massachussetts 02021
USA
Telephone: +1 781 401 5000
Fax: No general number
Website: www.reebok.com
Key: C / S

SERGIO TACCHINI

Sergio Tacchini Spa
Via Liberta 215
28043 Bellinzago
Novarese
Italy
Telephone: +39 32 192 4111
Fax: +39 32 192 4308
Website: www.sergiotacchini.com
Key: C / S

SPALDING

Spalding Inc
425 Meadow Street
Chicopee
Massachussetts 01021
USA
Telephone: +1 413 536 1200
E-mail@ consumer-
relations@spalding.com
Website: www.spalding.com
Key: R

TRETORN

Tretorn Försäljnings AB
Rönnowsgatan 10
PO Box 931
251 09 Helsingborg
Sweden
Telephone: +46 42 197120
Website: www.tretorn.com
Key: B

VÖLKL

Völkl (International) AG
Ruessenstrasse 6
6341 Baar
Switzerland
Telephone: +41 41 769 7310
Fax: +41 41 769 7392
Website: www.voelkl.com
Key: R / St / C

WILSON

Wilson Racquet Sports
8700 W. Bryn Mawr Avenue
Chicago IL 60631
USA
Telephone: +1 773 714 6713
Fax: +1 773 714 4581
Website: www.wilsonsports.com
Key: R / B / C / S / St

YONEX

Yonex Co Limited
3-23-13 Yushima
Dunkyo-ku
Tokyo 113-8543
Japan
Telephone: +81 3 3836 1221
Fax: +81 3 3832 0583
Website: www.yonex.co.jp
Key: R / St / C / S

EQUIPMENT MAKERS

Manufacturers Key:

SM = String Machines

DC = Diagonostic Centres

ES = Electronic Scoreboards

CRC = Court Rollers & Cleaners

S = Scorekeepers

SA = Stringing Aids

BM = Ball Machines

BH = Ball Hoppers

SCE = Soft Court Equipment

BS = Benches & Stands

W = Windscreens

NP = Nets & Posts

R = Retrievers

BD = Backdrops

LT = Line Tape

SC = Screens

ALPHA
New Tech Tennis
PO Box 201 896
Austin
Texas 78720-8417
USA
Telephone: +1 512 250 8417
E-mail:
    newtech@nettechtennis.com
Website: www.aplhatennis.com
Key: SM

BABOLAT
Babolat VS SA
93 rue André Bollier
69007 Lyon
France
Telephone: +33 4 7869 7869
Fax: +33 4 7869 7879
Website: www.babolat.com
Key: SM / DC

DEUCER
SGJ Limited
Half Mile House
Little Chesterton
Oxfordshire OX25 3PD
England
Telephone: +44 1869 24477
E-mail: info@deucer.net
Website: www.deucer.net
Key: ES

FORTEN SPORTS
Forten Sports
12320 Stowe Drive
Suite J Poway
California 92064
USA
Telephone: +1 858 628 5023
E-mail: info@forten.com
Website: www.forten.com
Key: CRC / S / N / SA

GAMMA
Gamma Racquet Sports
200 Waterfront Drive
Pittsburgh
Pennsylvania 15222
USA
Telephone: +1 412 323 0335
E-mail: gsi@gammasports.com
Key: SM / BH / S / CRC / SCE /
    BS / W / NP

JUGS
Jugs
PO Box 3126
Tualtin
Oregon 97062
USA
Telephone: +1 503 692 1635
Key: BM

LOBSTER
Lobster Inc
PO Box 2807
Toluca Lake
California 91610
USA
Telephone: +1 818-506-7200
Fax: +1 818-506-7474
E-mail: sales@lobsterinc.com
Website: www.lobsterinc.com
Key: BM

MASTER SPORTS
Master Sports
137 Chambeau Road
Fort Wayne
Indiana 46805
USA
Telephone: +1 219 471 0001
E-mail: info@mastersports.com
Website: www.mastersports.com
Key: BM / R / CRC

PLAYMATE
Playmate HW
PO Box 30399
Raleigh
North Carolina 27622-0399
USA
Telephone: +1 919 544 0344
E-mail: metaltak@msn.com
Website:
    www.playmatetennis
    machines.com
Key: BM / R

PRINCE
Prince Sports Group
One Sportsystem Plaza
Bordertown
New Jersey 08585
USA
Telephone: +1 609 291 5800
Fax: +1 609 291 5795
Website: www.bssusa.com
Key: BM / SM / R

SPORTS TUTOR
Sports Tutor Inc
3300 Winona Ave
Burbank
California 91504
USA
Telephone: +1 818 972 2772
Website: www.sportstutor.com
Key: BM

SUPERCOACH
Supercoach International
c/o Sports Equipment
    International Inc
11249 Woodcreek Drive
Carmel
Indiana 46053
USA
Telephone: +1 408 855 9644
Website: www.tennismachine.com
Key: BM

WILSON
Wilson Racquet Sports
8700 W. Bryn Mawr Avenue
Chicago IL 60631
USA
Telephone: +1 773 714 6713
Fax: +1 773 714 4581
Website: www.wilsonsports.com
Key: BM / NP / SC / B / LT

FOR EQUIPMENT SALES
see the following websites:

www.west.net/~yta
www.advantagetennis.com/links/
    manuf.htm
www.advantagetennissupply.com/

PLAYER MANAGEMENT COMPANIES

The big three are IMG, Octagon and SFX, who each represent a number of players. The rest all have a smaller selection of players on their books.

INTERNATIONAL MANAGEMENT GROUP IMG

Europe office:
Pier House
Strand on the Green
London W4 3NN
England
Telephone: +44 20 8233 5000
Fax: +44 20 7233 5001

USA office:
IMG Center
1360 East 9th St
Suite 100
Cleveland
Ohio 44114
Telephone: +1 216 522 1200
Fax: +1 216 522 1145
Website: www.imgworld.com

OCTAGON
(formerly Advantage International)
Main office:
81-83 Fulham High Street
London SW6 3JW
England
Telephone: +44 20 7862 0000
Fax: +44 20 8944 5710
Website: www.octagon.com

SFX
(a company amalgamating a number of smaller sports marketing agencies, of which ProServ was the main name in tennis)
SFX Sports Group
Suite 602
2665 South Bayshore Drive
Miami
Florida 33133
USA
Telephone: +1305 668 3266
Fax: +1 305 285 3279

AMI PROMANAGEMENT
370 Felter Ave
Hewlett
New York 11557
USA
Telephone: +1 516 569 8922

AMG SPORTS
9465 Wilshire Blvd
Beverly Hills
California 90212
USA
Telephone: +1 310 860 8999
Fax: +1 310 860 8100

BARCELONA MEETING POINT
Barcelona
Spain
Telephone: +34 3 205 5111

ELITE MANAGEMENT
31 Avenue Princesse Grace
98000 Monaco
Telephone: +377 9325 8634
Fax: +377 9216 0245
E-mail: elite@monaco.mc
Tennis contact:
   Elly van Veenandaal

GRAND SLAM SPORTS
Suite 4163
20533 Biscayne Blvd
Aventura
Florida 33180
USA
Telephone: +1 305 931 9250

ISC SPORTMANAGEMENT
Kinostr 21
5061 Salzburg-Elsbethen
Austria
Telephone: +43 662 630459
Fax: +43 662 630469
E-mail:
   office@isc-sportmanagement.at

ROBERT KAPLAN
145 East 18th St (Apt 1)
New York
NY 10003
USA
Telephone: +1 212 420 9190

MS CONSULTING GMBH
Bayernstr 383
5071 Salzburg
Austria
Telephone: +43 662 853 8780
MS stands for Michael Stich

PRO SPORTS INTERNATIONAL PSI
2905 Brookhaven View
Atlanta
Georgia 30319
USA
Telephone: +1 404 577 9242

SHARF MARKETING GROUP
Suite 203
822 Boylston St
Chestnut Hill
Massachussetts 02167
USA
Telephone: +1 617 566 7070

SPORTS MARKETING CONSULTANTS
A division of
   Interperformances Group
Suite 105-G
7025 Beracasa Way
Boca Raton
Florida
USA
Telephone: +1 561 417 8405
Fax: +1 561 417 8471
Website:
   www.smcsportsmarketing.com

TSM & PARTNERS
c/o Giauque Sport
   Management Consulting
Wallisellerstr 160
8152 Opfikon
Switzerland
Telephone: +41 76 366 6829

GLOBAL EQUIPMENT UMBRELLA ORGANISATIONS

TENNIS INDUSTRY ASSOCIATION
PO Box 7845
Hilton Head Island
SC 29938
USA
Telephone: +1 843 686 3036
Fax: +1 843 686 3078
Website: www.tennisindustry.org
President: Kurt Kamperman

WORLD FEDERATION OF SPORTS GOODS INDUSTRIES
La Maison du Sport
PO Box 480
1936 Verbier
Switzerland
Telephone: +41 27 775 3570
Fax: +41 27 775 3579
Website:
   www.wfsgi.org wfsgi@verbier.ch
President: Stephen Rubin

TENNIS JOURNALISTS' ASSOCIATIONS

INTERNATIONAL TENNIS WRITERS ASSOCIATION

The organisation for the most specialist tennis writers and broadcasters, strict criteria apply for members based around attending a given number of tournaments each year and a given number of Slams in a two-year period.
Contact:
Lynn Zanconato Evans
13 Avenue St Michel
98000 Monaco
Telephone: +33 4 9376 8416
Fax: +33 4 9376 8417
E-mail: Zanevans@compuserve.com

AUSTRALIAN TENNIS MEDIA ASSOCIATION

The umbrella organisation for Australian tennis writers and broadcasters, plus non-Australians based in Australia and nearby countries (one member in the Philippines).
Contact:
John Hogan
2 Caledonian Avenue
Winstone Hills NSW 2153
Australia
Telephone: +61 2 9288 2451
Fax: +61 2 9288 2439

LAWN TENNIS WRITERS ASSOCIATION

The umbrella organisation for British tennis writers and broadcasters, full membership limited to 40 at any one time.
Contact:
Henry Wancke
Cedar Lodge
Howe Road
Warlington
Oxford OX9 5ER
England
Telephone: +44 1491 612042
Fax: +44 1491 614104

UNITED STATES TENNIS WRITERS ASSOCIATION

Set up to tackle issues affecting tennis media in America, but full membership open to non-Americans.
Contact:
Liza Horan
810 Seventh Ave
New York NY 10019
USA
Telephone: +1 212 636 2723
Fax: +1 212 636 2730
E-mail: Liza@tennis.com
Website: www.tennis.com/ustwa

TENNIS RADIO NETWORK

Not an association as such, but a company set up by four radio journalists to bid for radio reporting contracts, and thus something of a magnet for tennis journalists who specialise in radio.
Contact:
Chris Bowers
5 Greenacres Drive
Ringmer
East Sussex BN8 5LZ
England
Telephone: +44 1273 813331
Fax: +44 1273 813331

TELEVISION RIGHTS

Television rights to the Grand Slam tournaments are handled by TWI for the Australian Open and Wimbledon, the French Tennis Federation for Roland Garros, and SwanTV for the US Open.

TWI

Trans-World International
23 Eyot Gardens
London W6 9TR
Telephone: +44 20 8233 5400
Fax: +44 20 8233 5401
Website: www.imgworld.com

SWANTV

Herb Swan
Suite 303
44 Canal Center Plaza
Alexandria
Virginia 22314
USA
Telephone: +1 703 360 0547
Fax: +1 703 360 7269
E-mail: swantv@aol.com

FRENCH TENNIS FEDERATION

see National Tennis Associations page 165.

TENNIS PHOTOGRAPHERS & PHOTOGRAPHIC AGENCIES

There are hundreds of professional photographers who photograph at tennis tournaments. Of those who are regularly on the tour, they can probably break down into three categories:

ALLSPORT

A worldwide photographic agency whose photographers take pictures of all sports and have some of the best photographers in tennis.
Contact:
Allsport Photographic Limited
Sport Pictures Agency
3 Greenlay Park
Prince George's Road
London SW19
England
Telephone: +44 20 8685 1010
Fax: +44 20 8648 5240
E-mail:
    allsportlondon@gettyimages.com
Website: www.allsport.com

PROFESSIONAL SPORT

A private agency specialising in tennis pictures run by the British photographer Tommy Hindley featuring his tennis photography and those of other freelance tennis photographers
Contact:
Professional Sport
18-19 Shaftesbury Quay
Hertford
SG14 1SF
England
Telephone: +44 1992 505000
Fax: +44 1992 505020
E-mail: pictures@prosport.co.uk
Website: www.prosport.co.uk

There are a number of award-winning freelance tennis photographers, of whom the best known are Russ Adams, Ron Angle, Gianni Ciaccia, Cynthia Lomb, Angelo Tonelli, and Paul Zimmer. To contact any of these, go through:
Paul Zimmer
Telephone: +49 711 471597
Fax: +49 711 475672
E-mail: paulzimmer@t-online.de

For historic tennis pictures, the following bodies have impressive photographic/picture collections:

INTERNATIONAL TENNIS HALL OF FAME

The Newport Casino
194 Bellevue Avenue
Newport
RI 02840
USA
Telephone: +1 401 849 3990
Fax: +1 401 849 8780
Website: www.tennisfame.com

WIMBLEDON LAWN TENNIS MUSEUM

All England Lawn Tennis Club
Church Road
London
SW19 5AE
Telephone: +44 20 8946 6131

TENNIS WEBSITES

Enter 'tennis' in your search engine and you'll find thousands of websites.

The following are the top official ones plus the biggest independents, but one or two letters different and you could well find an unofficial website that is just as informative.

Enter a top player's name and you have a good chance of travelling to their own personal fan club website.

www.advantage-tennis.com
A private British website but nevertheless a good source of tennis photographs, especially of the world's top top players.

www.atptennis.com
The ATP's own website. A good database for getting information about male players, though the amount of advertising can get irritating.

www.ausopen.org
The official website of the Australian Open. Has live scoring and is generally user-friendly.

www.daviscup.com
The official website of the Davis Cup. Has live scoring during Davis Cup weekends, and sometimes live commentary from a selected World Group tie; also features Davis Cup news between Davis Cup weekends.

www.ebay.com
Not a tennis website but an American auction website which sells tennis autographs and memorablia.

www.itftennis.com
The official website of the International Tennis Federation. Good database for information, though so comprehensive it takes some getting to know.

www.masters-series.com
The website for the ATP's top nine tournaments. Has live scoring on the top matches, though can be very slow.

www.racquettech.com
The website of Recquet Tech, the official publication of the United States Registered Stringers Association and arguably the best publication for questions of rackets and stringing.

www.roland-garros.com
The official website of the French Open. Has live scoring. Available in English and French.

www.sanexwta.com
The Sanex WTA Tour's own website and the premier resource for information on female players. Has just been revamped having proved rather slow – it's still a shade slow, but much more user-friendly.

www.tennis.com
The website of 'Tennis' magazine in the USA, it was one of the first and still one of the most up-to-date for regular features on tennis. Also a tremendous resource for just about everything connected with tennis.

www.tennisexpress.com
An independent shopping website with lots of sections from trivia to tips, jobs to shops, plus a directory offering lots of useful contacts.

www.tennisfame.com
The official website of the International Tennis Hall of Fame. Good for biographical information.

www.tennisjobs.com
A specialist website for jobs. Tends to over concentrate on coaching and facility directors, and is very USA-centric, but offers a resume/CV posting service.

www.tennisresortsonline.com
An independent website offering a critical guide to the world's best tennis resorts and tennis camps. The word 'world' is slightly misleading given that it is largely USA-based, but it does feature some non-US options and is a very good port of call if considering a tennis holiday.

www.tennisserver.com
A useful website for the consumer because although it wants to sell you things it does give a number of very useful hints about products through 'frequently asked questions' (FAQ) pages.

www.tennisweek.com
An offshoot of 'Tennis Week' magazine in America, it specialises in news from the tours, plus details about tennis on television and how to get tickets for tournaments.

www.usopen.org
The official website of the US Open. Has live scoring, and has expanded its live radio service during the US Open in the last couple of years.

www.wimbledon.org
The official website of The Championships, Wimbledon. Has live scoring, and its written reports during Wimbledon fortnight are good quality by internet standards and are regularly updated.

GLOSSARY

Tennis has its fair share of jargon. Here is a selection of the most commonly used terms.

ACE
A serve which wins the point without any part of the opponent's racket touching the ball (if it even snicks the edge of the opponent's racket it shouldn't be termed an ace).

BACKSPIN
See 'slice'.

BAGEL
A slang term meaning a 6-0 set. Comes from the fact that a bagel is a bread roll with a hole in it, therefore looking like a zero. By the same logic, other terms in less common usage include 'donut', 'goose egg' and 'Polo mint'. A 'double bagel' is a 6-0 6-0 result.

CHALLENGE ROUND
The practice common in the early days of lawn tennis of allowing the defending champion to go straight into the following year's final meant that the final was known as a challenge round.

It was abolished at Wimbledon for the 1922 championships, and in Davis Cup as late as 1972. (Some American tournaments still refer to the final as the 'challenge match').

DOUBLE SET (OR BREAK) POINT
A term which can sometimes mean different things in different parts of the English-speaking world. In America and Australia it clearly means two points to take the set (eg. being 5-3 40-15 up), but in British English 'two set points' (or break points) is the more commonly used term, with 'double break point' sometimes being used to mean a point for a double break (eg. 2-4 30-40).

FOLLOW-THROUGH
The part of a stroke after the strings have made contact with the ball.

A vital part of any stroke as without a good follow-through players frequently don't get the power out of their stroke, but in the powerful modern game a follow-through can't be too exaggerated or a player will lose valuable time before having to play the next stroke.

FOOT-FAULT
The infringement of a player's foot touching a part of the baseline before he/she has hit the ball on a serve.

HALF-VOLLEY
A shot played virtually at the moment the ball has hit the ground with the racket at ground level; occasionally the shot is played with the ball actually touching the ground. An emergency shot played to get a player out of trouble!

HANDS
A player is said to have 'good hands' if he/she can find lots of angles, is versatile on the volley, and has a good feel for the ball (see touch below). A natural doubles player frequently is credited with having 'good hands'.

HOST BROADCASTER
A television term referring to the company which has the contract with the tournament to provide the cameras not only for its own coverage but a 'feed' of pictures to all other companies showing the tournament in other countries.

IN-TO-OUT FOREHAND/BACKHAND
Sometimes known as 'inside out forehand' or 'off forehand'. A stroke in which the shot moves away from the side on which the player played the shot – in other words, an in-to-out forehand played by a right-hander heads off to the right (as the player looks) a little like a golfer's slice, while the right-hander's in-to-out backhand heads off to the left (as the player looks).

OFF FOREHAND
See 'in-to-out forehand/backhand'.

OPEN ERA
The era of tennis since early 1968 when the amateur and professional circuits came together to allow the best players to play in the most prestigious tournaments.

RACE
The name given to the ranking lists which start from zero at the start of the year (like season-based league tables or standings in other sports). The ATP race is officially called The ATP Champions Race followed by the year in question.

RUBBER
The name given to one of the five matches which make up a Davis Cup tie (comes from Bridge terminology).

RUN-BACK
The area between the baseline and the back fence. In championship tennis it must be a minimum of 6.4 metres (21 feet), but it can be as short as 5.5 metres (18 feet) in clubs and public parks (and for economic reasons frequently is).

SLAM DUNK
A term taken from basketball meaning to hit a smash with both feet well off the ground. Popularised in tennis by Pete Sampras for whom it is the most charismatic shot in his armoury.

SLICE
The way of hitting the ball that comes down across the back of the ball to send it flying through the air with a backward roll. This reduces the trajectory as the ball falls to the ground, and keeps the bounce low after impact with the ground (therefore good on low-bouncing courts like grass, and for approach shots).

STATS
Short for statistics, generally refers to the set of statistics released after a match detailing both players aces, double faults, winners, unforced errors, etc.

SWEET SPOT
The centre of the stringing on a racket and the area around it which gives players optimum contact when the ball strikes that part of the stringing. The modern composite rackets (such as graphite) have increased the size of the sweet spot.

TANK
A verb of tennis slang, meaning to deliberately lose a match but disguise the fact. Though few players will admit to it, they do tank matches, notably some tour events when they want to move on to the next city without having spent too long on court.

TOPSPIN
The way of hitting the ball that hits up the back of the ball to send it flying through the air with a forward roll. This reduces the trajectory as the ball falls to the ground, and sends it spinning rapidly and with a high bounce after impact with the ground (therefore good for lobs).

TOUCH
A word with two meanings: one refers to a player's feel for the ball, in particular how much sensitivity he/she can get when the ball makes contact with the strings (a 'touch player' is one who uses a lot of low-power but carefully weighted shots); the other is a call an umpire gives to denote the infringement when a player's racket touches the net while the ball is still live in a rally.

WILDCARD
A player who failed to qualify for automatic entry to a tournament because his/her ranking was too low is given a wildcard.

Wildcards are generally given to players of the host country, and occasionally to high-profile players who are on the comeback trail after injury or a loss of form. The best example is Goran Ivanisevic who was given a wildcard at the 2001 Wimbledon and won the tournament.

ALPHABET SOUP

Like in most walks of life there are masses of acronyms in tennis. Here are the most commonly used ones, with page references indicating where the body or feature behind the acronym is explained.

AELTC
ALL ENGLAND LAWN TENNIS CLUB
The full name for the club that hosts Wimbledon.
(see page 34)

ATP
ASSOCIATION OF TENNIS PROFESSIONALS
Originally Association of Tennis Professionals, but just ATP these days.
(see page 17)

ESP
ENTRY SYSTEM POSITION
The ATP's 52-week ranking system.
(see page 28)

FFT
FÉDÉRATION FRANÇAISE DE TENNIS
The French Tennis Federation.
(see page165)

IMG
INTERNATIONAL MANAGEMENT GROUP
The biggest player management agency.
(see page 54)

ITF
INTERNATIONAL TENNIS FEDERATION
(see page 20)

ITHF
INTERNATIONAL TENNIS HALL OF FAME
(see page 114)

ILTF
INTERNATIONAL LAWN TENNIS FEDERATION
The ITF before 'Lawn' was dropped in 1977.
(see page 20)

ITWA
INTERNATIONAL TENNIS WRITERS ASSOCIATION
(see page 59)

LTA
LAWN TENNIS ASSOCIATION
Governing body of British tennis.
(see page 165)

MIPTC
MEN'S INTERNATIONAL PROFESSIONAL TENNIS COUNCIL
(see page 17)

SFX
Doesn't stand for anything (rumoured to be some of the jumbled up initials of its founder), a company owned by the Clear Channel Group which includes the former ProServ, the third biggest player management agency.
(see page 54)

TMC
TENNIS MASTERS CUP
The name since 2000 of the men's end-of-year championship jointly owned by the ATP and ITF, which switches venue year-by-year.
(see page 17)

TMS
TENNIS MASTERS SERIES
The name given to the elite series of tournaments on the ATP tour since 2000, formerly known as the Super Nine.
(see page 17)

TPL
TENNIS PROPERTIES LIMITED
The company set up by the nine elite tournaments on the ATP tour to run their affairs; it is effectively – though not legally – a subsidiary of the ATP.
(see page 162)

USNLTA
UNITED STATES NATIONAL LAWN TENNIS ASSOCIATION
Forerunner of USTA – the 'National' was dropped in 1920 and 'Lawn' was dropped in 1975.
(see page 169)

USTA
UNITED STATES TENNIS ASSOCIATION
(see page 169)

WCT
WORLD CHAMPIONSHIP TENNIS
Lamar Hunt's professional circuit.
(see page 14)

WTA
WOMEN'S TENNIS ASSOCIATION
Originally Women's Tennis Association but these days it only appears as the Sanex WTA Tour.
(see page 18)

WTT
WORLD TEAM TENNIS
(see page 27)

TENNIS TOURNAMENT DIRECTORS

MEN'S TOUR

The following were the tournament directors on the ATP in 2001. As *The Book of Tennis* went to press, it was not clear which of these tournaments would disappear before the 2002 calendar was finalised.

They appear in the order in which they were held in 2001.

For the 2002 calendar, visit www.atptennis.com

DOHA
Ayman Asmy
Qatar Exxon Mobil Open
Qatar Tennis & Squash Federation
PO Box 4959
Doha
Qatar
Telephone: +974 409601
Fax: +974 483 1972
E-mail: asmy@qatar.net.qa

CHENNAI
Sheila Manniam
Gold Flake Open
c/o IMG
Bertschenackerstr 15
4014 Oberwil
Switzerland
Telephone: +41 61 403 1236
Fax: +41 61 403 1235
E-mail: smaniam@imgworld.com

ADELAIDE
Colin Stubs
The AAPT Championships
Colin Stubs Enterprises
479a Glenferrie Road
Melbourne
Victoria 3144
Australia
Telephone: +61 3 9822 4430
Fax: +61 3 9822 4848
E-mail: case@mire.net

AUCKLAND
Graham Pearce
Heineken Open
ASB Bank Tennis Centre
72 Stanley Street
Auckland
New Zealand
Telephone: +64 9 373 3623
Fax: +64 9 373 3625
E-mail:
    graham@aucklandtennis.co.nz

SYDNEY
Craig Watson
Adidas International
Sydney International
    Tennis Centre
Shirley Strickland Avenue
Homebush Bay
Sydney
Australia
Telephone: +61 2 9331 4144
Fax: +61 2 9360 0436
E-mail: cwatson@tennisnsw.com

AUSTRALIAN OPEN
Paul NcNamee
Tennis Australia
Melbourne Park National Tennis
Centre
Private Bag 6060
Richmond South
Victoria 3121
Australia
Telephone: +61-3-9286-1175
Fax: +61-3-9650-1040
E-mail:
    pmcnamee@tennisaustralia.
    com.au

MILAN
Franco Bartoni
Milan Indoors
147 Via di Casal Selce
00166 Rome
Italy
Telephone: 39-335/7001766
Fax: 39-06/66180895

BOGOTA
Manuel Mate
Cerveza Club Colombia Open
Calle 93-A #11-49
Santafe de Bogota, DC
Colombia
Telephone: +57-1/616-7556
Fax: +57-1/616-7440
E-mail: manumate@latino.net.co

MARSEILLE
Jean-Francois Caujolle
Open 13
Pampelonne Organisation
97-99, Avenue de Saint Antoine
13015 Marseille
France
Telephone: +33-6 1431 9108
Fax: +33 4/91519937
E-mail: open13@wanadoo.fr

COPENHAGEN
Peter Bastiansen
Copenhagen Open
Snaregade 14
1205 Copenhagen
Denmark
Telelephone: +45-33/127244
Fax: +45-33/937220

VINA DEL MAR
Alvaro Fillol
Chevrolet Cup by BellSouth
Luis Thayer Ojeda N 166 Of. 906
Providencia
Santiago
Chile
Telephone: +56-2/234-3788
Fax: +56-2/244-1056
E-mail: fillolsa@bellsouth.cl

BUENOS AIRES
Martin Jaite
Copa AT&T
Zapiola 1646 - 4 Piso 1426
Buenos Aires
Argentina
Telephone: +541-15-288-1125
Telephone: +541-14-773-3799
Telephone: +541-14-773-0911
Fax: +541-14-551-9033
E-mail: altenis@sinectis.com.ar

ROTTERDAM
Wim Buitendijk
ABN/AMRO World Tennis
Tournament
Spo mark BV
Ahoy' weg 10
PO Box 5552
3008 AC Rotterdam
The Netherlands
Telephone: +31-10/2933450
Fax: +31-10/2933459
E-mail: wimb@spomark.com

MEMPHIS
Tom Buford
Kroger St Jude
Racquet Club of Memphis
5111 Sanderlin Avenue
Memphis TN 38117
USA
Telephone: +1 901-765-4400
Fax: +1 901-682-4229
E-mail:
    tom.buford@racquetclubof
    memphis.com

SAN JOSE
Bill Rapp
Siebel Open
Compaq Center
525 West Santa Clara Street
San Jose CA 95113
USA
Telephone: +1 408-999-5764
Fax: +1 408-367-7040
E-mail: brapp@sjsharks.com

ACAPULCO
Lisette Trepaud Johnson
Abierto Mexicano de Tenis Pegaso
Blvd. M. Avila Camacho No 88-103
Col. Lomas de Chapultepec
DF 11000
Mexico
Telephone: +52-5/540-0102
Fax: +52-5/540-0088
E-mail: ltrepaud@mextenis.com

DUBAI
Jeff Chapman
The Dubai Tennis Championships
The Dubai Tennis Centre
Aviation Club
Dubai
UAE
Telephone: +971 4 828971
Fax: +971 4 828953
E-mail: maria.bizri@sportsworld.net

DELRAY BEACH
Mark Baron
Citrix Tennis Championships
Match Point Inc.
30 Northwest First Avenue
Delray Beach FL 33444
USA
Telephone: +1 561-330-6000
Fax: +1 561-330-6001
E-mail:
    mbaron@matchpointinc.com

SCOTTSDALE
Gus Sampras
Franklin Templeton Tennis Classic
11755 Wilshire Blvd
Suite 850
Los Angeles CA 90025
USA
Telephone: +1 310-473-0411
Fax: +1 310-473-3914
E-mail: gsampras@imgworld.com

INDIAN WELLS
Charlie Pasarell
Tennis Masters Series Indian Wells
78-200 Miles Avenue
Indian Wells CA 92210
USA
Telephone: +1 760-345-2055
Fax: +1 760-360-2606
E-mail: pmsport1@aol.com

KEY BISCAYNE/MIAMI
Cliff Buchholz
The Ericsson Open
150 Alhambra Circle
Suite 825
Coral Gables FL 33134
USA
Telephone: +1 305-446-2200
Fax: +1 305-446-9080

ESTORIL

João Lagos
Estoril Open
João Lagos Sports SA
Rua Fernao Mendes Pinto no 42
1400-146 Lisbon, Portugal
Telephone: +351-21/3034900
Fax: +351-21/3034933
E-mail: lagossports@mail.telepac.pt

CASABLANCA

El Kebir Haggouch
Grand Prix Hassan II
Federation Royale Marocaine
de Tennis
Parc de la Ligue Arabe
Casablanca
Morocco
Telelphone: +212-22/981262
Fax: +212-22/981265
E-mail: frmt@casanet.net.ma

MONTE CARLO

Francis Truchi
Monte Carlo Country Club
B.P. 342
98006 Monaco Cedex
Tel: +33-4/9341 3015
Fax: +33-4/9341 7816
E-mail: info@mccc.mc

ATLANTA

Bob O'Connor
Verizon Tennis Challenge
SFX Sports Group
410 Greenwich Avenue
Greenwich CT 06830
USA
Telephone: +1 203-629-2229
Fax: +1 203-629-5902

BARCELONA

Sixte Cambra
Open Seat Godo
Real Club de Tenis Barcelona 1899
c/o Ana Verges
Bosch I Gimpera, 5-13
08034 Barcelona
Spain
Telephone: +34-93/2052117
Fax: +34-93/2045010
E-mail: buzon@rctb1899.es

MUNICH

Rudi Berger
BMW Open
MTTC Iphitos E.V.
Aumeisterweg 10
80805 Munich
Germany
Telephone: +49-89/32209050
Fax: +49-89/32209055
E-mail: r.berger@iphitos.de

HOUSTON

Kris Young
US Clay Court Championships
Westside Tennis Club
1200 Wildcrest Drive
Houston TX 77042
USA
Telephone: +1 713-783-1620
Fax: +1 713-783-3731

MALLORCA

Alberto Tous
Mallorca Open
Participaciones en el Mundo del
Deporte s.l.
CL Can Oliva, 10
Principal dcha.
07003 Palma de Mallorca
Spain
Telephone: +34-971/721626
Fax: +34-971/495179
E-mail: atous@mallorcaopen.com

ROME

Adriano Panatta
Tennis Masters Series Roma
Federazione Italiana Tennis
Foro Italico
Viale dei Gladiatori, 31
00194 Rome
Italy
Telephone: +39-06/32639917
Telephone: +39-06/32639903
Fax: +39-06/32638552
Fax: +39-06/32638550
E-mail: romeopen.2001@tin.it

HAMBURG

Walter Knapper
Tennis Masters Series Hamburg
German Tennis Federation
DTB Rothenbaum Turnier GmbH
Haller Str. 89
20149 Hamburg
Germany
Telephone: +49-40/41178230
Fax: +49-40/41178333
E-mail: walter.knapper@t-online.de

DÜSSELDORF

Horst Klosterkemper
Arag ATP World Team
Championship
Rochusclub Turnier GmbH
Rolander Weg 15
40629 Düsseldorf
Germany
Telephone: +49-211/95960/9596232
Fax: +49-211/613435
E-mail:
klosterkemperh@messe-duessel
dorf.de

ST PÖLTEN

Hans Holzer
Internationaler Raiffeisen
Grand Prix
AMI Promarketing
Landhaus Boulevard - Top 21
3100 St Pölten
Austria
Telephone: +43-2742/258060
Fax: 43-2742/258070
E-mail:
eva.hammerschmidt@amipro.at

ROLAND GARROS

Executive Committee
Federation Francaise de Tennis
Stade Roland Garros
2, Avenue Gordon Bennett
75016 Paris
France
Telephone: +33-1/47434800
Fax: +33-1/46516724

LONDON
(QUEEN'S CLUB)

Ian Wight
Stella Artois Championships
Octagon Marketing
Octagon House
81-83 Fulham High Street
London SW6 3JW
England
Telephone: +44-207/8620000
Telephone: +44-207/8620045
Fax: +44-207/8620001
E-mail: ian.wight@octagon.com

HALLE

Ralf Weber
Gerry Weber Open
Gerry Weber Management &
Event GmbH
Neulehenstr. 8
33790 Halle/Westfalen
Germany
Telephone: +49-5201/185161
Fax: +49-5201/665128
E-mail: r.weber@gerryweber.de

S'HERTOGENBOSCH

Marcel Hunze
The Heineken Trophy
Octagon Marketing
Burghtstraat 25-B
6227 RR Maastricht
The Netherlands
Telephone: +31-43/3672424
Fax: +31-43/3672422
E-mail: marcel.hunze@octagon.com

NOTTINGHAM

Patrick Hughesman
The Lawn Tennis Association
The Queen's Club
Palliser Road
London W14 9EG
England
Telephone: +44-20/73817029
Fax: +44-20/73816
E-mail:
patrick.hughesman@lta.org.uk

WIMBLEDON

Christopher Gorringe
All England Lawn Tennis &
Croquet Club
Church Road
Wimbledon
London SW19 5AE
England
Telephone: +44-20/89469122
Fax: +44-20/89478752

BÅSTAD

Thomas Wallen
Telenordia Swedish Open
PR Event
Box 64
428 32 Kallered
Sweden
Telephone: +46-31/940250
Fax: +46-31/940251
E-mail:
thomas.wallen@swedishopen.org

NEWPORT

Mark Stenning
Miller Lite Hall of Fame Tennis
Championships
International Tennis Hall of Fame
194 Bellevue
Newport RI 02840
USA
Telephone: +1 401-849-3990
Fax: +1 401-849-8780
E-mail: mstenn4410@aol.com

GSTAAD

Jacques H. Hermenjat
UBS Open
Hermenjat Sports
Promenade 1
PO Box 394
3780 Gstaad
Switzerland
Telephone: +41-33/7488361
Telephone: +41-33/7488366
Fax: +41-33/7446630

AMSTERDAM
Piet Van Eijsden
Energis Open
Piet Van Eijsden Sport
Management
Gomarushof 76a
1216 HN Hilversum
The Netherlands
Telephone: +31-35/6231445
Fax: +31-35/6236470
E-mail: piet@energisopen.nl

STUTTGART
(outdoor)
Bernd Nusch
Mercedes Cup
Tennisclub Weissenhof e.V.
Parlerstrasse 102
70192 Stuttgart
Germany
Telephone: +49-711/1654382
Fax: +49-711/1654355
E-mail: nusch@mercedescup.de

UMAG
Slavko Rasberger
International Championship of
   Croatia
International Tennis Centre
Stella Maris
Savudrijska Cesta BB
51470 Umag
Croatia
Telephone: +385-52/741704
Fax: +385-52/7415
E-mail:
   slavko.rasberger@pu.hinet.hr

KITZBÜHEL
Hellmuth-Dieter Küchenmeister
Generali Open
Tennisclub Kitzbühel
Casino Stadion Kitzbühel
Schlossbergstrasse 2
6370 Kitzbühel
Austria
Telephone: +43-5356/72076
Fax: +43-5356/63311
E-mail:
   tennis@kitzbuehel.netwing.at

SOPOT
Ryszard Fijalkowski
Idea Prokom Open
Ul. Merlimego 2
02511 Warsaw
Poland
Mobile: +48-601/330833
Telephone: +48-22/8441297
Fax: +48-22/8441297
E-mail: rfijalkowski@poczta.fm

LOS ANGELES
Robert Kramer
Mercedes-Benz Cup
L.A. Tennis Center
PO Box 240015
Los Angeles CA 90024
USA
or
UCLA
420 Charles Young Drive West
Los Angeles CA 90024
USA
Telephone: +1 310-824-1010
Fax: +1 310-209-4750
E-mail: bobk@scta.usta.com

MONTREAL
(odd-numbered years)
Eugene Lapierre
Tennis Masters Series Canada
Tennis Canada
Bureau de Montreal
285 rue Faillon Ouest
Montreal
Quebec H2R 2W1
Canada
Telephone: +1 514-273-1515
Fax: +1 514-276-0070
E-mail:
   elapierre@tenniscanada.com

TORONTO
(even-numbered years)
Jane Wynne
Tennis Masters Series Canada
Tennis Canada
3111 Steeles Ave. W.
Downsview
Ontario M3J 3H2
Canada
Telephone: +1 416-665-9777
Fax: +1 416-665-9017
E-mail: iwynne@attglobal.net

CINCINNATI
Paul Flory
Tennis Masters Series Cincinnati
Chiquita Center
250 East 5th Street
Suite 1610
Cincinnati OH 45202
USA
Telephone: +1 513-651-3082
Fax: +1 513-651-3088
E-mail: Pflory@cincytennis.com

INDIANAPOLIS
Rob MacGill
RCA Championships
815 W. New York St
Indianapolis IN 46202
USA
Telephone: +1 317-632-4100
Fax: +1 317-634-9437
E-mail: rmacgill@btlaw.com

WASHINGTON
Jeff Newman
Legg Mason Tennis Classic
SFX Sports Group
5335 Wisconsin Ave NW
Suite 850
Washington DC 20015
USA
Telephone: +1 202-721-9515
Fax: +1 202-721-7201
E-mail: jeffrey.newman@sfx.com

LONG ISLAND
Kari Mutscheller
The Hamlet Cup
400 Post Avenue, Ste. 403
Westbury NY 11590
USA
Telephone: +1 516-876-0400
Fax: +1 516-876-7907
E-mail: karimutsch@aol.com

US OPEN
Arlen Kantarian
United States Tennis Association
70 West Red Oak Lane
White Plains NY 10604
USA
Telephone: +914-696-7000
Fax: +914-696-7019
E-mail: kantarian@usta.com

SALVADOR
Luis Felipe Tavares
Brasil Open
Av. Paulista 1754 5 andar
   01310-200
Sao Paulo SP
Brazil
Telephone: +55-11-253-8866
Fax: +55-11-253-8635
E-mail:
   luisfelipe.tavares@octagon.com

BUCHAREST
Dumitru Haradau
Gelsor Open
Fundatia Open Romania
Nicolae Caranfil Nr 19
Sector 1
Bucharest
Romania
Telephone: +40-1/2330402
Fax: +40-1/2243027
E-mail: open.romania@itcnet.ro

TASHKENT
Danny Gelley
President's Cup
c/o Israel Tennis Centre
PO Box 51
Ramat Hasharron 47100
Israel
Telephone: +972 3 645 6634
Fax: +972 3 645 6677
E-mail: tourn@tennis.org.il

SHANGHAI
Michael Luévano
Heineken Open
Ba-Shi Building (Room 1608)
525 Jianguo East Road
Shanghai 200025
China
Telephone: +86 21 6386 0864
Fax: +86 21 6386 0871
E-mail: mluevano@netvigator.com

HONG KONG
Carol Samuel
Salem Open
Unit 705-6 (7th floor)
Yardley Commercial Building
3 Connaught Road West
Sheung Wan
Hong Kong
China
Telephone: +85 2 2834 0060
Fax: +85 2 2838 8593
E-mail: salemopen@sportzite.com

TOULOUSE
Patrice Dominguez
Open de Toulouse
Groupe Jean-Claude Darmon
5, rue de Liege
75009 Paris
France
Telephone: +33-1/55071048
Fax: +33-1/55078159

PALERMO
Cino Marchese
Campionati Internazionali di
   Sicilia
C.M. Produzioni
Via delle Quattro Fontane, 21A
00184 Rome
Italy
Telephone: +39-06/4873557
Fax: +39-06/4743415
E-mail: cinomarchese@libero.it

TOKYO
Toshiro Sakai
Japan Open
1-1-1 Jin-nan Shibuya-ku
Tokyo 150-8050
Japan
Telephone: +81 3 3481 2321
Fax: +81 3 3467 5192

MOSCOW
Alexander Volkov
Kremlin Cup
Kremlin Cup office
16 Olimposky Prospect
Moscow 129090
Russia
Telephone: +7 095 956 3360
Fax: +7 095 956 3361
E-mail:
   alexander.katsnelson@
   russport.ru

LYON

Gilles Moretton
Grand Prix de Tennis de Lyon
Occade Sport
20 Route de Strasbourg
69300 Caluire
France
Telephone: +33-4/72272900
Fax: +33-4/72272910
E-mail: gmoretton@occade.com

VIENNA

Leo-Gunther Huemer
CA Tennis Trophy
Wiener Stadthalle
Vogelweidplatz 14
1150 Vienna
Austria
Telephone: +43-1/98100
Fax: +43-1/98100363
E-mail: l.huemer@stadthalle.com

STUTTGART

(indoor)
Markus Günthardt
Tennis Masters Series Stuttgart
World Sport Marketing GmbH
Hohe Strasse 18
70174 Stuttgart
Germany
Telephone: +49-711/228870
Fax: +49-711/2288712
E-mail:
  m_guenthardt@yahoo.com

BASEL

Roger Brennwald
Davidoff Swiss Indoors
Bettenstrasse 73
4123 Allschwil
Switzerland
Telephone: +41-61/485-9595
Fax: +41-61/485-9596
E-mail:
  davidoff@davidoffswissindoors.ch

ST PETERSBURG

Michael Rydnik
St Petersburg Open
Bolshaya Morskaya Street 19
Office 4C
St Petersburg 191186
Russia
Telephone: +7 812 326 8626
Fax: +7 812 326 8637
E-mail: info@spbopen.ru

STOCKHOLM

Per Hjertquist
If Stockholm Open
Kungliga Tennishallen
Lidingovägen 75
115 41 Stockholm
Sweden
Telephone: +46-8/50622400
Telephone: +46-8/54502600
Fax: +46-8/4591641
E-mail: phjertquist@imgworld.com

PARIS-BERCY

Gilles Jourdan
Tennis Masters Series Paris
Federation Francaise de Tennis
Stade Roland Garros
2 Avenue Gordon Bennett
75016 Paris
France
Telephone: +33-1/47434800
Fax: +33-1/46516724
E-mail: gjourdan@fft.fr

SANEX WTA TOUR

The following were the tournament directors on the Sanex WTA Tour in 2001.

As *The Book of Tennis* went to press, it was not clear which of these tournaments would disappear before the 2002 calendar was finalised.

They appear in the order in which they were held in 2001.

For the 2002 calendar, visit www.sanexwta.com

GOLD COAST

Liz Smylie
PO Box 637
Mermaid Beach
QLD 4218
Australia
Telephone: 61-7-5526-1755
Fax: 61-7-5526-1799
E-mail:
  fwilson@tennisaustralia.com.au
Website: www.tennisaustralia.com

AUCKLAND

Richard Palmer
Auckland Tennis Inc
72 Stanley Street
Box 2905
Auckland
New Zealand
Telephone: +64-9-3733-623
Fax: +64-9-3733-625
Website: www.aucklandtennis.co.nz
asbcentre@aucklandtennis.co.nz
rpalmer@aucklandtennis.co.nz

SYDNEY

Craig Watson
Tennis New South Wales
30 Alma Street
Paddington NSW 2021
Australia
Telephone: +61-2-9331-4144
Fax: 61-2-9360-4036
E-mail: cwatson@tennisnsw.com.au
Website:
  www.adidasinternational.com.au

HOBART

Steve Walker
Tennis Tasmania
PO Box 260
Newstead
Tasmania 7250
Australia
Telephone: +61-3-6334-4237
Fax: +61-3-6334-4564
E-mail:
  swalker@tennisaustralia.com.au
Website:
  www.tennisaustralia.com.au

CANBERRA

Janet Young
Tennis Australia
Private Bag 6060
Richmond South
Victoria 3121
Australia
Telephone: +61-3-655-1177
Fax: +61-3-9650-2743
E-mail:
  jyoung@tennisaustralia.com.au
Website: www.tennisaustralia.com

AUSTRALIAN OPEN

Paul NcNamee
Tennis Australia
Melbourne Park National
  Tennis Centre
Private Bag 6060
Richmond South
Victoria 3121
Australia
Telephone: +61-3-9286-1175
Fax: +61-3-9650-1040
E-mail:
  pmcnamee@tennisaustralia.
  com.au
Website: www.ausopen.org

TOKYO

(indoor)
Toshio Noji
UNO Inc
Tokyo Yohfuku Kaikan Building
13 Ichigaya Hachiman-cho
6th Floor
Shinjuku-ku
Tokyo 162-0844
Japan
Telephone: +81-3-5229-0266
Fax: +81-3-5229-0277
E-mail: ck-uno@adgnet.or.jp
Website: www.Toray-ppo.co.jp

PARIS

Regis Brunet
IMG
54 Avenue Marceau
75008 Paris
France
Telephone: +33-1-44-31-44-31
Fax: +33-1-44-31-44-32
E-mail: rbrunet@imgworld.com
Website:
  www.gazdefrance.com/open

NICE

Gilles Moretton
Tournoi De Tennis Feminin Nice
Occade Sport
20 route de Strasbourg
69300 Lyon Caluire
France
Telephone: +33 4-72-27-29-00
Fax: +33-4-72-27-29-04
E-mail: gmoretton@occade.com
Website: www.occadesport.com

DOHA

Ayman Azmy Galal
Khalifa International
   Tennis & Squash Federation
Maglis Al-Taawon St
Al-Dafna Area
Qatar
Telephone: +974-440-9666
Fax: +974-483-2990
E-mail: azmy@qatar.net.qa

OKLAHOMA CITY

Sara K. Forniciari
Sports Plus
7020 Heatherhill Road
Bethesda MD 20817
USA
Telephone: +1 301-229-5401
Fax: +1 301-229-2375
E-mail: sara@sportsplus.com

BOGOTA

Sandra Silva
Jesus Mendez Diaz
Calle 100 No 11 B 67
Bogota
Colombia
Telephone: +57-1-6103311
Fax: +57-1-6162388
E-mail: jmendez@colsanitas.com.co
Website: www.colsanitas.com

DUBAI

Bharat Godkhindi
Sportsworld Media Group
   Middle East LLC
PO Box 28474
Dubai Tennis Stadium
Al Gharoud
Dubai UAE
Telephone: +971-4-28-28-971
Fax: +971-4-28-28-953
E-mail: bharatg@sportsworld.net

SCOTTSDALE

Peter Tatum
IMG
2 Bryant Street
Suite 150
San Francisco CA 94105
USA
Telephone: +1 415-227-8000
   (ex 124)
Fax: +1 415-227-4288
E-mail: ptatum@imgworld.com
Website: www.scottsdaletennis.com

ACAPULCO

Ivan Brixi
Octagon
1751 Pinnacle Drive
Suite 1500
McLean
VA 22102
USA
Telephone: +1 703-905-3300
Fax: +1 301-905-4495
E-mail: ivan.brixi@octagon.com

INDIAN WELLS

Gavin Forbes
IMG Center
Suite 100
1360 East 9th Street
Cleveland OH 44114
USA
Telephone: +1 216-522-1200
Fax: +1 216-522-1145
E-mail: gforbes@imgworld.com
E-mail:
   ssimon@championships-cup.com
Website:
   www.champions-cup/evert.html

MIAMI

Butch Buchholz
150 Alhambra Circle
Suite 825
Coral Gables FL 33134
USA
Telephone: +1 305-446-2200
Fax: +1 305-446-9080
E-mail: cmb@verinet.com
Website: www.ericsson-open.com

PORTO

Paulo Cordoso
Apartado 328
4481-912 Vila Do Conde
Portugal
Telephone: +351-252-240620
Fax: +351-252-240629
E-mail:
   pcardoso@nortenis.jazznet.pt

AMELIA ISLAND

John Arrix
Kaleidoscope Sports &
   Entertainment
136 Madison Avenue
8th Floor
New York NY 10016
USA
Telephone: +1 212-779-6600
Fax: +1 212-779-8861
E-mail: jarrix@ksesport.com
Website: www.blchamps.com

ESTORIL

Joao Lagos
Joao Lagos Sports SA
Rua Fernao Mendes Pinto 42
1400-146 Lisboa
Portugal
Telephone: +351-21-303-4900
Fax: +351-21-303-4933
E-mail: lagossports@mail.telepac.pt

CHARLESTON

Lisa Thomas
Family Circle Cup
416 King Street
Charleston
SC 29403
USA
Telephone: +1 843-720-5265
Fax: +1 843-723-8355
E-mail: lthomas@gjusa.com
Website: www.familycirclecup.com

BUDAPEST

Jeno Marky
Kiralyok utja 105
1039 Budapest
Hungary
Telephone: +36-1-240-8616
Fax: +36-1-240-8416
E-mail:
   9123 markeyjeno@matavnet.hu

HAMBURG

Walter Knapper
DTB Rothenbaum Turnier GmbH
Hallerstrasse 89
20149 Hamburg
Germany
Telephone: +49-40-41178-0
Fax: +49-40-41178-222
E-mail: knapper@dtb-tennis.de
Website: www.dtb-tennis.de

BOL

Antun Plenkovic
Zlatni Rat
21420 Bol
Croatia
Telephone: +385-21-635-142
Fax: +385-21-635-120
E-mail:
   antun.plenkovic@bolladies.hr
Website: www.bolladies.hr

BERLIN

Eberhard Wensky
German Tennis Federation
LTTC Rot-Weiss eV
Gottfried-von-Cramm-Weg 47-55
14193 Berlin
Germany
Telephone: +49-30-89-57550
Fax: +49-30-89-575552
E-mail:
   germanopen@rot-weiss-berlin.de
Website:
   www.german-open-berlin.de

ROME

Adriano Panatta
Sergio Palmieri
Foro Italico
Viale dei Gladiatori 31
001904 Roma
Italy
Telephone: +39-06-3263-9917
Fax: +39-06-3263-8552
E-mail: romeopen@katamail.com
Website: www.federtennis.systex.it

ANTWERP

Serge Haubourdin
Jan Kempfer
Department Sport & Recreation
Desguinlei 17-19
2018 Antwerpen
Belgium
Telephone: +32-3-242-9841
Fax: +32-3-242-9850
Website: www.belopen.com

STRASBOURG

François Cade
Directeur SIIG
Universités de Strasbourg
4 rue Blaise Pascal
67000 Strasbourg
France
Telephone: +33-3-90-24-11-78
Fax: 33-3-90-24-11-77
E-mail:cade@siig.u-strasbg.fr
Website:
   www.webcity.fr/internationaux-
   de-tennis-feminin

MADRID

David Serrahima
   or Fernando Soler
IMG Espana
Via Augusta n 200 4th Floor
08021 Barcelona
Spain
Telephone: +34-93-200-3456
Fax: 34-93-200-5924
E-mail: dserrahima@imgworld.com
E-mail: fsoler@imgworld.com

ROLAND GARROS: PARIS

Stephane Simian
Fédération Française de Tennis
Stade Roland Garros
2 Avenue Gordon Bennett
75016 Paris
France
Telephone: +33-1-47-43-4800
Fax: +33-1-46-51-6724
Website: www.rolandgarros.org

BIRMINGHAM

Marjory Howie
 or John Feaver
The Lawn Tennis Association
Queen's Club
West Kensington
London W14 9EG
England
Telephone: +44-20-7381-7022
Fax: +44-20-7381-6050
E-mail: marjory.howie@lta.org.uk
E-mail: john.feaver@lta.org.uk
Website: www.lta.org.uk

TASHKENT

Yona Yair
Danny Gelley
Israel Tennis Center
Kfar Hayarok Intersection
Ramat Hasharon 4721000
Israel
Telephone: +972-3-645-6613-6634
Fax: +972-3-645-6677
E-mail: tourn@tennis.org.il
Website: www.tourntennis.org.il

EASTBOURNE

John Feaver
The Lawn Tennis Association
Queen's Club
West Kensington
London W14 9EG
England
Telephone: +44-20-7381-7000
Fax: +44-20-7381-5965
E-mail: john.feaver@lta.org.uk
Website: www.lta.org.uk

S'HERTOGENBOSCH

(formerly Rosmalen)
Marcel Hunze
Al Benelux BV
Burghstraat 25B
6227 RR Maastricht
The Netherlands
Telephone: +31-43-3-67-24-24
Fax: +31-43-3-67-24-22
E-mail: marcel.hunze@octagon.com
Website: www.heinekentrophy.nl

WIMBLEDON

Christopher Gorringe
The All England Lawn
 Tennis & Croquet Club
Church Road
Wimbledon
London SW19 5AE
England
Telephone: +44-20-8944-1066
Fax: +44-20-8947-3354
Website: www.wimbledon.org

PALERMO

Oliviero Palma
Country Time Club
Viale dell Olimpo 5
90149 Palermo
Italy
Telephone: +39-091-454886
Fax: +39-091-684-1644
E-mail: countrytime@iol.it
Website: www.trinacria.it/country

VIENNA

Peter Michael Reichel
Kienzlstr 13
4600 Wels
Austria
Telephone: +43-7242-63747
Fax: +43-7242-51981
E-mail: office@matchmaker.at
Website: www.matchmaker.at

KNOKKE-HEIST

Leslie McCormack
IMG - Axis Center
Burlington Lane
London W42 TH
England
Telephone: +44-208-233-5300
Fax: +44-208-233-5301
E-mail: lmccormack@imgworld.com
Website: www.sanex.net

STANFORD

Peter Tatum
IMG
2 Bryant Street
Suite 150
San Francisco
CA 94105
USA
Telephone: +1 415-227-8000
 (ex 124)
Fax: +1 415-227-4288
E-mail: ptatum@imgworld.com
Website:
 www.bankofthewestclassic.com

SOPOT

Ryszard
Fijalkowski
9 Merliengo Str
02-511 Warsaw
Poland
Telephone: +48-22-844-12-97
Fax: +48-22-844-12-97

CASABLANCA

Mjid Mohamed
Federation Royale Marocaine
 de Tennis
Parc De Lalique Arabe
Casablanca
BP 15794
Morocco
Telephone: +212-2-2981262
Fax: +212-2-2981265

SAN DIEGO

Raquel Giscafre
Promotion Sports Inc
7720B El Camino Real
Suite 436
Carlsbad
CA 92009
USA
Telephone: +1 760-438-9220
Fax: +1 760-438-9656
E-mail:
 raquel@promotionsports.org
or Jane Stratton at
E-mail: jane@promotionsports.org

BASEL

Thomas Wirz
PreCon Ladies Open - P4T AG
Gundeldingerstrasse 170
4053 Basel
Switzerland
Telephone: +41-61-367-9376
Fax: +41-61-367-9372

LOS ANGELES

Gus Sampras
IMG
11755 Wilshire Blvd
Suite 850
Los Angeles
CA 90025
USA
Telephone: +1 310-473-0411
Fax: +1 310-473-3914
E-mail: gsampras@imgworld.com

TORONTO

(odd-numbered years)
Jane Wynne
National Tennis Centre
3111 Steeles Avenue West
Downsview
Ontario M3J 3H2
Canada
Telephone: +1 416-665-9777
Fax: +1 416-665-9017
E-mail: jwynne@tenniscanada.com
Website: www.tenniscanada.com

MONTREAL

(even-numbered years)
Eugene Lapierre
Tennis Canada
Bureau de Montreal
285 rue Faillon Ouest
Montreal
Quebec H2R 2W1
Canada
Telephone: +1 514-273-1515
Fax: +1 514-276-0070
E-mail:
 elapierre@tenniscanada.com

NEW HAVEN

Anne Person Worcester
Pilot Pen
45 Yale Avenue
New Haven
CT 06515, USA
Telephone: +203-776-7331
Fax: +203-772-4647
E-mail: swax@pilotpentennis.com
E-mail: apwsports@home.com
Website: www.pilotpen.com

US OPEN: FLUSHING MEADOWS

Arlen Kantarian
United States Tennis Association
70 West Red Oak Lane
White Plains NY 10604
USA
Telephone:+914-696-7000
Fax: +914-696-7019
E-mail: kantarian@usta.com
Website: www.usopen.org

WAIKOLOA

Eric Kutner
4 Marcia Court
Troy
New York 12180
USA
Telephone: +1 518-274-1674
Fax: +1 413-480-7400
E-mail: eric@tesports.com

BAHIA

Paulo Carvalho
Av. Paulista
1754-5 andar
Sao Paulo
Brazil
Telephone: +55-11-253-8866
Fax: +55-11-253-8635
E-mail:
 paulo.carvalho@octagon.com

QUEBEC CITY

Jacques Herisset
Club de Tennis Avantage
1080 Rue Bouvier
Quebec (QC) G2K 1L9
Canada
Telephone: +1 418-627-3343
Fax: 418-623-8720
Website: www.challengebell.com

TOKYO

(outdoor)
Nobuo Ariyoshi
Sports Marketing Division
Dentsu Inc
1-11 Tsukiji
Chuo-ku
Tokyo 104-8426
Japan
Telephone: +81-3-5551-7043
Fax: +81-3-5551-2253

BALI

Kevin Livesey
Unit 72-2 Seri Duta Condominium
Jalan Gallagher
Taman Duta
50480 Kuala Lumpur
Malaysia
Telephone: +603-252-1450
Fax: +603-252-4215
E-mail: kevanie@pc.jaring.my

LEIPZIG

Ivan Radosevic
SCI Sport Consulting International
Menzelstrasse 24
67061 Ludwigshafen
Germany
Telephone: +49-621-58-77-44-5
Fax: +49-621-56-39-48
E-mail: scisport@compuserve.com
Website:
  www.sparkassencupcompuserve.
  de/leipzig

MOSCOW

Aleksei Selivanenko
Trans Marketing Group
Myasnitskaya Ul. 22-1
Suite 6/7
Moscow 101000
Russia
Telephone: +7-095-92309812/
  2137/2711
Fax: +7-095-924-6427
E-mail:
  aleksei.selivanenko@russport.ru
Website: www.kremlincup.ru

TOKYO, JAPAN

Sanji Arisawa
Japan Tennis Association
Kishi Mem. Park 4F
1-1-1 Jinnan
Shibuya-ku
Tokyo 150-8050
Japan
Telephone: +81-3-3481-2511
Fax: +81-3-3481-2510

FILDERSTADT

Dieter Fischer
TennisSportshalle Filderstadt
Sportzentrum Plattenhardt 70794
Filderstadt
Germany
Telephone: +49-711-775151
Fax: +49-711-7776690

SHANGHAI

Michael Luevano or
  Charles Humphrey Smith
Room 1703
17th Floor
525 Jianguo Road
East Shanghai
China
Telephone: +86-21-6386-0864
Fax: +86-21-6386-0871
E-mail: mluevano@netvigator.com
E-mail: chsinnet@aol.com
Website:
  www.heinekenopen.china.com

ZÜRICH

Beat Ritschard
Octagon (Switzerland) AG
Im Werd 8
8952 Zürich-Schlieren Switzerland
Telephone: +41-1-738-9000
Fax: 41-1-738-9001
E-mail:
  office@swisscom-challenge.com
Website:
  www.swisscomchallenge.com

BRATISLAVA

Igor Moska -
  General Sectretary STA
Junacka 6
832-80 Bratislava
Slovakia
Telephone: +421-7-49249-262
Fax: +421-7-49249-533
Fax: +421-7-49249-561
E-mail: stg@stg.sk
Website: www.stg.sk

LINZ

Peter Michael Reichel
Matchmaker Gesellschaft für
  Sportcommunication
Kienslstr 13
4600 Wels
Austria
Telephone: +43-7242-63747
Fax: +43-7242-51981
E-mail: office@matchmaker.at
Website: www.matchmaker.at

LUXEMBOURG

Danielle Koster
Residence Miro II
14 rue Francois Cigrang
4068 Esch-sur-Alzette
Luxembourg
Telephone: +352-55-7902
Fax: +352-57-0631
E-mail: iwtp@neacom.lu
Website: www.seatopen.lu

MUNICH

Bill Dennis
Global Tennis
PO Box 4039
Salisbury
MD 21803-4039
USA
Telephone: +1 410-543-1515
Fax: +1 410-860-2087

SURABAYA

Kevin Livesey
Unit 72-2 Seri Duta Condominium
Jalan Gallagher
Taman Duta
50480 Kuala Lumpur
Malaysia
Telephone: +603-252-1450
Fax: +603-252-4215
E-mail: kevanie@pc.jaring.my

PATTAYA CITY

Geoffrey Rowe
49/42 Soi Onnuj 53
Onnuj-Latkrabang Rd
Pravet District
Bangkok 10250
Thailand
Telephone: +66-2-321-7541
Fax: +66-2-721-2979
E-mail: rowe@ksc.th.com

THE INDEX

BROUGHT TO YOU BY...

If you have enjoyed *The Book of Tennis* you might be interested to know about *Get-A-Grip*, the book of grips and strokes coming soon from JWM Publishing. British professional coach Paul Seymour has devised the most complete analysis of grips and strokes ever undertaken. Did you know there are well over 250 strokes played to world class standard, yet it takes only seven grip positions to produce all of them? Look out for *Get-A-Grip*, or check out our website for details.

About the author

Chris Bowers was born in Heswall, in the north-western English county of Cheshire.

His first sporting interest was cricket, but with a tennis club only a short lob away he soon directed his playing energies into the sport and a life-long passion for tennis had begun. Although a poor match temperament caused the peak of his playing career to be the quarter-finals of the Cheshire under-14 junior circuit, surely his finest hour came aged 16 when he and three school friends broke the world under-18 marathon doubles record when they played 44 hours of non-stop tennis!

Chris studied at the University of East Anglia in southern England. His college days included teaching English for a year in the south-western corner of Germany, where he supervised the school's two tennis teams in an area already getting excited about two highly promising local kids, Boris Becker and Steffi Graf.

After graduating in 1983, he became a newspaper journalist with the Thomson Regional Newspapers group, initially on the Evening Chronicle newspaper in Newcastle upon Tyne, north-eastern England, and then for three years on the Wokingham and Bracknell Times series west of London. In 1986 he turned to radio, a move which took him to Switzerland to work with the Swiss world service Swiss Radio International. After that he spent 18 months working in news and sport for BBC Radio in London.

In 1990, inspired by his concern for and belief in the environment, Chris quit journalism to run an environmental organisation he had helped set up, the Environmental Transport Association. This also involved work for a Brussels-based European environmental lobby group, the European Federation for Transport and Environment, with whom he is still involved.

But by 1992 he was getting itchy feet to go back to journalism, and when he one day lobbed himself the question 'what is my dream job?' the answer was obvious: reporting on tennis. Since then, he has toured the globe as a regular freelance contributor to BBC radio, the European television sports channel Eurosport, and several newspapers, magazines and internet sites. He also runs the Tennis Radio Network, an alliance of radio and television commentators who report from top events around the world.

Although music and theatre compete for his attentions, Chris finds his greatest pleasure beyond the run of the mill forehands and backhands, when tennis produces moments of great theatre, like in the Davis Cup or a gripping final set of a Grand Slam match.

He and his partner Louise live in southern England and have a daughter, Tamara, who was born just before *The Book of Tennis* went to press.

About the editor and publisher

Jeff Wayne was born in Forest Hills, New York. His parents, Cathie and Jerry, met at the 1939 World's Fair, Long Island, not far from the current site of the US Open.

From age five Jeff took piano lessons and was taught tennis by Jerry – a former college player turned singer/actor/writer/theatrical producer, who in 1953 played romantic gambler Sky Masterson in the original West End production of 'Guys and Dolls', bringing the Wayne family to the UK.

After four years they returned to New York, then California in 1960, where Jeff graduated High School and College. He played keyboards in local bands, captained and played No1 for both Grant High and LA Valley College, and graduated with a journalism degree before switching to music.

In 1966, Jerry offered him the opportunity to compose the score for his upcoming West End production 'Two Cities' based on Charles Dickens's 'A Tale Of Two Cities'. Returning to the UK, Jeff's musical career truly began.

Following 'Two Cities', Jeff composed advertising, television, radio and film music and produced three UK Top Five David Essex albums, No1 UK singles 'Hold Me Close' and 'Gonna Make You A Star', USA No1 'Rock On' (NME winner Best Produced Single) and 'Stardust', title track from the David Putnam film.

In 1978, Jeff's musical version of 'The War Of The Worlds' was released, achieving international success, multi million sales, hit singles 'The Eve Of The War' and 'Forever Autumn' and two Ivor Novello Awards. The Best Recording in Science Fiction and Fantasy followed (the judges included Steven Spielberg, George Lucas, and Alfred Hitchcock).

Since 'The War of the Worlds' Jeff's work has included the Who's film 'McVicar'; television movie 'The Knowledge'; ITV's The Big Match; World of Sport, and World Cup; TVam's 'Good Morning Britain'; BBC's '60 Minutes'; and London radio station LBC. His musical work 'Spartacus' was also released featuring Anthony Hopkins, Catherine Zeta Jones, and Ladysmith Black Mambazo and conducted music from 'The War of the Worlds' with the London Symphony Orchestra and Choir in Gothenburg, Sweden, and the Royal Albert Hall, London..

Jeff's compositions have been recorded by: Apollo 440, the London Symphony Orchestra, Human League, Acker Bilk, Orbital, Justin Hayward, Todd Terry, N-Trance, Dario G, Sakin & Friends, Tilt, Hybrid, and performed to by gymnasts, jugglers, dancers, ice skaters, magicians, fire eaters and animals!

On court, Jeff has won at club, county, and national level including, the British National Indoor Veterans singles and doubles titles, and the National Clay Court doubles. In 1992 he partnered Great Britain Davis Cup captain Roger Taylor at the European Veterans Championships. 1999 saw Jeff represent Great Britain competing for the Austria Cup in Spain, and achieved an ITF world ranking in his age group. He recently completed 12 years as Hertfordshire county men's captain.

Jeff has also played pro-am tournaments including for: Muscular Dystrophy, Olympic Games Fund Raising, and Save The Children.

Jeff married Geraldine, a company director at JWM Group, in 1977. They live in Hertfordshire, England, and have four children: Anna-Marie an actress, Jemma studying at Newnham College, Cambridge, Zeb juggling 'A' levels, rugby, and DJ'ing, and already at nine, Joab, keen to be the world's best tennis player.

Above: Chris Bowers interviewing Pete Sampras for Eurosport

Right: Jeff Wayne age 17, captain and No1 for Grant High School, North Hollywood, California